Crisis
in Representation

Anonymous, Robespierre Guillotining the Executioner. Ca. 1794.

Crisis in Representation

Thomas Paine, Mary Wollstonecraft,
Helen Maria Williams, and the
Rewriting of the French Revolution

Steven Blakemore

Madison • Teaneck
Fairleigh Dickinson University Press
London: Associated University Presses

Associated University Presses
440 Forsgate Drive
Cranbury, NJ 08512

Associated University Presses
16 Barter Street
London WC1A 2AH, England

Associated University Presses
P.O. Box 338, Port Credit
Mississauga, Ontario
Canada L5G 4L8

The paper used in this publication meets the requirements
of the American National Standard for Permanence of Paper
for Printed Library Materials Z39.48–1984.

Library of Congress Cataloging-in-Publication Data

Blakemore, Steven.
   Crisis in representation : Thomas Paine, Mary Wollstonecraft,
Helen Maria Williams, and the French Revolution / Steven Blakemore.
    p. cm.
   Includes bibliographical references and index.
   ISBN 0-8386-3714-0 (alk. paper)
   1. France—History—Revolution, 1789–1799—Foreign public opinion.
2. France—History—Revolution, 1789–1799—Historiography.
3. France—History—Revolution, 1789–1799—Literature and the
revolution. 4. Paine, Thomas, 1737–1809—Views on French
Revolution. 5. Wollstonecraft, Mary, 1759–1797—Views on French
Revolution. 6. Williams, Helen Maria, 1762–1827—Views on French
Revolution. I. Title.
DC158.8.B55 1997
944.94—dc20
                                              96-38535
                                                CIP

In Memoriam
Karen Jean Blakemore
(13 August 1953–18 May 1962)

Contents

Abbreviations

Works cited throughout this study are identified by the following short titles in the text and notes:

Analytical Review: Mary Wollstonecraft, *Analytical Review* (1788–97), in *The Works of Mary Wollstonecraft*, vol. 7, edited by Janet Todd and Marilyn Butler, 13–502. 7 vols. New York University Press, 1989.

CW: *The Complete Writings of Thomas Paine*, 2 vols., edited by Philip S. Foner. New York: The Citadel Press, 1945.

Enquiry: Edmund Burke, *A Philosophical Enquiry into the Origin of Our Ideas of the Sublime and Beautiful* (1757). Edited by J. T. Boulton. New York: Columbia University Press, 1958.

The Female Reader: Mary Wollstonecraft, *The Female Reader; or Miscellaneous Pieces in Prose and Verse; Selected from the Best Writers, and disposed under proper heads; for the Improvement of Young Women* (1789), in *Works*, 4:53–350.

The French Revolution: Mary Wollstonecraft, *An Historical and Moral View of the Origin and Progress of the French Revolution and the Effect it has produced in Europe* (1794), in *Works*, 6:1–235.

Letter: Thomas Paine, *Letter to George Washington* (1796), in *The Complete Writings of Thomas Paine*, 2 vols. edited by Philip S. Foner. New York: The Citadel Press, 1945.

Letters: Helen Maria Williams, *Letters from France* (1790–96), 2 vols., edited by Janet M. Todd. Delmar, New York: Scholars' Facsimiles & Reprints, 1975.

Letters in Sweden: Mary Wollstonecraft, *Letters Written During a Short Residence in Sweden, Norway, and Denmark* (1796), in *Works*, 6:237–364.

Reflections: Edmund Burke, *Reflections on the Revolution in France* (1790), edited by Conor Cruise O'Brien. Harmondsworth: Penguin Classics, 1986.

Rights of Men: Mary Wollstonecraft, *A Vindication of the Rights of Men, in a Letter to the Right Honorable Edmund Burke; Occasioned by his Reflections on the Revolution in France* (1790), in *Works*, 5:1–78.

Acknowledgments

I am very grateful to the following friends and colleagues who responded to portions of this book: Frances Ferguson, Daniel E. Ritchie, Nicola Watson, Fred Hembree, Matthew Bray. I owe a special debt of gratitude to John E. Faulkner for generously reading versions of the manuscript and replying to numerous queries.

Introduction

Iɴ an anonymous print, *Robespierre, guillotining the Executioner after having guillotined all the French,* a wilderness of guillotines confronts the viewer from all angles, as if the Terror cuts from all sides and directions. The guillotines are repetitive replicas, each representing the sanguinary history of heads cut off in the same way and with the same result. The letter affixed to each guillotine labels the collective group or class that has been executed: members of the Committee of Public Safety, Jacobins, Cordeliers, Brissotins, Girondins, Hebertists, nobles, priests, the elderly, women and children, and so on. Only Robespierre, sitting on a tomb, lives to behead the penultimate executioner, miming the latter's role and executing the revolutionary logic that ends with friends and enemies tumbled together in anonymous resemblance, funereally represented by the obelisk bearing the legend, "Here lies all France." From one perspective, the print is an ironic representation of Robespierre's view of himself: the Incorruptible purifying *la patrie* of the corrupt body politic—his severe revolutionary reason embodied in the precise geometric shape of the guillotine(s) reproducing the repetitive deaths of the Republic of Virtue, now multiplied and equated with a Republic of Death—an egalitarian fraternity compelled to die for the nation, finally one and indivisible. Divided heads and bodies paradoxically unify Robespierre's republic; private bodies represent the corrupt body politic, purged in a repetitive ritual of ideological genocide.

From another angle, the Revolution has been distorted into its opposite—the inverted liberty bonnet piked at the top of the obelisk (replacing the traditional Liberty pole) represents another missing head and the insane logic of liberty turned upside-down, immolated in the Incorruptible's holocaust. Resting his feet on two dialectical Constitutions, the suppressed "Liberal" Constitution of 1791 and the suspended "Jacobin" Constitution that was supposed to have replaced it, Robespierre "tramples" on both—their fates are also the same. In the end, the Revolution's history is headless. The only heads, besides Robespierre's, are the back of the executioner's soon-to-be decapitated one, and below, the detached face

of an anonymous victim who lies beside anonymous knees, his
(or her?) slight mouth turned down into a stern frown resembling
Robespierre's. In turn, Robespierre's fate will soon resemble
theirs. Robespierre ultimately seems to be both cause and effect
of the egalitarian republic that finally conforms to the logic of his
ideological obsessions. The ambiguous thrust of the print suggests
that either the Incorruptible will somehow manage to guillotine
himself, ensuring the impossibility of human corruption, or that
Robespierre will remain, among guillotines and corpses, the self-
fulfilling monument of the dead body politic. Published circa 1794,
the print embodies a Thermidorian perspective that protests the
Revolution's repeated betrayal by Robespierre—the ironic counterrevolutionary murderer of the French nation.

The anonymous print expressively encapsulates various themes
appearing in books and pamphlets written by British and American
writers who had supported the French Revolution in the jubilant
days of 1789, but who were compelled to revise their original representations once the Revolution began to spin out of control. In
repetitive readings framed around Robespierre, the Guillotine, and
the Terror, there are a series of binary contrasts that nevertheless
complement each other: past and present, purity and corruption,
similarity and difference, beginnings and ends, vision and revision,
revolution and regression. In the voluminous, contradictory representations of the Revolution, these and other binary polarities repetitively identify each other, and themes of resemblance and
repetition become primary modes by which the Revolution is con-
tinuously written and revised. Themes of representation and misrepresentation correspondingly match those of resemblance and
difference. Confronted with their prior explanations, revolutionary
writers were confronted with a crisis in representation—attempting to reconcile their original visions with a Revolution they
no longer recognized. The result was a re-visioning of a Revolution
they had to reimagine and rewrite.

In the tumultuous, electric atmosphere of the 1790s, the Revolution was being written even as it was unfolding, and so a new era
of human history seemed immediately present to the Revolution's
contemporary witnesses. Thus to write the Revolution's history
was to participate concurrently in the creation of its meaning, especially for those writers who saw the Revolution as a transforming
idea regenerating the world. But when the idea turned into rebellious flesh and blood, the same writers had to rewrite the Revolution's significance, revising its history and the previous texts that
retrospectively suggested that the Revolution had been fatally mis-

read. The Revolution's history, its "past," became a problem to be written "out."

From the beginning, of course, the French Revolution had been represented as an apocalyptic event that would regenerate the world, an explosion of transforming energy, unprecedented in human history. Supporters and opponents of the Revolution saw it at different times as an astonishing phenomenon bearing no resemblance to the past, and yet both tried to make it intelligible by connecting it to the past's recognizable history. Antirevolutionaries✗ such as Edmund Burke saw it as a second Fall, an eruption of heretical ideologies (formerly suppressed) into the traditional European world. Revolutionaries saw it initially as an extension of the Enlightenment and the progressive principles that would transform that inherited world. In writing about the Revolution, both sides tried to explain its significance in terms of recognizable English history: the contested debate over the Revolution's meaning was simultaneously a debate over England's or, in the case of Thomas Paine, America's meaning. Three previous revolutions impinged on the writing of the French Revolution: the Puritan Revolution of the 1640s, the Glorious Revolution of 1688, and the American Revolution of 1776.

The French Revolution hence revivified the ideological battles of the seventeenth century, allowing British dissidents to promote the old radical agenda (extended suffrage, parliamentary reform, and religious freedom) in the seemingly new language of natural rights and the French Revolution. The American Revolution was yet another "text" used to read the paradigms of the past into the ongoing French Revolution. A historical paradigm is, as Hayden White notes, "the model of what a set of historical events will look like once they have been explained."[1]

But when the historical paradigms no longer corresponded to the phenomena they were explaining, they had to be subsequently replaced or revised, resulting in a variety of intertextual revolutions—not only the readings and revolutions of the past, but the many French Revolutions represented in their Girondin and Jacobin versions—and the other competitive readings of a protean Revolution contradictorily reified and represented as a unified bloc. Most writers engaged in writing the Revolution believed, not surprisingly, that his or hers was the true French Revolution. For the Revolution's supporters, to write the French Revolution was to participate in the creation of a new transcendent history, but without the correspondent vocabulary to express its confusing transformations. Thus, in I. A. Richards's terms, an English *vehicle* illuminated the French *tenor.*

Writing the "new" Revolution in the traditional language of radical British discourse, contemporary writers turned to the reactionary past as an explanation, once the Revolution seemed to deviate and rebel against their original representations. Consequently, they rewrote revolutionary difference as regressive similarity, resembling the reactionary past they had previously rejected. The Revolution that appeared as a radical break from history and the commencement of a new time began to resemble reactionary past(s): linear progression into a utopian future turned into cyclical repetitions of the "Gothic" past.

Using the example of the reactionary past as an explanation for present revolutionary violence, they ironically implicated the Revolution (and themselves) in the repetitive regressions of the past. Rather than constituting a rejection of oppressive history, the Revolution suddenly seemed to resemble and repeat that history. Even before the Terror, the paradigm of the contaminated past had been used to explicate present revolutionary violence. In the *Rights of Man* (1791), Thomas Paine explained why French citizens were suddenly parading decapitated heads affixed to spikes:

> [they had learned] it from the governments they live under; [they retaliated against] the punishments they had been accustomed to behold. The head stuck upon spikes, which remained for years upon Temple Bar, differed nothing in the horror of the scene from those carried about on spikes at Paris; yet this was done by the English government. . . . In France, under the former government, the punishments were not less barbarous. Who does not remember the execution of Damien, torn to pieces by horses? The effect of those cruel spectacles exhibited to the population, is to destroy tenderness, or excite revenge, and by the base and false idea of governing men by terror, instead of reason, they become precedents.[2]

For Paine, repressive England resembles France's Old Order, and repetitive imitation of past "spectacles" explains the aberrant present.

In *Letters on the Revolution of France* (1791), another writer, Thomas Christie, reformulated Paine's parallel by responding to the contemporary question ("But how come the mobs in France to be so cruel in their vengeance?") with the appropriate answer:

> Their superiors set them the example. . . . The *Bastille* had accustomed them to condemn and punish without trial or accusation; the

frequent repetition of *public capital punishments* . . . had familiarized them with putting men to death; the *gibbets* of the State pointed to the *laterne,* and the *racks, stakes,* and *wheels* of established authority, had fatally habituated them to shut their ears against the cries of the dying, and to abuse the bodies of the dead.[3]

Both Paine and Christie assumed that this would change once the Revolution had triumphed in the hearts and minds of the people and probably would have been perplexed that their representations could be retrospectively read to point not to the past but to the repetitive future. Paine's reference to "spectacle" and Christie's reference to "repetition" would subsequently haunt revolutionary imaginations and memories.

The three writers I deal with—Thomas Paine, Mary Wollstone-craft, and Helen Maria Williams—illustrate the crisis in represen-tation confronting writers who had previously committed themselves to a revolution that was suddenly unrecognizable. From 1789 through 1792, the Revolution's contradictions had been princi-pally explained in terms of an external counterrevolution without, and an internal counterrevolution within. Both counterrevolution-ary models consequently explained the Revolution's responsive ex-cesses. This formulation, however, became more problematic once revolutionary factions began accusing one another of betrayal and apostasy. Since Paine, Wollstonecraft, and Williams shared a quasi-Girondist perspective of the Revolution—the dominant perspective of the Revolution's British and American admirers—they were confronted with yet another representational crisis once the Jacob-ins took power and, in effect, proscribed both the Girondins and their "texts." While the ci-devant Counterrevolution could initially explain controversial events such as the October Days of 1789, the overthrow of the French monarchy (10 August 1792), and even the September Massacres, the conventional explanations had to be revised, especially after the execution of Louis XVI (21 January 1793), the declaration of war by France on Great Britain (1 Febru-ary), and the purge of the Girondins from the National Convention (31 May–2 June). The commencement of the Terror was the culmi-nating event that precipitated an unavoidable crisis for the Revolu-tion's British and American advocates.

Paine, Wollstonecraft, and Williams were thus principal partici-pants in the ongoing revision of the French Revolution, not only because of their contemporary prominence and their previous pro-revolutionary writing, but because they were living in revolution-ary France during the Terror. The crisis in representation was, for them, intensely personal: in 1793, Paine and Williams were arrested and imprisoned, and Wollstonecraft, at times, feared for her life. The Revolution no longer corresponding to their previous representations compelled them to confront confusing, and seemingly inexplicable, contradictions. These contradictions, however, ensued not only from the Revolution itself, but from their earlier intertextual wars with Edmund Burke—a subject I pursue in a concurrent book and whose themes I continue to explore in this one.

In *A Vindication of the Rights of Men* (1790), Wollstonecraft, for instance, had attacked Burke's aesthetic treatise, *A Philosophical Enquiry into the Origin of our Ideas of the Sublime and Beautiful* (1757) and its ideological connection with Burke's *Reflections on the Revolution in France* (1790).[4] Since Burke had contrasted the sublime and beautiful via a gendered ideology centering on traditional distinctions between men and women, masculinity and femininity, Wollstonecraft perceptively understood that Burke, in the *Reflections,* had recast his aesthetic values into a political critique of the French Revolution. Consequently, she linked both the *Reflections* and the *Enquiry* in a countercritique of both. Likewise, Helen Maria Williams, as we will see, responded to both the *Enquiry* and the *Reflections* in her *Letters from France* (1790–96). Burke's writings subsequently presented another representational crisis for both women, given their earlier criticisms and the Revolution's post-1792 course.

With regard to Paine, he and Wollstonecraft had criticized Burke for writing counterrevolutionary tragedy rather than true history, and yet they both produced their own theatrical versions of the French Revolution. This constituted another kind of crisis and repetition—the writing "out" of the French Revolution in terms of their previous criticisms of Burke's *Reflections.* This writing "out"—in the simultaneous sense of erasure and exposure—characterizes certain intertextual junctures in the writings of Wollstonecraft and Williams, in (for instance) their respective versions of *Macbeth:* the theme of guilty regicide and "bloody hands" pertains, as will be seen, to their revisions of the revolution of 1789. While Burke was not always the focal point of the Revolution's supporters, he represented a constant reference point for their ongoing revisions.

My principal focal point, however, is how the crisis in representation compelled all three writers to reconceive the Revolution through strategies and themes of repetition. For these (and other) writers, the crisis was also one of faith, and hence it is important to emphasize that while they criticized and rewrote problematic aspects of the Revolution, none of them renounced the Revolution *in toto,* as James Mackintosh had done, a decade after the publication of *Vindiciae Gallicae* (1791). It was, in fact, through thematic repetitions that they were able to maintain their faith in a true, albeit betrayed, revolution. At the same time, however, their revisions constituted an allusive critique of their earlier representations. By contextually contradicting their previous pronouncements, Wollstonecraft's and Williams' revisions of the Revolution became a way of "unsaying" what they had previously written. In this sense, their rewriting of the Revolution was also a way of unwriting it.

Paine was always the exception: constitutionally incapable of critically contradicting himself, he rewrote the French Revolution by representing its contradictions and betrayals as contradictions and betrayals of himself. His historical contribution to the revolutionary debate was the creation of himself as the rebellious, Ur-revolutionary writer. In his works, Paine depicted himself as the author of the American Revolution and the Painean principles that "caused" the French Revolution. He thus emerged textually as the founding father of both revolutions. As Ur-revolutionary author, Paine explained the Terror as a personal betrayal of himself and the enlightened principles that had created both revolutions. He hence linked Robespierre's terrorist regime with George Washington's Federalist faction—both of which he believed had conspired to imprison him and hence betray the two revolutions he had ideologically established. Both betrayals constituted, for him, a reactionary return to the oppressive powers he had opposed in 1776. In response, Paine always returned to his creations of 1776 and 1789, and his strategies of repetition allowed him to rewrite his place within the "text" of both revolutions. This entailed the linguistic assassination of revolutionary rivals and founding fathers, and, in this context, his neglected *Letter to George Washington* (1796) constituted a crucial ideological move—allowing him to rewrite himself as the true father of both revolutions. Reexamining the *Letter to George Washington,* the *Rights of Man,* and his earlier American writings, I explore how Paine repetitively re-creates himself through a series of textual parricides that culminate thematically in *The Age of Reason* (1794).

Wollstonecraft, in contrast, explained the Revolution's contradictions through the reactionary history of the past. In *An Historical and Moral View of the French Revolution* (1794), she participated in the formulation of classic explanations of the Terror and revised her previous representation of the October Days in the *Rights of Men* (1790). Wollstonecraft endeavored to reconcile her idea of a "progressive" revolution with the reality of the regressive Terror, and her revision of the Revolution was again revised in *Letters Written in Sweden, Norway and Denmark* (1796), her final revolutionary assessment.[5]

Although Helen Maria Williams is not as well known today as her canonical contemporaries, her *Letters from France,* in the 1790s, were a significant text in the revolutionary debate. In contrast to Paine and Wollstonecraft, she openly represented the Revolution as a theatrical event, replotting its history through the genres of literature. Like Wollstonecraft, the repetitious past, for her, reexplained a revolution contradicting her prior scripts. Her specific rewriting of the Revolution provides a classic example of how subsequent passages contextually recall and contradict previous pronouncements, creating an intertextual juncture where the "past" is rewritten.

The present book complements the one dealing with the intertextual wars of the 1790s. In that book, I discuss Wollstonecraft's previous representations of the Revolution in both *Vindications* and Paine's conception of himself as the author of world revolution. Read together, both books provide key passages of figuration within a variety of eighteenth-century texts. Given the voluminous factors and materials involved in anything having to do with so large a subject as the French Revolution, the present book is specifically restricted to how three principal authors responded to the Terror and the events that contradicted their previous writings, in a crisis that compelled them to rewrite both the Revolution and themselves as well. The texts I analyze impinge on a specific historical moment, and while there are innumerable social and political factors as well as factors of gender and class, other than those I discuss—factors signifying different things to different people— my modest endeavor is to suggest a starting point where these and a variety of other figurations may be incorporated into what has become the ongoing text of the French Revolution. For the writers I revisit, the crisis in representation had to be resolved by explaining the tragedy of 1793, and the revolution whose trajectory they had plotted in light of 1789 had to be revised by returning to the past as a prelude to the present and future.

To rewrite is to return paradoxically to former materials that are reconceived anew. Like a palimpsest, previous signatures and traces are invisibly present, albeit erased or contradicted. While rewriting a revolution suggests a recognition and hence a correction of "error," the writers I consider ultimately re-right the Revolution, re-explaining its apparent contradictions. They return to re-present the Revolution, not as a renunciation of their revolutionary faith, but as a way of reclaiming both their faith and the Revolution. Since their lives in revolutionary France influenced their subsequent revisions, I have included short biographical chapters, especially because their personal histories are often pertinent to their revisions as well as the historical contexts underwriting their discourse.

At the beginning of the *Eighteenth Brumaire of Louis Bonaparte* (1852), Karl Marx noted that revolutionaries tend to represent themselves in the old language and roles of radical tradition, repeating farcically the revolutionary past. If, as Marx insisted, the "tradition of all the dead generations weighs like a nightmare on the living," the pro-revolutionary writers of the 1790s returned to a different (counter)revolutionary tradition to re-explain a revolution they had originally represented. For every writer engaged in the revolutionary debate, the struggle over the meaning of the Revolution's history was a struggle to control its textual representation. Texts, like the print of Robespierre and the guillotines, pose a variety of conflicting questions. In the interstices of the writings I examine, the assertion of the Revolution's betrayal turns into the question of whether the Revolution is itself part of the past it re-presents. In complex, significant ways, Wollstonecraft, Paine, and Williams re-crystallized a historical problem that has, for the past two centuries, engaged writers of other revolutions as well.

Crisis
in Representation

1

In the Beginning: Thomas Paine's Two Revolutionary Careers

In a novel based on the life of Mary Wollstonecraft, Frances Sherwood imagines Thomas Paine boisterously proclaiming, "I am the Revolution."[1] This proclamation does, in fact, well up in Paine's writings on both the American and French Revolutions, and to understand Paine's conception of the latter, it is necessary to consider first his conception of the former, for they are both linked inextricably in his mind. Like Wollstonecraft and Williams, Paine had a quasi-Girondist interpretation of the French Revolution. Like both, he linked the Revolution's betrayal to Jacobin terror, but he also insisted that it was a personal betrayal of himself, since he had personally made the Revolution possible by creating its causal, ideological conditions. His conception of the Revolution is essentially a self-encompassing vision of himself: Paine believed that he had also created the American Revolution, which "caused" the French Revolution and all the pan-European revolutions that he imagined flowing from his Ur-revolutionary words. His emphasis on himself throughout his writings impinges on his obsessive self-representations and self-conceptions. In this context, after a brief biographical survey of his life following the American Revolution, I proceed to establish the links in Paine's mind between himself and the American and French Revolutions. In the subsequent chapters, I discuss both his critique of Edmund Burke and his defense of the French Revolution and then move chronologically to his *Letter to George Washington* (1796) and Paine's revision of his place in the American Revolution, concluding thematically with *The Age of Reason* (1794)—the culmination of Paine's conception of himself as the creator of world revolution. Since Paine's emphasis on America is central to his causal conception of the French Revolution, this focus necessarily dominates several chapters: Paine's vision of the French Revolution is ultimately a vision of himself as the revolutionary creator of America—a creator who exposes counterrevolutionary traitors and erases competitive revolutionary "founders," emerging as both the first and the last originator of the modern revolutionary era.

I

Paine's political life began after he arrived in America in 1774. Previously unhappy and unsuccessful in England, he subsequently fought against his native country when war broke out in 1775, helping turn American public opinion against England with *Common Sense* (1776) and sustaining the ideological revolt with *The American Crisis* essays (1776–83). Throughout the war, Paine generously gave both his money and himself to the American war effort, serving as volunteer aide-de-camp to General Nathanael Greene and as congressional secretary to the Committee for Foreign Affairs. After the successful completion of the war, however, Paine felt he was owed financial compensation for his services to the American "cause," and he complained that he was being treated shabbily by the country he had helped liberate. American "ingratitude" became a recurrent theme in both his letters and writings. Although George Washington and others had tried to push a petition in Congress (buried by Paine's enemies) granting him financial aid, Paine did receive other forms of financial assistance, so when he left for Europe in April 1787 to promote his plan to build a single-arch bridge across the Schuylkill river near Philadelphia, Paine was relatively well off. He had previously sought opportunities to leave America, and it would be another fifteen years before he returned. In the spring of 1787, he was, in effect, beginning his second revolutionary career, for the energies that would turn into the French Revolution were just beginning to rumble.

When he arrived in Paris in May 1787 to promote his plan for the bridge, Paine was helped by Thomas Jefferson (the resident U.S. Minister to the French government) and the Marquis de Lafayette (whom Paine had known in America), both of whom were instrumental in introducing him to influential French contacts. More importantly, the day before Paine arrived in France (25 May), the Assembly of Notables had been suddenly dissolved, radically politicizing public discourse. Paine sensed the new change in French public opinion and, convinced that the French had begun "to think," decided to turn this change into a new amicable understanding between the peoples of France and England, as well as to avert a war between both countries over Holland. With this in mind and with Thomas Jefferson's introductory help, he sent a letter to and then had a subsequent conversation (in August) with the Abbé Morellet, a confidant of Loménie de Brienne, who had recently replaced Charles Alexandre de Calonne as Minister of Finance. Paine summarized his conversation with Morellet in a memorandum and sent it to him. Morellet, in turn, showed the letter "to the minister and answered in writing with Brienne's knowledge."[2] After learning that the French Academy of Sciences had endorsed his plan for the bridge, Paine left for London, hoping to receive similar approval from the British Royal Academy and carrying with him the memorandum he had written Morellet as well as a positive response from both Morellet and Brienne. The letter from Morellet subsequently figured in the *Rights of Man*.

During his three months in London (September–November), Paine met Edmund Burke. After returning to Paris in December, he was back in London (mid-June 1788) still promoting his bridge. He was also involved in British politics, becoming, with Jefferson's help, the unofficial minister to Great Britain, circulating among British politicians and sending, via Jefferson, political information he thought would benefit American interests. During this time, he renewed his acquaintance with Burke, visiting him for a week at his home. Burke helped Paine promote his bridge and introduced him to influential members of the Whig opposition. Although both Burke and Paine had different self-interested motives (Burke and the Portland Whigs wanted to reestablish closer contacts with America; Paine wanted useful political information), they both enjoyed each other's company. They also misjudged each other—a misjudgement underscored in the *Rights of Man*.

Meanwhile, the French Revolution was accelerating, even though, by the summer of 1789, Paine had not anticipated the explosive events of July. He was soon, however, enthusiastic with its course and possibilities. Writing to George Washington on 16 October 1789, shortly after the October Days, Paine was looking forward to returning to France, since "a share in two revolutions is living to some purpose."[3] By late November he was back in Paris. He had not forgotten Burke, sending him a glowing account of the Revolution's progress in a letter (17 January 1790) that would also figure in the *Rights of Man*.[4]

On 9 February 1790 Burke attacked the Revolution in a speech in Parliament, and Paine was surprised to learn that he soon intended to publish his meditations on the Revolution in a forthcoming pamphlet. Although Paine had already begun a book on the

French Revolution, he returned to London in order to respond to Burke in a book that eventually became the *Rights of Man.* Apparently believing that Burke's forthcoming attack on the Revolution constituted an attack on himself, when he arrived in London in late March 1790, he waited impatiently for Burke's *Reflections* to appear. In the interval, Paine claimed that he met occasionally with Burke and that they both had agreed not to discuss the French Revolution, since Paine intended to reply to Burke's pamphlet. Paine was also meeting with Burke's political enemies, including those Burke would later call New Whigs, who were supporting the Revolution.

Burke's *Reflections* appeared on 1 November 1790, and Paine immediately started the first part of the *Rights of Man,* which appeared on 16 March 1791. Returning to Paris sometime between 7 March and 7 April, he worked through the spring on the second part of the *Rights of Man.* In Paris, he met with liberal republicans such as Condorcet, the Abbé Sieyès, and Nicolas de Bonneville, cofounder of the *Cercle Social,* which Paine would later associate with. Shortly after the royal family's flight and capture at Varennes (21 June), Paine and four French men (including Condorcet and Brissot) formed a Republican Club and started a brief journal, *Le Républicain,* which opposed the restoration of Louis and espoused the transformation of France into a republic. On 1 July, Paine and another member of the Republican Club plastered the walls of Paris and the doors of the National Assembly with a fiery manifesto Paine had written, advocating a republic.

On 4 July Gouverneur Morris, who would soon be the American Minister in Paris, wrote in his diary that Paine was "inflated to the eyes and big with a litter of revolutions."[5] Indeed, on 2 July 1791 Paine had returned to England, hoping to inspire revolutions in England and Ireland. On 4 November he proposed a famous toast to "the Revolution of the World," but he sensed that English public opinion was turning against France and suspected, correctly, that the English government was trying to harass him.

On 16 February 1792 the second part of the *Rights of Man* was published and was, like the first, a resounding success. While the English government had ignored part one, which had also criticized, *inter alia,* the British constitution, it decided to make an example of Paine, informing him on 21 May that he was to appear in court on 8 June. Paine was not intimidated and continued giving antigovernment speeches; on 6 June he addressed an open letter to Henry Dundas, the Home Secretary, welcoming government prosecution and ridiculing the English government. For unexplained reasons, the government, on 8 June, postponed Paine's trial until December.

On 10 August the French monarchy was effectively overthrown when a prefabricated mob stormed the Tuileries and the royal family fled to the National Assembly. On 19 August Lafayette, to whom Paine had dedicated part two of the *Rights of Man* and who had tried, unsuccessfully, to move his army against Paris in the days following 10 August, abandoned the Revolution and was captured by troops from Austria, with whom France had been at war since April. While Paine approved of the monarchy's overthrow, he was stunned by the ensuing September Massacres (2–6 September 1792) and later recalled how they were used by the Revolution's enemies to influence British public opinion.

Meanwhile, electoral assemblies in France had chosen deputies for the newly formed National Convention, and Paine was selected, on the third ballot, to represent the department of Calais, along with Robespierre and three others. Previously, on 26 August, the National Assembly had officially made him an honorary French citizen of the new French republic. Consequently, Paine left for Calais on 12 September. When he arrived in France, Paine was given a rousing welcome and immediately threw himself into French politics and plans for a world revolution. In late September Paine and John Frost, an English attorney and a member of the English prorevolutionary Society for Constitutional Information, advised and provided information to John Oswald, a Scottish radical and soon-to-be commander of the First Battalion of Pike-Bearers (Oswald later died fighting the rebels in the Vendée). On 30 September Oswald, in what David Erdman calls "a nicely orchestrated presentation," addressed the Jacobin Club, informing its members about the counterrevolutionary activities of Peter Thellusson, identified as the French Consul in London. Oswald hoped to provoke a diplomatic incident by having Thellusson recalled or returned to France. According to Oswald, whose source was Paine and Frost, Thellusson was discrediting the Revolution and trying to prevent arms from being sent to France by English admirers. Erdman notes that "Oswald, advised by Paine and Frost, must have realized that action upon this accusation would be likely to initiate a series of perilous diplomatic events that might lead to war—and an English Revolution."[6]

Paine's enthusiasm for revolution was also expressed in his association with Nicolas de Bonneville, a Parisian intellectual and co-founder of the *Cercle Social* (1790–93), a revolutionary club and publishing company. Conventionally, Bonneville and *Cercle Social*

members have been characterized as a group of liberal intellectuals intent on reinterpreting the Enlightenment in wake of the
French Revolution. Recent scholarship, however, suggests a more
radical role. Bonneville, for instance, envisioned the *Cercle Social*
as an elite intellectual vanguard that would prepare the European
people for a series of apocalyptic revolutions. In 1789 Bonneville
saw his new journal, *Le Tribun du Peuple,* "as a 'circle of light,'
whose writers were to transform the world by constituting themselves as 'simultaneously a centre of light and a body of resistance.'"[7] Bonneville envisioned closed circles of purified
intellectuals who would help regenerate the world by initiating the
ideological revolution against despotism.

In the first issue of *Bouche de Fer* (October 1790), the principal
journal of the Social Circle, Bonneville had promoted a "'different
superior power'" that would "conduct censorship and denunciation
in defense of the revolution. Its mission was 'universal surveillance' on behalf of that 'multitude of good citizens who are not yet
enlightened enough to know what they desire.'" There seems to
have been a series of correspondent revolutionary clubs in Utrecht,
Geneva, Genoa, Philadelphia, and finally London, "where
Bonneville had lived and written just prior to the Revolution and
where a printing press and formal branch of the Social Circle were
founded under 'one of our English franc-brothers'—John Oswald"[8]—Paine's fellow revolutionary in Paris who had given the
speech to the Jacobins on 30 September 1792. Although it is possible that Paine had earlier met Bonneville and other future members
of the Social Circle such as Oswald and Brissot in London, he
cooperated with Social Circle members in the campaign for a republic following the king's capture at Varennes (21 June 1791), and
his name appeared on the title page (his portrait was featured on
the frontpiece) of the May 1792 issue of *La Chronique de Mais,*
another Social Circle publication, four months before he left London for Paris.[9] Since the National Convention had declared war
on Austria on 20 April, Paine apparently endorsed the Girondin
war effort: his name replaced that of Collot d'Herbois, who disapproved of the war.[10] On 25 September, less than two weeks after
Paine's arrival in France, Bonneville published Paine's latest essay,
Address to the People of France, in which Paine suggested that
French armies would liberate countries oppressed by "despots"
(*CW,* 2:539–40). In October, Paine was writing for the *Chronique
de Mais.* Although Paine subsequently insisted he was not a parti-
san of any revolutionary party, the Social Circle was, in fact,
aligned with the Gironde (several Social Circle publications were

secretly funded by the Roland government in 1792), a fact that would soon cause him problems.

On 11 October the National Convention selected Paine and seven Frenchmen to write a new Constitution for the French republic. In the same month, Paine met with Edward Fitzgerald, an influential Irishman who had come to Paris seeking his aid in abetting a revolution in Ireland. On 19 November the National Convention issued its controversial decree declaring that the French nation would help all peoples wishing to recover their liberty. On 4 December Paine endeavored to interest Pierre Lebrun, Minister of Foreign Affairs, in a revolutionary plan: France would contribute two hundred thousand pounds sterling and Irish revolutionaries would commence an Irish revolution. Cautiously interested, Lebrun approved a secret trip by Colonel Eleazer Oswald, an Irish-American officer whom Paine had known during the American Revolution, to see if the Irish people were ready for a revolution (they were not). David Erdman notes that Eleazer Oswald "had been assigned" as Paine's "secret-service aide" and had traveled earlier to London, in October 1792, to see if the English were also ready for a revolution.[11] This suggests that Lebrun had given Paine authority to use Oswald as a French intelligence agent. Paine was deep in the revolutionary game.

By November 1792 a group of British republicans in Paris had organized and begun to initiate activities ranging "from military involvement to amateur or official spying." This was the infamous "British Club," of which Paine was a member. In November 1792 the British Club, in conjunction with the French government, was making grandiose plans for a world revolution that would overturn all oppressive governments. Paine's task was to write a universal republican Constitution and to "cooperate with the war office to supply French assistance for an insurrection in Dublin."[12] Paine had previously argued that universal principles would spread inevitably throughout the world, but he had apparently decided that these principles could be accelerated and advanced with some pointed force.

On 18 December 1792 Paine was tried and convicted *in absentia* in London for his "seditious" attack on the British government in the *Rights of Man*. On 11 January 1793 Paine and Robert Merry, both members of the British Club, proposed that the Club send an address to the National Convention requesting a war to liberate the British people. The proposal was voted down by one vote, but a "second address" was later presented to the Convention.[13]

During this time, Louis XVI was being tried for treason against the French nation. In the *Rights of Man,* Paine had rebuked Burke for worrying needlessly over the French king's safety, informing him that the French Revolution constituted an attack on despotic principles, not on an individual person (*CW,* 1:256). The discovery of the *Armoire de Fer,* the secret box containing documents compromising the king, in November 1792, changed this idealistic formulation. Although he voted with the majority in the National Convention to try the king, Paine argued against his execution, proposing that he should instead be exiled to America (but detained in France until the war's end), where he could be reeducated and enlightened. On 19 January 1793 Paine had another address translated and read to the National Convention, but Jean-Paul Marat interrupted the reading twice, once to protest that Paine should not be allowed to vote on the king's death since he was a Quaker (he was not) and hence presumably against capital punishment, and again to insist that the words being read were not really Paine's (they were; see Paine, *CW,* 2:556–58). Louis was guillotined on 21 January. Paine never again mentioned his trial or death.

On 1 February the National Convention declared war on Britain and Holland, but power had shifted from the Girondins to the Mountain, and Paine realized belatedly that he had made enemies by associating himself with Girondist positions. On 18 March French troops under General Dumouriez, whom the Girondins had earlier embraced as "their" general, were defeated by the Austrians. Dumouriez defected to Austria on 5 April. The next day, the National Convention named the nine members who would compose the Committee of Public Safety.

In the same month, Paine complicated his situation by taking on Jean-Paul Marat who, as president of the Parisian Jacobin Club, had sent a letter to all the provincial clubs, urging that "traitors" within the National Convention be murdered. In conjunction with Brissot, Paine tried to discredit Marat by suggesting that his republican beliefs were suspect and by exaggerating a suicide attempt by William Johnson, an Englishman and fellow boarder in Paine's house, who supposedly had killed himself, believing that Paine had been targeted for death by Marat. Unfortunately for Paine, Johnson lived, even though he was reported dead in Brissot's newspaper, *Le Patriote.* All this figured in the trial of Marat, who had been charged by his Girondist enemies in the Convention with a series of crimes and who proceeded to make Paine's misrepresentations an issue rather than his own threats. It was an awkward affair for Paine, who, under cross-examination, modified or contradicted himself on various points. On 24 April Marat was acquitted by judges appointed by the Girondists and then was carried shoulder-high from the court back to the Convention by his enthusiastic followers. Paine had inadvertently helped to discredit his own Girondist friends.

Suddenly, Paine was pessimistic about the French Revolution. In a letter to Thomas Jefferson (20 April 1793), he observed that had "this Revolution been conducted consistently with its principles, there was once a good prospect of extending liberty through the greatest part of Europe; but I now relinquish that hope"; indeed, "as the prospect of a general freedom is now much shortened, I begin to contemplate returning home" to America (*CW*, 2:1331). On 6 May he wrote Georges-Jacques Danton, lamenting "the distractions, jealousies, discontents, and uneasiness that reign among us, and which, if they continue, will bring ruin and disgrace on the Republic." Paine was especially concerned with Jacobin denunciations of twenty-two Girondist deputies in the Convention and was apparently attempting a reconciliation with Marat, whom he had written on the same day "but not on the same subject" (*CW*, 2:1335–38).

On 31 May the Parisian sections surrounded the National Convention, and the Convention's members were soon forced to expel the twenty-two proscribed Girondist deputies, who were arrested and later executed. On the same day, Paine had approached the Convention and was warned away by Danton, who told him his name might also be added to the list of endangered Girondists. Paine subsequently dated the Revolution's fall on 31 May (see *CW*, 2:600, 606).

Disillusioned and depressed, Paine retired from the Convention, trying to remain unnoticed. Although he had indirect contact with the Committee of Public Safety, which had sought his advice on American affairs, Paine decided in the autumn of 1793 to return to America, as he informed Bertrand Barère, a Committee member, on 5 September. By 3 October however, he was still in Paris, where he was denounced in the Convention, along with Girondist leaders, as a traitor to the Revolution. In the same month, Robespierre had written an ominous memorandum: "Demand that Thomas Paine be decreed of accusation for the interests of America as well as of France."[14] Through Barère and others, Robespierre probably knew that Paine intended to return to America and, consequently, decided to have him imprisoned, apparently fearing that he would harm Franco-American relations.

Paine subsequently claimed that he had expected to be arrested and that he was not surprised when agents of the Committee of

General Security arrived and eventually conducted him to the Luxembourg prison on 28 December. (He finished the first part of *The Age of Reason* shortly before his imprisonment and completed the second part after his release.) In late February 1794, French authorities prohibited all communication with prisoners; consequently, Paine had no contact with anyone outside for six months. He later recalled that between the middle of March 1794 and the fall of Robespierre, life in the Luxembourg was one of tension and horror—prisoners being continually removed, executed, and, fancifully, that he himself had been marked for execution but had providentially escaped when the door to his room (etched with a number in chalk) had been marked while the door was open (the door opened "outward and flat against the wall"), so the fatal number appeared on the "inside" when it was closed at night "and the destroying angel passed by it" (*CW*, 2:921).[15] In June Paine caught a fever and was delirious for five weeks. He later speculated that the illness had probably saved him from the guillotine. Fortunately, some fellow inmates and the prison physician attended him, and he recovered just before Robespierre's fall (29 July 1794). In August he was relieved to learn that Gouverneur Morris had been replaced by the new American Minister, James Monroe.

Paine wrote a series of letters to Monroe, asserting his claim to American citizenship and urging him to work for his liberation. On 4 November Monroe finally effected Paine's release. He had been imprisoned ten months and nine days.

Invited as a temporary guest, Paine spent the next year and a half in Monroe's house. Although he had opportunities to return to America, Paine chose to stay, informing Samuel Adams by letter (6 March 1795), that "as I am embarked in the Revolution, I do not like to leave it till it is finished" (*CW*, 2:1375). Paine now had time to brood over the reasons for his imprisonment, becoming convinced that Robespierre's terrorist regime and Washington's "Federalist" administration had conspired to silence him—a subject I will later consider in detail.

Because Paine continually railed against the American President and American foreign policy (for example, Federalist policy exemplified in the Jay Treaty) from the home of the American Minister, an embarrassed and compromised James Monroe (who privately shared Paine's views) asked him to desist. Paine temporarily acquiesced but then began again. Monroe felt further compromised when he began suspecting that Paine was leaking confidential information that Monroe had given him, in order to ingratiate himself with the French government. In a letter to James Madison (5 July

1796), Monroe complained that he had not expected such "ingratitude" from Paine[16]—the thematic word Paine associated with Washington's "betrayal." In the spring of 1796, Monroe had finally asked him to find other lodgings.

For the remainder of his time in France, Paine was generally supportive of whatever government happened to be in power. Although he had various opportunities to return to America, he remained in France until 30 October 1802, when, invited by Thomas Jefferson, the American President, and encouraged by a "republican" administration in America, he returned to his adopted country and quickly began redefining himself in relation to the two revolutions he believed he had fathered. This exercise in self-definition, however, had begun as early as 1776 when Paine began conceiving himself as the creator of the American Revolution and continued in his conception of himself as the creator of the French Revolution. Both creations begin with the creation of Thomas Paine.

II

When Paine first arrived in America in 1774, he began to reinvent himself anew. He changed his name from Pain to Paine and in 1776 connected himself with the incipient American Revolution, consummating the break with his native country. With the publication of *Common Sense* (1776) and the *American Crisis* essays (1776–83), Paine formulated a new political identity, continually defining himself in terms of his revolt and opposition to England, a country representing the postlapsarian past he wanted to expunge. In *Common Sense,* he developed a political parable in which kings and hereditary succession are equated with "original sin" and hence the political fall of the old European world (*CW,* 1:5, 10, 12–14). He dated a new time and a new thinking, beginning with the battles of Lexington and Concord (17–18), and referred to the "birthday of a new world," insisting that he and the Americans "have it in our power to begin the world over again" (45). Later, in the *Rights of Man,* he traced pristine revolutionary origins to "the case and circumstances of America," which "present themselves as in the beginning of the world." Hence, in the "inquiry into the origin of government," there is no need "to roam . . . into the obscure field of antiquity," since "[w]e are brought at once to the point of seeing government begin, as if we had lived in the beginning of time" (1:376). It is a myth of origins that he took literally. To Paine, there was a factual connection between the birth of a new nation and the rebirth of Thomas Paine, present at the Creation.

When he refers to his three major works—*Common Sense* (1776), the *Rights of Man* (1791–92), and *The Age of Reason* (1794–95), he frequently places them in context of his political birth and the origins of a new revolutionary world. He envisions his Trinitarian oeuvres creating a new revolution in America, France, and Europe. In *The Age of Reason,* he refers to *Common Sense* and his realization "that a revolution in the system of government would be followed by a revolution in the system of religion" (*CW,* 1:465). By revealing timeless "principles" creating the conditions for political change, Paine conceived himself as the creator of a new political world in which he had the privileged position of founding father. Throughout his writings, he is consumed with his own legitimate sources which he contrasts with his enemies' bastard origins.

By 1790 Paine saw the French Revolution as a reflection, a repetition of the American Revolution he believed was reproducing a series of world revolutions originating from principles he had established in 1776. In a letter to George Washington (21 July 1791), Paine feels "that principle is not confined to time or place, and that the ardor of Seventy-six is capable of renewing itself"—i.e. his commitment to a second revolution (*CW,* 2:1319). Paine connects these consanguineous revolutions through metaphors of repetition and reflection—through the similarities with which he conceives and hence sees them. But when these similarities turn into differences, he angrily seeks to explain the discrepancies as a treacherous betrayal of the principles he had produced.

In the *Rights of Man,* the French Revolution originates in America: French soldiers fighting in the American Revolution carry the principles of the Revolution back to France, creating the psychological conditions for the French Revolution (see *CW,* 1:299–301). Indeed, as David Wilson notes, the *Rights of Man* is as much about the American Revolution as it is the French Revolution.[17] America as a "cause" of the French Revolution was, of course, a cultural commonplace shared initially by "the friends of liberty" in both America and Europe. Richard Price, for instance, concludes his *Discourse on the Love of Our Country* (1789) with a dramatic image of light reflected from America to France, where it turns into a liberating blaze which "lays despotism into ashes and warms and illuminates Europe."[18] In the *Rights of Man* (1792), Paine announces that from "a small spark kindled in America, a flame has arisen not to be extinguished" (1:398). After he returned to America in 1802, Paine referred to himself as the "spark" of 1776.

In contrast, those who deplored the French Revolution denied it had any similarities with the American Revolution. John Quincy Adams, for example, translated a pamphlet by Friedrich von Gentz, who stressed the dissimilarities between both Revolutions. Adams felt that the pamphlet had absolved the American Revolution "from the disgraceful imputation of having proceeded from the same principles as the French."[19]

For Paine, however, the luminous link between both Revolutions was himself. Consequently, the language he uses to represent both is reflexively repetitious. In *Common Sense,* he proclaimed that the "cause of America is in a great measure the cause of all mankind"—"the sun never shone on a cause of greater worth" (*CW,* 1:3, 17). In a letter to Henry Laurens (14 September 1779), he declares it was the universal "Cause itself that irresistibly engaged me in [America's] support" (2:1178). Likewise, it is Paine's connection to the American "cause" that links him to the French Revolution. In the *Rights of Man* (1791), he remarks that every "country in Europe considers the cause of the French people as identical with the cause of its own people, or rather, as embracing the interests of the entire world" (1:247). In his *Address to the People of France* (1792), "the cause of France is the cause of all mankind" (2:538; cf. 540, 1315). He sees both Revolutions as a universal struggle between darkness and light, and he sees himself reflected in both through the universal principles (representative, republican government and the rights of man) that produced them. Using a language of resemblance and correspondence, Paine conceives himself as the original "cause" of both Revolutions.

In this context, he traces the origins of both revolutions to a psychological revolution implicitly initiated by himself. In *Common Sense,* he refers to the psychological transformation of the American mind—"a new method of thinking has arisen"—constituting a radical break from the past and the commencement of a new political era (*CW,* 1:17)—a thinking and a commencement reified in *Common Sense.* In the third *American Crisis* (1777), he refers to "the progress which independence has made on the minds of the different classes of men" (1:89), tracing this progress to three principal causes that produced the war of "independence"—causes appearing, not coincidentally, as compelling "reasons" for independence in *Common Sense* (see 1:19, 22, 25–27, 30, 33, 35, 41, 44). In his *Letter to the Abbé Raynal* (1782), Paine announces the consummation of the psychological revolution: "Our style and manner of thinking have undergone a revolution more extraordinary than the political revolution of the country" (2:243). The allusion to his own role as the producer of this revolution via *Common Sense* is repeated a decade later when he refers to the *Rights of Man* (1791) as a "work, written in a style of thinking and expression different to what had been customary in England" (1:348). In his letter on *Constitutional Reform* (1805), he informs the people of Pennsylvania that by "the event of the [American] Revolution we were put in a condition of thinking *originally*" (2:1003; my emphasis)—the adverb simultaneously suggesting a new manner of thinking as well as a return to the original principles proclaimed by Paine in 1776. Throughout his works, Paine causally connects political revelation to linguistic liberation, suggestively contending that his liberating words prepared both the Americans and the French for their respective revolutions.

In the *Rights of Man,* he notes that the French Revolution is the "consequence of a mental revolution previously existing in France"; indeed, "the mind of the nation had changed beforehand, and the new order of things had naturally followed the new order of thoughts" (*CW,* 1:298). He traces this mental revolution to Enlightenment writers and "a spirit of political inquiry [which] began to diffuse itself through the nation at the time the dispute between England and the then colonies of America broke out" (299): that is, the time Paine started producing his own enlightened works. Indeed, in his characterization of previous enlightened writers (Montesquieu, Voltaire, Rousseau and the Abbé Raynal, Quensay, and Turgot), he qualifies his praise by observing that (because of the time in which they were living) these writers could only go so far. Finally, however, the "spirit of political inquiry" exploded in 1776 (1:299).

Since Paine sees the French Revolution reflected in the American Revolution, he repetitiously makes the same points about both. For instance, he wrote his *Letter to the Abbé Raynal* (1782) to correct what he believed were erroneous impressions about the American Revolution expressed in Raynal's *Révolution d' Amérique,* which had appeared in English translation in 1781. Paine informed Raynal that the American people "cannot again go back to ignorance and prejudice. The mind once enlightened cannot again become dark. There is no possibility, neither is there any term to express the supposition by, of the mind *unknowing* anything it already knows"; consequently, America cannot be conquered because her mind cannot be conquered: it is impossible to recall "her back to her former condition of thinking" (*CW,* 2:244,

254). Similarly, in the *Rights of Man* (1791), Paine tells a benighted Edmund Burke, who had also written what Paine believed to be an erroneous book about the French Revolution, that "though man may be *kept* ignorant, he cannot be *made ignorant*": "it is impossible to put the mind back to the same condition it was in before it saw . . . There does not exist in the compass of language, an arrangement of words to express so much as the means of effecting a counter-revolution. The means must be an obliteration of knowledge; and it has never yet been discovered how to make a man *unknow* his knowledge, or *unthink* his thoughts" (1:320). Paine, in effect, connects counterrevolution in America and France with the impossible endeavor to expunge the liberating knowledge he himself has revealed.

Likewise, in his *Address to the Addressers* (1792), Paine links the inquisitional endeavor of the English government to ban the *Rights of Man* with the futile censorship that caused the Old Regime in France to fall: once "thought" gets "abroad in the world," it "cannot be restrained, though reading may" (*CW,* 2:481). Paine had made this point earlier in the *Rights of Man:* once "principles" are "abroad in the world . . . no force can stop them. Like a secret being told, they are beyond recall" (1:444).[20] These thoughts and principles are of course part and parcel of Paine's revealable "knowledge" that cannot be suppressed or "recalled."

In the fourth of *The Forester's Letters* (1776), Paine had observed that when "precedents fail to spirit us, we must return to the first principles of things for information; and *think,* as if we were the *first men* that *thought*" (*CW,* 2:83). Although Paine occasionally observed that he had merely discovered universal principles latently present in human history, he also created a self-perpetuating fiction making himself not only the discoverer but the originator of these principles. In his conception of himself as creator of world revolution, Paine initially conceived himself as one of "the first men," but he subsequently began linguistically eliminating rivals that existed, in his mind, as "originators" or founding "fathers," so that, in the end, he remained the sole creator of the modern revolutionary world. Paine used this self-creating fiction to crystallize his vision of revolution as well as to explain counterrevolutionary "apostasy" and "betrayal."

From 1787 to 1793 Paine continually referred to America, insisting, at one point, that he had America "constantly" in his "mind in all [his] publications" (*CW,* 2:694). On 16 March 1790, he informed an anonymous correspondent that he wished "most anxiously" to see his "much loved America. It is the country from whence all reformation must originally spring" (2:1286). Indeed, this was his principal thesis during the initial stage of the French Revolution: American (that is, "universal") principles would effect a regenerative world revolution. In the March 16 letter, he notes that he will be leaving Paris for London, carrying "the key to the Bastil[l]e," which Lafayette had given him to "present to General Washington" and which he intends to send "by the first American vessel to New York" (2:1285–86). The symbolism is significant, since Lafayette, the Hero of Two Worlds, returns to Washington, via Paine, the "key" opening despotism's prison. As the crucial link between the American and French worlds, Paine sees himself as the liberating key of both revolutions. In a letter to George Washington (1 May 1790), Paine fleshes out the metaphor: "I feel myself happy in being the person through whom the Marquis has conveyed this early trophy of the spoils of despotism, and the first ripe fruits of American principles transplanted into Europe, to his master and patron. . . . That the principles of America opened the Bastille is not to be doubted; and therefore the key comes to the right place" (2:1303). Since Paine thinks of himself as the discoverer and revealer of American principles, he becomes the liberating link between both Revolutions—"the person through whom" Lafayette returns the original "principles" opening both revolutions.

In the *Rights of Man,* he allusively refers to his role in both revolutions as the revealer of the liberating principles transforming the world: America shocked despotism, existing as "the only spot in the political world, where the principles of universal reformation could begin" (*CW,* 1:354). The American Revolution "led to a discovery of the principles, and laid open the imposition, of governments" (1:360). Alluding to himself as the Columbus of the new political world, revealing error and discovering principles (cf. 1:488; 2:750), when he celebrates America as the original source of world reformation, Paine celebrates himself as the principal source of world revolution.

In his role of discoverer and revealer of universal principles hidden and suppressed by despotism, Paine employs metaphors of provenance and priority, through an argument from origins establishing his privileged position as the discoverer of principles having "no connection with time" (*CW,* 2:483)—principles that are prior to the prescriptive traditions of his antirevolutionary enemies. As early as *Common Sense,* he contrasted the evil "origins" of despotic kings and governments with the new beginning he prophesied for America: "We have it in our power to begin the world over again. A situation, similar to the present, hath not happened since the days of Noah until now. The birthday of a new world is at hand" (*CW*, 1:45). The allusion implicitly posits a revolutionary Jehovah cleansing the corrupt world by creating it anew. Beginning by envisioning the regeneration of America and the world as a collective national endeavor, Paine's messianic vision culminated with himself as the exclusive creator of the new revolutionary world.

By 1802, in a series of open letters addressed *To the Citizens of the United States,* he was promoting himself as the sole survivor of both revolutions and hence the only existing originator. In his eighth and final letter (1805), which he subsequently described as "the most important of any I have published" (*CW*, 2:1468), Paine returned to his beginning as the creator of America, quoting himself in *Common Sense* and thus associating his "first" words with America's creation:

> It was the opportunity of *beginning the world anew* . . . and of bringing forward a *new system* of government in which the rights of *all* men should be preserved that gave *value* to independence. The pamphlet *Common Sense,* the first work I ever published, embraced both those objects. *Mere* independence might at some future time, have been effected and established by arms, *without principle,* but a *just* system of government could not. In short, it was the *principle,* at *that* time, that produced the independence; for until the principle spread itself abroad among the people, independence was not thought of, and America was fighting without an object. Those who know the circumstances of the times I speak of, know this to be true. (2:956)

Paine sees himself as both liberator and destroyer, for the principles he reveals regenerate the new world through the destruction of the old world. But in order to present himself as the source of world revolution (a revolution starting with America and spreading to France, Europe, and beyond), he had to eliminate linguistically any rivals or competitors, whether it was his principal linguistic rival—God and the Bible—or Washington, the "father" of his country. There is, as we will see, a connection between Paine's linguistic assassinations and his logocentric conception of himself as the author of world revolution.

III

Looking back and contemplating himself in the wake of two revolutions, Paine contended that his books had created both. But his original self-conception started with his creation of the American Revolution. In a letter to Henry Laurens (14 January 1779), he suggested that *Common Sense* created the conditions for American independence, noting a cause-and-effect relationship between its publication and *The Declaration of Independence,* which followed "six months after it." Indeed, without *Common Sense,* Paine believed that "the Congress would not now have been sitting where they are" (*CW,* 2:1163). In a letter to the Speaker of the House of Representatives (7 March 1808), Paine informed him that he doubted if "independence would have been declared" without *Common Sense* (2:1495). In *The Age of Reason* (1794), he noted the same causal connection between *Common Sense* and American independence: "I wrote 'Common Sense' . . . and published it the first of January, 1776. Independence was declared the fourth of July following" (1:497). Since *Common Sense* actually appeared on 10 January, Paine suggests that he inaugurated a new political era starting on the first day of the new year. In a letter to the United States Senate (21 January 1808), Paine asserts that *Common Sense* "awakened America to a declaration of independence" (2:1490). In his final will (18 January 1809), Paine refers to *Common Sense* awakening "America to a declaration of independence on the fourth of July following, *which was as fast as the work could spread through such an extensive country*" (2:1498; my emphasis). In the thirteenth *American Crisis* (1783), Paine had connected "the cause of America" with his literary, political identity: "It was the cause of America that made me an author" (1:235). In *The Age of Reason* (1794), he noted that he would "never have been known in the world as an author on any subject whatever had it not been for the affairs of America" (1:497). By 1802, he was still producing these procreant themes: America was the "place of my political and literary birth. It was the American Revolution that made me an author" (2:926; cf. 992). But the real connection, for Paine, was his original authorship of the revolution he created.

In a letter to Robert Morris (20 February 1782), Paine was "thinking and ranking [himself] among the founders of a new Independent World" (*CW,* 2:1207); in a letter to the Continental Congress (October 1783), he refers to the satisfaction he derived "from the idea of being ranked among the founders of a New Empire raised on the principles of liberty and liberality," but he suggestively narrows the field of founding fathers by observing that *Common Sense* changed American thinking and hence made the Revolution possible (2:1228–29; cf. 1241, 1255).

In the *Rights of Man,* Paine is still preoccupied with his own beginning as the founder of the free world. After referring to his old-world origins in England, he moves "from such a beginning" (*CW*, 1:405) to his new unprecedented status of literary, political creator: "I have not only contributed to raise a new empire in the world, founded on a new system of government, but I have arrived at an eminence in political literature, the most difficult of all lines to succeed and excel in, which aristocracy, with all its aids, has not been able to reach or to rival" (1:405–6). This is followed by a triumphant footnote proclaiming that he thinks independently without relying on other people's opinions and books. He then proceeds with a self-congratulatory reference to *Common Sense*, a pamphlet whose success "was beyond anything since the invention of printing" (406)—presumably including the Bible. Paine's point is that the principles he revealed (published) made both Revolutions possible. He thus sees himself as the focal point where both Revolutions intersect, for just as the French Revolution reflects the principles of the American Revolution, so the *Rights of Man* reflects principles established in *Common Sense*.

In his first letter *To the Citizens of the United States* (1802), he notes that the "principles" of the *Rights of Man* "were the same as those in 'Common Sense;'" and the *Rights of Man*, like *Common Sense*, "had the greatest run of any work ever published in the English language" (*CW*, 2:910). Referring to the *Rights of Man*, in May 1792, Paine refers to himself "as the author of . . . one of the most useful and benevolent books ever offered to mankind" (2:444); in June 1792, he declares that he does not believe that "there are found in the writings of any author, ancient or modern, on the subject of government, a spirit of greater benignity, and a stronger inculcation of moral principles than in those which I have published" (2:446; cf. 461).

Paine's celebration of himself as the author of books producing revolutions also makes him the *author*, "the person who originates or gives existence to anything," of these revolutions (*OED*, definition #1; definition #6 is "The Creator"). His denigration of other "authors" and books is at one with his effort to exclude or linguistically suppress any rival source or founder. In a conversation with Paine (8 July 1791), Étienne Dumont, a Genevan who had been Mirabeau's secretary, was astounded by his self-conceit: "He believed that his book on *The Rights of Man* could take the place of all the books of the world, and he said to us quite sincerely that if it were in his power to demolish all the libraries in existence he would do it without hesitation so as to destroy all the errors of which they were the depository—and with *The Rights of Man* begin a new chain of ideas and principles. He knew by heart all his own writings and knew nothing else."[21] Paine's proclamation of himself as the author of a new political world generated his revisionist strategy to expunge or "read out" of existence anyone he felt threatened his privileged position. His obsession with his own origins coincided with his obsession with the origins and sources of his antirevolutionary enemies. In the *Rights of Man* (1791), for instance, he thematically bastardized and "belated" Burke's sources and origins: the British constitution and the authoritative documents Burke cites in the *Reflections*.[22] He berated Burke for concealing the ominous origin of the traditional authority he celebrated—the illegitimate English constitution was the bastard child of William the Conqueror and the Norman Yoke. Thus, for a "monarchial talker," like Burke, "[a] certain something forbids him to look back to a beginning, lest some robber . . . should rise from the long obscurity of time, and say, *I am the origin!*" (*CW*, 1:319). Paine asserted the superiority of his "historical" account of the French Revolution, which he opposed, to Burke's "theatrical" fiction. He focused on origins and "causes" that Burke suppressed in order to underscore this distinction and to showcase Burke's counterrevolutionary tragedy. In this context, I want to consider Paine's account of the Bastille's fall and the October Days of 1789 before reconsidering the ways in which he eliminates textual enemies and rivals. For Paine, superior revolutionary history exposes the fiction of Burke's counterrevolutionary drama.

2

Paine's Revolutionary Comedy: The Bastille and October Days in the *Rights of Man*

Paine's version of the Bastille's fall and the October Days of 1789 comprehends a thematic contrast to the suppressions, distortions, and misrepresentations in Burke's *Reflections*. Like other revolutionary respondents, he focuses on the October Days to highlight the difference between Burkean theater and revolutionary history, and he amplifies Burke's "silence" on the Bastille to show how Burke suppresses inconvenient facts. In addition, he condemns Burke for not dealing with the Revolution's "commencement or progress." This is because, according to him, Burke does not understand the origins of the Revolution; consequently, Burke was astonished when it "burst forth" (*CW*, 1:298). In contrast, Paine contends the Revolution was "the consequence of a mental revolution previously existing in France," and he traces this revolution to "the writings of the French philosophers" and the American Revolution. He also provides an account of the events leading up to and prefiguring the Revolution—the financial crisis, the Assembly of Notables, the calling of the States General; in short, a series of causal events that Burke fails to mention (see 290–313).

But Burke had, in the *Reflections*, presented his version of the Revolution's origins and commencement, referring, just as Paine does, to the Enlightenment as an ideological source. In addition, he refers to the growth of "a great monied interest," the economic expansion of the bourgeoisie, as a cause of the Revolution (*Reflections*, 209–10), which, coupled with the influential power of a new class of intellectuals—the "Men of Letters" who revolutionized public opinion by discrediting the institutional values of the Old Order—made the Revolution a reality (211–14). He also refers to the class suicide of French nobles who "countenanced too much that licentious philosophy which has helped to bring on their ruin" and the unnatural separation of new money and old landed wealth, which created unnecessary resentment and distinctions (244–45).

He criticizes revolutionaries who cite as "causes" historical injustices that are disguised pretexts for their own injustices (247–48; see 173–74 for other causes). By contending that Burke does not deal with the commencement or the "causes" of the Revolution, Paine misrepresents Burke by suppressing what Burke says these causes are. Both Burke and Paine, of course, select those facts and events that support the thesis they want to push. Burke, not surprisingly, is more interested in enumerating the causes of the Revolution's inevitable failure. Paine castigates Burke for ignoring or suppressing facts or causes because Burke's facts and causes are not his.

Paine focuses on the events of 14 July because, for him, this epochal date marks the start of the real revolution prepared by the prior mental revolution. In contrast, he notes that "through the whole of Mr. Burke's book I do not observe that the Bastille is mentioned more than once," except for a couple of slight references Paine later acknowledges in a footnote (see *CW,* 1:259–60). Burke, indeed, does not deal with the fall of the Bastille—an event and "tower" that had immense symbolic significance for revolutionaries. (Paine acknowledges the Bastille's symbolic significance when he writes "the downfall of it included the idea of the downfall to despotism" [261].) Before the Revolution, however, it had already been decided that the Bastille was, in effect, useless and needed to be destroyed to make way for urban development. Burke considered the Bastille's fall unimportant. In a letter to an anonymous correspondent, in January 1790, he noted that they both knew that "the destruction of the *Bastile,* of which you speak, . . . was a thing in itself of no consequence whatever":

> The *Bastile* was at first intended as a citadel undoubtedly; and when it was built, it might serve the purposes of a citadel. Of late, in that view, it was ridiculous. It could not contain any garrison sufficient to awe such a city as Paris. As a prison, it was of as little importance. Give despotism, and the prisons of despotism will not be wanting, any more than lamp-irons will be wanting to democratic fury.[1]

Burke did not deal with the Bastille's destruction because, unlike Paine, he did not consider 14 July as the beginning of the physical revolution, which he dates on 6 October 1789, with the invasion of the king's palace at Versailles and the forced removal of the royal family to Paris (*Reflections,* 175).

Paine, nevertheless, dwells on the events leading up to 14 July and focuses on the Bastille to reveal the real reason for Burke's silence: Burke is callously unmoved by despotism's suppressed victims—the victims languishing in the prison the Revolution opens (*CW,* 1:260). He contends that Burke cares only for the theatrical sufferings of anachronistic kings and queens; thus, in his famous aphorism, Burke "pities the plumage, but forgets the dying bird" (260). Paine, however, does something characteristic of the revolutionary historiography of the time: he refers to abstract victims without mentioning the real victims; he celebrates the opening of the Bastille and the symbolic fall of despotism without mentioning the specific victims liberated on 14 July. It is not coincidental that Paine is also silent about despotism's flesh-and-blood victims, since there were only seven prisoners when the Bastille was taken: four forgers, tried and convicted; two lunatics, shortly returned to an insane asylum; and one nobleman incarcerated, at his family's request, for libertinism. This fact does not fit Paine's revolutionary script, so after one commiserating glance, he proceeds with his narrative. While he insists that Burke's "hero or heroine must be a tragedy-victim expiring in show, and not the real prisoner of mystery, sinking into death in the silence of a dungeon" (260), he himself exploits Enlightenment and revolutionary clichés dealing with the mysterious tragedy victims of the Bastille, silently expiring in despair.

Throughout the *Rights of Man,* Paine contrasts "the sober style of history," which he implicitly writes (*CW,* 1:269), with Burke's "theatrical representation" (258). He refers to Burke's "tragic paintings," his artful manipulation of facts to produce "a weeping effect," his demonization of the Revolution through "horrid paintings"—all illustrated in his "theatrical exaggerations for facts" (258–59, 267). Burke "should recollect that he is writing history and not *plays;* and that his readers will expect truth, and not the spouting rant of high-toned declamation" (259). In the *Reflections,* Burke had also accused Richard Price and other revolutionary sympathizers of producing melodramatic revolutionary drama: "There must be a great change of scene; there must be a magnificent stage effect; there must be a grand spectacle to rouze the imagination" (156). Allusively contrasting his response with the response of Richard Price exulting over the king's humiliation in the *Discourse,* Burke says he would "be truly ashamed" if he shed tears over the dramatic enactment of "such a spectacle" on stage, while exulting over it "in real life": "I should be truly ashamed of finding in myself that superficial, *theatric sense of painted distress,* whilst I could exult over it in real life" (*Reflections,* 175, my emphasis). Paine, in effect, ascribes to Burke the very thing Burke rejects:

"that superficial, theatric sense of painted distress." This suggests that Burke's condemnation of revolutionary drama provided Wollstonecraft, Paine, and others the terms with which they condemn Burke. Since Paine is also selectively rewriting the Revolution so that it accords with his interpretation of facts, the distinction between Burke and himself disappears within the context he himself establishes.

Paine's language, for instance, illustrates that he is also producing drama; the imagery he selects to highlight the significance of the Bastille's fall is both theatrical and artful: "The mind can hardly *picture* to itself a more tremendous *scene* than which the city of Paris *exhibited* at the time of the taking of the Bastille" (*CW*, 1:261, my emphasis). Likewise, "the representative system of government . . . presents itself on the open theater of the world" (373). Earlier, referring to the *Declaration of the Rights of Man*, his imagery is equally dramatic: "we see the solemn and majestic spectacle of a nation opening its commission . . . to establish . . . a scene so new, and so transcendently unequalled by anything in the European world" (1:317). Commenting on this passage, Tom Furniss notes, "That [Paine] repeats precisely what he repudiates Burke for shows how Paine works within the same paradigms as his adversary—especially when he tries to construe the Revolution as good rather than bad drama."[2]

Having accused Burke of selectively emphasizing or suppressing facts, Paine does the same, authoritatively citing the figure of twenty-five to thirty thousand foreign troops that surrounded Paris in July 1789—a figure he received in a letter from Thomas Jefferson (11 July 1789). He ignores, however, Jefferson's account of the events of 12 July (in a letter to Paine dated 13 July): a mob threw stones at the "German cavalry," provoking the cavalry to counterattack.[3] In Paine's version, "the Prince de Lambesc, who commanded a body of German cavalry . . . insulted and struck an old man with his sword," and the enraged French, "remarkable for their respect of old age," then "attacked the cavalry" with stones (*CW*, 1:263). Paine's preference for the revolutionary version clashes with his previous rebuke to Burke for ignoring the authoritative Thomas Jefferson—"an authority which Mr. Burke well knows was good" (1:261).[4]

Something similar happens in his account of the October Days, for what links his version of the fall of the Bastille and the October Days is his contention that Burke intentionally suppresses the "causes" of both events. He notes that he "cannot consider Mr. Burke's book in scarcely any other light than a dramatic performance; and he must, I think, have considered it in the same light himself, by the poetical liberties he has taken of omitting some facts, distorting others, and making the machinery bend to produce a stage effect" (CW, 1:267–68). Referring to Burke's "account of the expedition to Versailles" (Burke does not deal with the 5 October "expedition"), Paine insists that Burke begins his account by "omitting the only facts, which, as causes, are known to be true; everything beyond these is conjecture, even in Paris" (268). Paine then reveals the "causes" that Burke conceals—the causes that provoke the "people" into reacting: "It is to be observed throughout Mr. Burke's book, that he never speaks of plots *against* the Revolution; and it is from these plots that all the mischiefs have arisen. It suits his purpose to exhibit consequences without their causes. It is one of the arts of the drama to do so" (268). Since Paine establishes the principal criterion he uses to condemn Burke's book—the concealment of "causes"—he thematically compromises himself by making concealment an issue, since he engages in the very concealments he condemns. Jerome D. Wilson and William F. Ricketson observe that "Paine gives a very detailed account of events that led to the march as well as to the events in Versailles"[5]; Paine, however, excludes embarrassing events contradicting his version of "sober" history.

While he concedes that "the expedition to Versailles . . . still remains enveloped in . . . mystery" (CW, 1:268), he concentrates on the known causes: the "uneasiness" caused by the king's failure to sanction the *Declaration of the Rights of Man* and the August 4th Decrees (268–69), as well as secret machinations by the Revolution's enemies to provoke the march in order to use it as a pretext— hoping that the king would flee to Menz, "where they expected him to collect a force" and oppose the Revolution (270). In one ambiguous clause, Paine also implies that the patriotic crowd might have been infiltrated by enemies of the Revolution acting as *agents provocateurs* (270; 3rd par.). Although the last "cause" is conjectural, Paine's principal cause, in the revolutionary version he cites, is the trampling of the national cockade by the *Garde du Corps* in the banquet of 1 October (269). This, according to him, was the primary reason why the crowd gathered on 5 October—they marched to Versailles "to demand satisfaction" for the insult to the cockade, but "all this Mr. Burke has carefully kept out of sight" (269). In the *Reflections,* Burke had argued that the Convention Parliament of 1689 had gone out of its way to keep "from the eye" any hint of radical democracy in the Glorious Revolution (102). Paine suggests allusively that Burke similarly "keeps out of sight"

anything embarrassing or inconvenient (see also *CW*, 1:319, 434).
But Paine himself keeps out of sight one of the cardinal causes
of the march—at least as important as the bruised cockade—the
scarcity of bread in Paris. Paine evidently did not want to contend
that the scarcity of bread (a rather glaring omission) was a counterrevolutionary plot (a popular explanation for the "Great Fear" in
July 1789) to starve the people, so he suppresses this material
cause and concentrates on an indignant people marching to Versailles to vindicate the national cockade and the rights of man.
Indeed, the omissions in his account of the Bastille (the actual
prisoners) and 5 October (the scarcity of bread) underscore the
ideological nature of his narrative, since these "facts" do not fit
the story he is telling. Like Burke, he is often more interested in
ideological explanations rather than "material" ones.

In his narration of both events, Paine sees the Revolution in
terms of its political symbols—the attack on the Bastille is an attack on a symbol of despotism (*CW*, 1:261); the insult to the national cockade constitutes an attack on the Revolution, provoking
the march to Versailles. In addition, Paine either misses or keeps
out of sight Burke's reason for omitting the events of 14 July and
5 October: dating the Revolution's commencement on 6 October,
a revolution "which may be dated from that day" (*Reflections*,
175), Burke is not interested in the events of 14 July and 5 October.
These events do not figure in his antirevolutionary script. It would
be difficult for Paine to attack Burke's interpretation of when the
Revolution actually began (and hence what is really important)
because he could only counter with his own interpretation. He
hence ascribes motives that explain why Burke really conceals the
evidence that he contrastingly reveals.

In Paine's march to Versailles, there are other omissions that
color his narrative. For instance, no one in his revolutionary crowd
has any sort of weapon—no pikes, no muskets, or cannons—the
latter celebrated in contemporary prints commemorating the
march. Hence he does not mention that the "very numerous body
of women, and men in the disguise of women, collected around the
Hôtel de Ville" (*CW*, 1:270) had also ransacked the Hôtel, coming
away with weapons and ammunition. Nor does he mention the
forced recruitment of other women in Paris or on the road to
Versailles.[6]

When he discusses how Lafayette, as commander of the National
Guard, "set off after them" (*CW*, 1:270), he fails to mention that
Lafayette tried to stall for hours and was reluctantly compelled by
his own troops to go to Versailles[7]—another remarkable omission,

since Paine cites Lafayette as one of his personal sources (*CW*, 1:270, n. 1). Paine also omits that once the crowd arrived at Versailles, hundreds of women invaded the National Assembly, creating momentary havoc, nor does he mention the king's meeting with a small delegation of the women, whom he charmed. In Paine's sanitized narrative, all threatening violence is "kept out of sight," so it does not conflict with his narration of events.

When he discusses the events of 6 October, there are more glaring omissions. For instance, in his version, a member of the despised *Garde du Corps* appeared at a palace window, early in the morning, and insulted and then fired on the people who remained in the streets below—the cause of the people rushing "into the palace in quest of the offender" and pursuing *Garde* members "to the apartments of the King" (*CW*, 1:271). The crowd, however, had pursued the guards to the *queen's* apartments—the locale where Burke stages his tragic scene in the *Reflections* (164).[8] Moreover, Paine does not mention the bodyguards that were murdered before the mob reached the queen's apartment—something he would obviously have contested if he doubted it (cf. *Reflections*, 164). He again suppresses inconvenient facts contradicting the script he is writing.

The queen and the murdered bodyguards do appear elliptically in the next paragraph: "On this tumult, not the Queen only, as Mr. Burke has represented it, but every person in the palace, was awakened and alarmed; and M. de Lafayette had a second time to interpose between the parties, the event of which was, that the *Garde du Corps* put on the national cockade, and the matter ended, as by oblivion, after the loss of two or three lives" (*CW*, 1:271).

Paine's account of the queen merely "awakened and alarmed," just like everyone else, curiously omits any reference to Burke's account of the queen leaping from her bed and barely escaping as a frenzied revolutionary mob breaks in and pierces her bed with a hundred sharp strokes (*Reflections*, 164). Since Paine is specifically contrasting his representation with Burke's, his silence on Burke's specific representation is again telling, since he evades rather than contests it. In the second part of the *Rights of Man*, he tasks Burke for not refuting the "principles" contained in the first part: "I am enough acquainted with Mr. Burke, to know, that he would if he could" (*CW*, 1:349)—a statement that could be appropriately applied to himself. Likewise, he omits the fact that the queen then fled to the king's quarters and that Lafayette (and members of the National Guard) had "interpose[d] between the parties" to prevent the retreating guards from being massacred, not to break up a fight between two contending forces. In addition, the ambiguous allusion to "the loss of two or three lives" is a belated reference to the murdered bodyguards, whose heads were soon affixed to pikes. Paine underscores the silences in his text by having "the matter ended, as by oblivion," after the ambiguous "loss of two or three lives." This "oblivion" corresponds to the suppression of facts and causes that Paine insists Burke keeps "out of sight" (269).

Paine's facts are not Burke's facts. But since he makes a thematic issue out of revealing Burke's dishonest "silences" and contesting Burke's fabricated "facts," he exposes his own vulnerable representation to the same criteria. If, according to Paine, Burke suppresses "causes" and emphasizes "consequences," Paine, in addition to concealing causes, suppresses embarrassing consequences. Moreover, by making Burke's suppressions and distortions of facts examples of Burke's intellectual dishonesty, Paine's language betrays itself in acknowledging the forgetfulness, the "oblivion" by which so many details are conveniently changed or forgotten. Indeed, Paine knew that language can betrayingly reveal what is being suppressed or concealed. In an essay on the *Origin of Freemasonry* (1805), he anticipated what later became known as the Freudian slip: "It sometimes happens, as well as in writing as in conversation, that a person lets slip an expression that serves to unravel what he intends to conceal" (*CW*, 2:833–34).

One of the most remarkable omissions in Paine's narrative emphasis on "causes" is the conspicuous absence of the Duc d'Orleans, who, it was widely believed, had secretly financed and incited the crowd that marched to Versailles. The official inquiry conducted by the *Châtelet,* published in September 1790, had suggested "a vaguely defined Orleanist plot."[9] Indeed, Lafayette as well as the French court believed this, and, consequently, the Duc d'Orleans was exiled to London (21 October 1789–July 1790) on the pretext that he was on a secret mission to discover plots against the king! Lafayette, one of Paine's sources, informed the duke that he was being exiled. Moreover, Paine had referred to Orleans as a possible cause in his January (1790) letter to Burke—the letter he reproaches Burke for not heeding in the *Rights of Man* (*CW*, 1:244, 261, 297). In the letter, Paine informed Burke that "the March to Versailles has yet some mystery in it. I believe the Duke of Orleans knows as much of this business as any body knows. It certainly produced a Rupture between him and the Marquis de la Fayette. The Truth is that the Duke submitted to the proposal made to him of leaving the Kingdom. I am in this respect confident of the Authority I speak from. The Duke and the Marquis had some interviews . . . and it was agreed to cover his departure by an appearance of business."[10] Paine's "authority" is Lafayette himself—the restorer of peace and reconciliation in the *Rights of Man*. Orleans's presence, of course, would have complicated Paine's sanitized account of the patriotic crowd marching to Versailles to vindicate the national cockade. Thus two conspicuous causes are forgotten in Paine's representation: the scarcity of bread in Paris and the reputed role of the Duc d'Orleans.

After the "oblivion" of the palace invasion, Paine proceeds with his narrative: "During the latter part of the time in which this confusion was acting, the King and Queen were in public at the balcony, and neither of them concealed for safety's sake, as Mr. Burke insinuates" (*CW*, 1:271). But Burke insinuates nothing of the kind, since he refers to the royal family's "concealment" during the time the revolutionary mob was rampaging through the palace—not during their subsequent balcony appearance—a "scene" that Burke dispenses with, moving immediately to their forced journey to Paris (see *Reflections*, 164–65). Paine, one would think, could have made a stronger case by stressing that Burke, once again, conceals "causes," since, in Paine's narrative, the balcony is the scene of reconciliation, where the king freely chooses to return with his people to Paris. But by having the king and queen appear "in public at the balcony," Paine also dispenses with the solitary appearance of the apprehensive queen, who was, during a dangerous moment, compelled by the hostile crowd to appear alone on the balcony—a moment saved when Lafayette then appeared, bowed, and kissing the queen's hand, won the crowd over.

In Paine's next paragraph, everything is happily resolved: "Matters being thus appeased, and tranquillity restored, a general acclamation broke forth, of *Le Roi à Paris* . . . The King to Paris. It was the shout of peace, and immediately accepted on the part of the King. By this measure, all future projects of transporting the King to Metz, and setting up the standard of opposition to the Constitution, were prevented, and the suspicions extinguished" (*CW*, 1:271). In Paine's version, the king chooses freely to return to Paris, urged by the encouraging shouts of the patriotic crowd, rather than the intimidating insistence of the mob yelling, "*Le Roi à Paris*." Given Paine's emphasis on causes, it is again remarkable that he can suggest the king's return was not compelled by the insistent crowd that caused it.[11]

In addition, Paine omits the journey from Versailles to Paris, which Burke exaggeratingly highlights in the *Reflections*, where "the royal captives" are slowly led in triumph by a frenzied revolutionary mob (preceded by the piked heads of the murdered guards) for six harrowing hours (165). In one sentence, Paine has the royal family arriving in Paris and greeted "by M. Bailley, the Mayor of Paris" (*CW*, 1:271). Shortly after, he refers to the "procession from Versailles to Paris" in which "not an act of molestation was committed during the whole march," even though there were at least three hundred thousand people accompanying the king in the procession (272). Since Paine writes his sober history as a comprehensive contrast to Burke's fanciful drama, emphasizing Burke's distortions and suppressions of facts and events, his decision not to contest Burke's exaggerated script indicates that there were enough embarrassing details to compromise his revolutionary comedy—the happy ending of 6 October. For instance, if he had contested Burke's narrative, he would have had to address the guards' decapitated heads "stuck upon spears" (*Reflections*, 164–65)— heads that are "out of sight" in his own narrative. In addition, he would presumably have had to address what the (inflated) crowd of three hundred thousand was doing for six hours, for while there was no physical "molestation" of the royal family, the crowd carried a variety of weapons and sang insulting songs culminating in their cry that they were bringing "the baker, the baker's wife, and the baker's errand boy" back to Paris.[12] Paine consistently omits or forgets any suggestion of intimidation or coercion.

This becomes ironic when he chastises Burke for condemning Jean-Sylvain Bailly for calling 6 October "un bon jour," since, according to Paine, Bailly was referring to the "peaceful termination" of "the arrival of the King at Paris" (*CW*, 1:272). We have seen, however, that Burke's 6 October is certainly not Paine's and vice versa. As Frans De Bruyn notes, "history writing is as much a narrative or dramatic art as the writing of plays"; thus when Paine assigns "appropriate 'facts' and 'causes,'" he "ineluctably commits himself to his own narrative or version of events. He cannot do otherwise, for the effort to understand discrete historical events inevitably involves him in the articulation of a plot or story."[13]

After closing his "account of the expedition to Versailles," Paine cites the radical pro-revolutionary newspaper, the *Révolutions de Paris,* as a principal source for his version of the October days: "An account of the expedition to Versailles may be seen in No. 13, of the 'Révolution[s] de Paris,' containing the events from the 3rd to the 10th of October, 1789" (*CW*, 1:272, n. 8). One would assume that his source tendentiously confirms the story he tells, and to some extent it does: there is no mention of Lafayette's reluctance to march to Versailles (something Paine could have confirmed from Lafayette himself) or the invasion of the queen's apartment. But it is again precisely what is not seen in Paine's account that is revealing. For instance, *Révolutions de Paris* does mention the lack of food (that is, flour and bread) as a cause of the march; it mentions the crowd of women who went to the Hôtel de Ville, threatened to hang people from the lamppost, threw stones at the soldiers impotently protecting the Hotel, soldiers who retired, allowing "our brave amazons" (*nos braves amazonnes*) to enter and ransack the Hotel, taking away guns, ammunition, and cannons. In Versailles, it reports on a delegation of the women informing the National Assembly of the need of bread and mentions the king's meeting with another delegation and his sad acknowledgement of the lack of food. It reports that two of the king's bodyguards were injured on 5 October in altercations with the National Guard. It reports Lafayette arriving and telling the king that he has been sent to protect the king because he is not safe. On page 20, there is an engraving of the people (armed with pikes and cannon) who surround the royal family just before the latter are forcibly conducted to Paris.[14] In their detailed discussion of the October Days, Darline Levy and Harriet Applewhite reproduce the engraving as well as a translation of the caption accompanying it: "The National Guard of Paris and Versailles, numbering more than 20,000, not counting the more than 12,000 men and women, armed with various weapons, who complained to the King about the lack of bread in the capital, pressing the King to establish his residence in Paris."[15]

The *Révolutions'* account of 6 October is also telling. In the early morning of 6 October, it is the crowd gathered outside that provokes a bodyguard inside the palace to fire, killing a National Guard, providing the crowd the opportunity to invade the palace and search for the culprit. Erroneously believing they have found him, they take an innocent man outside, cut off his head, and affix it to a pike, which is then paraded to Paris. In various other places of the palace, the crowd arrests other members of the bodyguard, and one, trying to calm the crowd, is piked to death. A third one is killed by a National Guard who is forced by the enraged crowd to decapitate the victim. Another mob ransacks the bodyguards' quarters, while others continue looking for other guards and head towards the king's apartment. Later, when the royal family appears on the balcony, the king is so emotionally distressed that he cannot speak. When he does speak, he addresses the crowd with tears in his eyes and begs them to rescue his beleaguered bodyguards.[16] In the very source Paine cites, there appears the causal bread, the intimidating weapons, and the decapitating violence that are all kept out of sight in his march to and from Versailles. By making an issue out of Burke's fabricated drama and his own objective history, the distinction between Burke and himself implodes. By highlighting Burke's concealments of details he wants kept out of sight, he reveals his own concealments by ironically making concealment an issue: he exposes his own concealments precisely when he is revealing Burke's.

In one of his mocking condemnations, Paine characterizes Burke's method of producing bad counterrevolutionary drama: "Mr. Burke brings forward his bishops and his lantern, like figures in a magic lantern, and raises his scenes by contrast instead of connection" (*CW*, 1:272). But this is also Paine's method of writing revolutionary drama, for he casts Burke into the role of textual counterrevolutionary villain and proceeds to contrast his reactionary "scenes" with his own progressive ones. Paine's "causes" are counterrevolutionary conspiracies and insults that contrastingly provoke the revolutionary heroes he celebrates: Lafayette, the vanquishers of the Bastille, the National Assembly, and the vindicated rights of man. He brings forward his revolutionary heroes, like figures in a magic lantern, and connects his scenes through contrasts.

Paine's critique hence provides the very terms for reading his comedic drama: his representation of the *Reflections* mirrors his own reading of the Revolution—the suppressed origins and causes kept out of sight. His emplotment of revolutionary history as comedy reflexively complements Burke's antirevolutionary tragedy— both write "out" the "other" French Revolution. Paine poses again as the revealer of causes and hence asserts his authoritative control over the Revolution's rewriting. But it is Paine's rewriting of himself that is fundamentally central to his conception of the American and French Revolutions. Having announced the reflective triumphs of both revolutions in the *Rights of Man,* he subsequently explained their betrayals in his *Letter to George Washington.* Because the meaning of both revolutions is at one with the history of Thomas Paine, the *Letter to Washington* constitutes a crucial ideological move in Paine's discourse, since, as we will now see, counterrevolutionary betrayal legitimizes Paine's claim to be the true author of both revolutions.

This chapter, for different reasons, also appears in *Intertextual War: Edmund Burke and the French Revolution in the Writings of Mary Wollstonecraft, Thomas Paine, and James Mackintosh* (Fairleigh Dickinson University Press, 1997.)

3

Revisionist Patricide: Thomas Paine's *Letter to George Washington*

THOMAS Paine's *Letter to George Washington* (1796) is one of the most overlooked and underrated works of his *oeuvre*. It has been conventionally read as a polemical piece that Paine had written after being imprisoned in revolutionary France—convinced that Washington had personally betrayed him by acquiescing in his incarceration during the Terror.[1] The *Letter,* however, constitutes a crucial ideological move by Paine to rewrite himself as the author of both the American and French Revolutions. Throughout his writings, Paine engages in a series of linguistic assassinations of "founding fathers" in an endeavor to (author)ize himself as the Ur-source of linguistic revolution, repeatedly empowering himself through the texts in which he rewrites himself as the Ur-Creator. This was his predominant personal fiction, and *The Letter to Washington* particularly underscores the intertextual links between public texts and private histories. In this chapter, I explore the rhetorical strategies that underwrite Paine's *Letter* (and texts) through the historical truth Paine insists he is writing. Because Paine inscribes a variety of historical contexts in the *Letter,* I begin by providing the immediate context (Paine's imprisonment in France and the historical circumstances coloring the *Letter*) and then refocus my thesis before proceeding to show how other Painean texts also impinge on the writing (and reading) of the *Letter.* I conclude with a close analysis of Paine's *Letter* and its place within his revolutionary *oeuvre*. The *Letter,* as we will see, emerges as a founding document in Paine's presentation of himself as the linguistic creator of world revolution.[2]

I

After the second part of the *Rights of Man* was published in February 1792, Paine moved to France (September 1792), where he was imprisoned in the Luxembourg (December 1793–November 1794) and emerged subsequently convinced that Robespierre and Washington were responsible and had conspired to silence him. The memorandum written by Robespierre ("Demand that Thomas Paine be decreed of accusation for the interests of America as well as of France") was, for him, testimonial proof that the Federalist and Jacobin "factions" had mutual conspiratorial interests. In a letter to James Madison (24 September 1795), Paine initially contended that Robespierre had interpreted Washington's silence as implicit approval of his imprisonment, speculating that Washington and the Federalists had wanted him imprisoned either "to gratify the English government" or to turn American public opinion against the Revolution—or perhaps to prevent him from denouncing Washington's Federalist administration (*CW,* 2:1380). Robespierre and the Jacobins, in turn, wanted him incarcerated so that he would not return to America and reveal their betrayal of the Revolution in France.

Once released, Paine had brooded obsessively on his own "betrayal," approving an undeclared naval war (1795–96) between France and America that resulted in the capture of hundreds of American ships having traffic with England and publishing an essay in a Parisian newspaper (12 September 1798) in which he provided the French government practical advice on how to conquer America: rather than invade on land as the British had fruitlessly done in the American Revolution, proceed up the coast of America, starting with Savannah, with a fleet of gunboats—the "master blow would be to finish at Halifax" and then "move down to New Orleans, take possession of the port of Natchez, call on the friends of liberty [that is, those Americans supporting the French Revolution and opposing the Federalists] in the back ports of the United States, from Kentucky to the Southern limits of English America." Paine was, in effect, proposing a second American Revolution with, as in the first, French assistance.[3]

It is within this context that Paine's *Letter to George Washington* (1796) has been conventionally read: an embittered Thomas Paine—after suffering and fearing for his life—emerges from prison (his health affected) and learning of Robespierre's memorandum and the "Federalist" Jay Treaty, becomes obsessed with the idea that he had been personally betrayed by Washington. All this is undoubtedly true, but there are other crucial contexts that directly impinge on the writing and the reading of the *Letter.* Although Paine's *Letter* has been given scant attention, it is thematically pertinent to his self-conception as founding father of the

American and French Revolutions as well as his role as the original writer of world revolution. Given what he feels were his invaluable services to the American Revolution, Paine angrily accuses Washington of "traitorous" ingratitude—an indictment connected with earlier complaints of American ingratitude. His ambivalence towards his adopted country (which he associates with Washington) resonates throughout the *Letter,* allowing him to establish a conspiratorial link between Robespierre's "Jacobin" regime and Washington's Federalist "faction": by doing "nothing" to effect Paine's release, Washington conspired with Robespierre to keep Paine "silent"—a conspiratorial "betrayal" that coincides with the betrayal of both Revolutions. This conspiratorial thesis allows Paine to engage in a radical revision and erasure of Washington's role and place in the American Revolution and, causally, to reaffirm his own role and place within the French and American Revolutions. In one of the most reflexively intertextual letters of the postrevolutionary period, Paine, in effect, writes Washington out of the Revolution while writing himself into his place as America's founding father.

II

In "Familial Politics: Thomas Paine and the Killing of the King," Winthrop D. Jordan shows how Paine, in *Common Sense,* turns George III into a "pretended father" who cruelly slays his American children and hence turns the American revolt into an act of symbolic regicide.[4] In his *Letter to George Washington* (1796), Paine engages in a more elaborate patricide—discrediting the false, treacherous father whom he himself replaces as America's true father.

In the *Letter,* Paine accuses Washington of presumptuously taking major credit for the Revolution's success and of flattering himself with "pompous encomiums." Consequently, "it is fair to examine" Washington's "pretensions" (*CW,* 2:717–18). Since Washington, Paine decides, in contrast to himself, did nothing politically, Paine proceeds to examine what he did militarily—for on this hinges Washington's unmerited fame (718). Not surprisingly, Paine concludes that Washington also did "nothing" militarily— any military successes were due to other American commanders (718–21).

Paine was, in effect, rewriting the fifth *American Crisis* essay (21 March 1778), in which he had praised Washington's generalship in context of American military successes. In a letter to Washington (31 January 1779), Paine had taken "the liberty" of mentioning that he had published the fifth *Crisis,* "at the time some discontents from the army and the country last winter were doing you great injustice": "I hoped that by bringing your former services in view to shame them out, or at least to convince them of their error" (*CW,* 2:1167). Likewise, in November 1802 Paine published his third letter *To the Citizens of the United States,* in which he claimed to have written the fifth *Crisis* to prevent the so-called Conway Cabal—the conspiracy of Washington's enemies to remove him as commander of the Continental Army—from doing just that. According to Paine, the "complaint" against Washington at that time was "that *he did nothing*" (2:922, Paine's emphasis; cf. 956). But it is also Paine's complaint, since in the *Letter to Washington* and other subsequent publications, he accuses Washington of doing nothing to get him released from prison and of previously "*doing nothing*" militarily in the war (2:718, Paine's emphasis again). The 1802 letter (to United States citizens) reveals that Paine was using the same complaint of the Conway Cabal in 1778 to discredit Washington's leadership—the very thing he was supposedly opposing in the fifth *Crisis.* Likewise, in Paine's *Letter to Washington,* one of the generals who gets credit for doing something militarily is Horatio Gates (718–19)—the general the Conway Cabal had pushed for Washington's position.

There is, additionally, a series of similarities between the fifth *Crisis* and the *Letter to Washington* that associates Washington allusively with America's enemies and betrayers. The first part of the *Crisis,* for instance, is also an open letter, albeit to the commander of the British forces, "General Sir William Howe" (*CW,* 1:106). In the *Crisis,* Paine taunts Howe with the very criticism he later uses against Washington: Howe did nothing—"unmilitary and passive," he hid himself "sleeping away the choicest part of the campaign in expensive inactivity" (1:115–16). Likewise, Washington, in Paine's 1796 *Letter,* "slept away [his] time in the field . . . and [had] but little share in the glory of the final event. It is time, Sir, to speak the undisguised language of historical truth" (2:695). There is, in addition, another connective context to Paine's references to both Howe and Washington's "sleeping." In 1777 Charles Lee, an American general and a military rival who wanted to replace Washington as commander of the Continental Army, was captured by British forces "while sleeping away from his army in an inn kept by a pretty widow."[5] In the fifth *Crisis,* Paine brilliantly projects this suppressed American embarrassment onto the British commander. In the *Letter to Washington,* this allusive context establishes yet another resemblance between Washington and a rival enemy. But Paine's own resemblance to the ungrateful Washington he is describing ironically subverts "the undisguised language of historical truth" he insists he is writing.

His "historical truth" is a radical revision of what he had previously written, turning General Washington into the metaphoric equivalent of General Howe: the commanding general of America's army suddenly resembles the commanding general of America's enemy. In this intertextual juncture, Paine metaphorically turns Washington into the "cold blooded traitor" that he had accused him of being in his letter (24 September 1795) to James Madison (*CW*, 2:1380). Washington thus "betrays" a resemblance to the enemy and in doing nothing militarily and in signing the Jay Treaty betrays his country and, of course, Thomas Paine. But Paine's "undisguised language of historical truth" also revealingly betrays and exposes his celebratory account of Washington in the fifth *Crisis* as a retrospective lie.

Indeed, the textual similarities highlight a discrepancy he himself had pointed to in his 1802 letter *To the Citizens of the United States:* his contention that he wrote the fifth *Crisis* to defend Washington from the charge he was doing nothing, even though Paine actually knew that "the black times of '76 were the natural consequence of [Washington's] want of military judgement"—deciding it was better to muddle on with Washington rather than distract the army into opposing "parties" (*CW*, 2:922). By suggesting that he had actually lied to protect Washington and America, Paine redirects the reader to the fifth *Crisis,* where he can see the similarities between Washington and Howe and realize that Paine is connectively accusing them both of the same thing. His defense, in retrospect, turns into an attack inscribed in the rewriting of Washington's role (and the fifth *Crisis*) in the "letters" of 1796 and 1802. Likewise, the fifth *Crisis* intertextually intersects and impinges on the revisionist writing and reading of both the *Letter to Washington* (1796) and the third letter *To the Citizens of the United States* (1802). Paine's retrospective emphasis on historical intentionality (Paine protecting the inactive Washington in the *Crisis,* disguising Washington's military role and the military crisis Washington had created) belies his insistence on historical truth, since he subsequently subverts his prior representation of Washington in the *Crisis,* rewriting both Washington and himself.

Moreover, Paine (in the *Letter to Washington*) subtly links Washington's "betrayal" with Benedict Arnold's "defection," even though he seemingly contrasts Washington's common "constancy" with Arnold's inconstancy (*CW*, 2:718). But the entire *Letter* is an extended exposé of Washington's inconstancy: the hypocritical, "*treacherous friend*" (713) who betrays America and France via the Jay Treaty (708); the inconstant President who leaves Paine languishing in prison; the double dealer whose private and public relations reveal the contradiction between what he publicly professes and what he privately does; the dubious military commander who endangers his country by doing nothing; in short, the treacherous betrayer who resembles another inconstant betrayer of his country—Benedict Arnold. Washington hence resembles enemies and betrayers (Howe, Lee, Arnold), just as Paine, as we will see, comes to resemble the "traiterous" Washington. (Washington, "the cold blooded traitor" [2:1380], felt personally betrayed by Arnold, whom he had befriended and assisted, just as Paine felt personally betrayed by Washington, whom he "betrays" in the *Letter.*) The deceptive contrast between Washington's "constancy" and Arnold's "inconstancy" disappears in a textual assault exposing Washington's voluminous betrayals. The theme of betrayal is, however, curious from the Thomas Paine who textually associates himself with the Conway Cabal and hence betrays his former commander and the friend who had helped him receive economic compensation for his services to America. It resembles the thematic "ingratitude" with which he accuses Washington and is doubly curious coming from the traitorous patriot who, in 1798, had proposed an invasion of America in *Le Bien informé*.

There is another "traitorous" link between the fifth *Crisis* and the *Letter to Washington*. In the *Crisis*, Paine provides an overview of American military successes from 1776 to 1778, but in the *Letter* he provides a selective overview of the same events in terms of Washington's failures. Throughout the *Letter*, he blames Washington for his "silence" and hence his betrayal of Paine, but a comparison of both military accounts underscores Paine's own silences. Suddenly what were Howe's failures in the *Crisis* (for example, Long Island in 1776) are Washington's (cf. *CW*, 1:111 with 2:719). In the *Letter*, Paine omits references to Washington's military successes (successes mentioned in the *Crisis*), especially Trenton and Princeton (see 1:112). There is another telling intertextual context. In *Letter to the Abbé Raynal* (1782), Paine had accused Raynal of misrepresenting American military successes at Trenton, Princeton, and Long Island by either omitting them or skipping over the relevant facts (2:222–27). American successes were due, Paine insists, to Washington's superior "generalship" (2:224). In the *Let-*

ter to Washington, Paine engages in the very omissions he had earlier accused Raynal of committing.

With regard to Washington's leadership, Paine, in the *Crisis,* refers eulogistically to the "superiority of [Washington's] generalship, as will ever give it a place in the first rank in the history of great actions." In the "close struggle of life and death" in 1776, the "unabated fortitude of a Washington prevailed," saving "the spark [of human freedom] that has since blazed in the north with unrivalled lustre" (*CW,* 1 : 112, 114). Presenting Washington as the savior of America ("suspended by a thread"), Paine feels "a triumph of joy at the recollection of [America's] delivery, and a reverence for the characters which snatched her from destruction. To doubt *now* would be a species of infidelity, and to forget the instruments which saved us *then* would be ingratitude" (113).

But this is precisely what he does in *The Letter to Washington:* "reverence for" Washington's "character" is changed into character assassination, and in the revisions and suppressions he "forgets" everything he previously wrote, constituting the very "ingratitude" the *Crisis* indicts and which he projects, in the *Letter,* onto Washington.[6] Paine's texts return to haunt him; hence he engages in an exorcisory rewriting of Washington's role in American history. It is as if, in his patricidal assault, he writes "out" his own covert sense of ingratitude. The language of forgetfulness and ingratitude, in the *Crisis,* returns in terms of Washington's ingratitude in forgetting Paine. Referring to his imprisonment, in the third letter *To the Citizens of the United States,* Paine recalls that "my only hope then rested on the Government of America, that it would *remember me.* But the icy heart of ingratitude, in whatever man it be placed, has neither feeling nor sense of honor" (*CW,* 2 : 922). "Ingratitude," as he noted in 1786, "has a short memory" (2 : 397).[7]

III

During the War of Independence, Tories had accused the American colonists of ingratitude—the unnatural ingratitude of American "children" toward their English "parent"—a strong, symbolic relationship Paine had attacked in *Common Sense* (1776). Gratitude was also, according to Montesquieu and other Enlightenment writers, the primary motive for obedience in a republican government and, consequently, its founding principle. In 1789 American "gratitude" to France became a cardinal issue for republicans during the first Federal Congress, which convened in New York in April. By

1793 Federalists were arguing that since revolutionary France had guillotined Louis XVI—the man responsible for French aid—the debt of gratitude was not owed his murderers. In turn, republicans argued that gratitude was owed to the office or country, not the man—an ironic "English view of gratitude and of inherited obligation," which Paine and other revolutionaries had formerly rejected. Thus there was a historical, semantic context that colored the usage of both *gratitude* and *ingratitude* in the eighteenth century.[8]

Ingratitude is of course the word Paine had hurled at Washington ever since his release from the Luxembourg: private ingratitude to Paine and public ingratitude to France. The word occurs frequently in his writings, and it functions as a thematic indictment in the *Letter to George Washington* (see *CW*, 2:691, 693, 695, 701, 721). In the *Letter,* Washington's "treachery" and "ingratitude" to Paine is conflated with his treachery and ingratitude to France. Paine, for instance, quotes approvingly the French government's official response to the Jay Treaty: "*that the French Republic had rather have the American Government for an open enemy than a treacherous friend*" (*CW*, 2:713, Paine's emphasis; cf. 712, 715). Likewise, Washington is "treacherous in private friendship" and "a hypocrite in public life" (723; cf. 706). Thus it "is as well the ingratitude as the pusillanimity of Mr. Washington, and the Washington faction, that has brought upon America the loss of character she now suffers in the world" (721)—a loss of character corresponding with Paine's character assassination of Washington as the embodiment of the Federalist "faction" and hence the false embodiment of America.

In this sense, Paine's attack was both a personal attack and an assault on the public myth of Washington as the primary founding father—a mythical Washington already accepted by his contemporaries as the historical Washington as well.[9] Indeed, Paine's attack on Washington corresponds to his attack on George III in *Common Sense*. In the latter, Paine "rejected the hardened, sullen-tempered Pharaoh of England for ever; and disdain the wretch, that with the pretended title of *Father of His People* can unfeelingly hear of their slaughter, and composedly sleep with their blood upon his soul" (*CW*, 1:25, Paine's emphasis). Paine always returns to 1776, and in the 1796 *Letter,* I suggest, he attacks yet another "father figure"—the "pretended" father who coldly betrays his country and friends. If *Common Sense* is the symbolic regicide of the false royal father, the *Letter to Washington* constitutes the revisionist patricide of the "false" democratic father. In addition, Paine's parricidal rage generates another connective theme in the *Letter:*

Washington's "ingratitude" to Paine and France is associated with America's ingratitude to Paine and France.

Writing to Jefferson in April 1797, Paine informed him that France was "enraged" with America's "ingratitude and sly treachery," referring to the "mean, ungrateful, and treacherous conduct of her administration" (*CW*, 2:1387, 1389). France's "rage" is, of course, also Paine's rage, and his accusation that America had been ungrateful to France (in light of French aid during the American Revolution) issues from earlier complaints that America had also been ungrateful to him.[10]

During and after the War of Independence, Paine continually tried to obtain economic compensation from both the Continental Congress and the individual American states—compensation he felt he deserved, given his endeavors during the war.[11] In letters to friends, including Washington, he frequently refers to American "ingratitude" (see, for instance, *CW,* 2:1185, 1224, 1227, 1233–34, 1244, 1348, 1357). Writing to a Committee of the Continental Congress (October 1783), Paine reviews his many services to the American "cause" and refers, throughout, to American ingratitude, noting, towards the letter's end, that the "cold conduct of America towards me for my past services has disabled me from rendering those I now wish to do," rendering "the character of America as unfavorable to letters and literary studies" (2:1241). By 1795 there was a connection in Paine's mind between American ingratitude during and after the war and American ingratitude during his imprisonment, and the connection was that in both cases America did *nothing* for Paine—the charge with which he castigates Washington in the "letters" of 1796 and 1802. Likewise, just as, following the Revolutionary War, Paine argued that America's failure to compensate him reflected on America's "character," so in his letters to James Monroe during his imprisonment, he contended that America's failure to get him released also reflected on America's character—in both instances he suggested that world opinion would be shocked by America's ingratitude to one of her principal liberators (see 2:1203, 1206, 1224, 1227, 1244, 1356–57, 1359, 1361, 1363). Similarly, in the *Letter to Washington,* Washington's ingratitude reflects pejoratively on Washington's character.

The language he uses in the 1780s to indict America's ingratitude is the same he uses in the 1790s to indict Washington's ingratitude. This linguistic identification of Washington with America (and in this period Washington was, in many ways, America) illustrates that in attacking Washington, Paine was also attacking America. In the 1783 letter to the Continental Congress, for instance, Paine's reference to America's "cold conduct" (*CW,* 2:1241) reappears later in references to Washington's cold conduct. (On 30 November 1781, Paine had written Washington a letter complaining of America's "cold" treatment [2:1203].) In his letter to Madison (24 September 1795), Paine accuses Washington of conducting a "cold and callous line of office" and of acting "the part of a cold blooded traitor" (2:1380). In the 1796 *Letter,* Washington is "cold"; he commits a "cold deliberate crime of the heart"; his "cold and unmilitary conduct" and "cold defense" almost loses America (2:698, 710, 695, 719).

Likewise, there is a connection between what Paine feels America owes France and what America owes him. In his letter to Jefferson (1 April 1797), the language he uses to represent France's rage reflects his own rage and resentment: "You ought not to be surprised if in the issue of this business [the Jay Treaty], France should demand reimbursement for the expense she was at in supporting the independence of America, for *she feels herself most rascally treated for that support*" (*CW,* 2:1390, my emphasis; cf. 1392, last two lines, and 1395). This suggests that just as he identifies America with Washington's ingratitude and treachery, so he identifies France with his own rage and demands for reimbursement. In a letter (26 April 1797) to "Citizen Skipwith" (Fulwar Skipwith, the U.S. Consul General in Paris), Paine angrily quotes an "official letter" from Timothy Pickering, the American Secretary of State, which had appeared in a Boston newspaper. In the letter, Pickering denies that America is obligated to France "for her services during the War" or that France is "entitled" to American "gratitude." Such sentiments, Paine notes, will "widen the breach between America and France" (2:1392; cf. 614). Indeed, there was also a widening breach between Paine and America, culminating in his 1798 invasion proposal.

The connection between both Paine's and France's "aid" to America appears again in the *Letter to Washington.* Engaging in a series of self-conscious comparisons, Paine informs Washington that "[t]he part I acted in the American Revolution is well known," associating himself with France and the crucial "aid" that saved America: "I know also that had it not been for the aid received from France, in men, money, and ships, that your cold and unmilitary conduct (as I shall show in the course of this letter) would in all probability have lost America; at least she would not have been the independent nation she now is" (*CW,* 2:695). Quoting a letter he had previously written Washington (22 February 1795), Paine tells him that "I do not hesitate to say that you have not served

America with more disinterestness, or greater zeal, or more fidelity, than myself, and I know not if with better effect" (2:707)—an assertion first made in his letter to James Madison (24 September 1795) and later in his third letter *To the Citizens of the United States* (2:1380, 922). It is ironic, of course, to watch Paine boasting publicly of his disinterested services to America and then privately insisting on compensation for these services, especially as he had praised Washington in the *Rights of Man* for serving America without pay (1:381). Even more ironic is his insistence that he is militarily superior to Washington, since he did something in the war while Washington did nothing.

After the Revolution, Paine contends he continued extending revolutionary "principles" (in France) while Washington "rested at home," just as during the war he "slept away [his] time in the field" (*CW,* 2:707, 695). He suggests that Washington is jealous of his revolutionary activity and that is one reason why, when Paine was imprisoned, Washington "folded [his] arms" and "forgot" his "friend" and "became silent" (707). Thematically, one notes, Washington's conspiracy of *silence* is the equivalent of *doing nothing* in the war (718).[12]

Referring to Washington's "vanity" and his habit of expending "so many fine phrases upon himself," he reprobates the "pompous encomiums" Washington "so liberally pays to himself," which might lead a "stranger" to "suppose" that Washington "had generated, conducted, completed, and established the Revolution: in fine, that it was all his own doing" (*CW,* 2:695, 717–18). Paine, however, proceeds to do exactly this, praising himself as the real hero of the Revolution. Indeed, his description of the absurd, megalomaniacal Washington is an appropriate description of himself. After reviewing Washington's nonexistent military career, Paine contends that, consequently, by the end of 1780, "the establishment of the Revolution, was a thing of remote distance" (720).

He then presents himself as one of the principal saviors of the American Revolution, relating how, when the country was broke and in desperate straits, he and Colonel John Laurens went to France and persuaded its government to provide a loan (ten million *livres*), a present (six million *livres*), and "a fleet of not less than thirty" ships, which would be sent at France's expense, "as an aid to America" (*CW,* 2:721). (Laurens, at one point, wrote Washington that the "gift" of six million *livres* was due to "the exalted opinion which the [French] Ministers have of your Excellency and everything which comes from you"; see Flexner, *Washington,* p. 156.) On 25 August 1781, Laurens and Paine returned to

America with 2,500,000 *livres* and two ships filled with supplies.[13] He then announces the climactic result: "And it was by the aid of this money, and this fleet, and of Rochambeau's army, that Cornwallis was taken; the laurels of which have been unjustly given to Mr. Washington. His merit in that affair was no more than that of any other American officer" (2:721; note that Paine is the only surviving American savior: Laurens died in 1782, and the other "aid" is foreign). Suddenly, Washington's victory at Yorktown (the climactic battle of the Revolution) is revealed to be due to indispensable foreign aid and, of course, the personal aid of Thomas Paine.

But in directly celebrating his mission to France and the correspondent victory at Yorktown, Paine is again taking revisionist liberties. There are, for instance, a series of omissions and suppressions, beginning with the fact that Paine was neither directly nor officially involved with Laurens' mission to obtain French aid, while Washington was. After "diplomatic channels" had failed in gaining additional aid, the Continental Congress, using "Washington as if he were President," instructed him "to send a personal envoy." (Paine mentions Congress's role but not Washington's, *CW*, 2:720.) Washington selected Laurens, who was, in addition to being a trusted military aid, also fluent in French.[14]

Paine also fails to mention that, in mid-January 1781, he and Laurens spent three days conferring with Washington, who gave Laurens detailed instructions on the specific aid he was to request or that, while in France, Laurens was reporting to Washington; in other words, he does not mention that Washington was in charge of overseeing the entire mission.[15] More blatantly, Paine does not mention that he himself had nothing to do with the successful acquisition of French aid. When they arrived in France, Paine (who spoke no French) stayed initially in Nantes, while Laurens proceeded to Paris, where he began negotiations with French officials. When Paine arrived in Paris, he, to use his own phrase, did nothing—linguistically isolated, he socialized with other Americans, although David Freeman Hawke suggests that he drafted Laurens' "reports back to Congress and to the French Ministers."[16]

After Laurens negotiated future French aid, with Benjamin Franklin's artful assistance, he and Paine returned to America, arriving in Boston on 25 August, accompanied by two transports loaded with military supplies and 2,500,000 *livres*.[17] Although Paine had absolutely nothing to do with the successful acquisition of this aid, his self-association with Laurens in the *Letter to Washington* and in other accounts of the "mission" (see, for example, *CW*, 1:407; 2:959, 1233–34, 1490) make it seem as if he was also instrumental in bringing back the aid that supposedly saved America. In the *Letter to Washington,* for instance, while he carefully disappears when mentioning the acquisition of the aid in France, he reappears at John Laurens' side, bringing the crucial assistance to America: "Colonel Laurens and myself returned from Brest . . . taking with us . . . the money given, and convoying two ships with stores" (2:721).

Paine, in effect, disingenuously suppresses Washington's role, while he suggestively inflates his own nonexistent role. In addition, he implies that his providential mission was also connected to the crucial arrival of De Grasse's French fleet, which arrived in the Chesapeake "at the same time" that he and Laurens arrived in Boston (*CW,* 2:721; the fleet arrived 5 September 1781). Since, according to Paine, the French had agreed "to send a fleet of not less than thirty sail of the line" (721), he suggests a causal relation between Laurens' negotiations and the fleet's arrival. But the French had agreed to nothing of the sort: they had their own national interests and had decided earlier (in May) that De Grasse's West Indies fleet would be sent to the Chesapeake. The other fleet, commanded by Barras, which "afterwards" joined De Grasse's fleet also had nothing to do with the "Laurens-Paine" mission, as Paine implies (721).[18] Finally, in listing the third cause ("Rochambeau's army") for the victory at Yorktown and the hence unmerited "laurels of which have been unjustly given to Mr. Washington" (721), Paine neglects to mention that Washington had persuaded Rochambeau to link his army with the Americans at Yorktown and that Washington (through a series of elaborate decoys and ruses) had made it possible for both the French and American armies (the latter conspicuously unmentioned) to march 450 miles and arrive, unmolested, at Yorktown.

Earlier in 1781, however, Paine had acknowledged Washington's role at Yorktown. In a letter to Jonathan Williams (26 November 1781), he refers to Cornwallis and his men being "nabbed nicely in the Chesapeake" (*CW,* 2:1201). Four days later (30 November), he writes Washington, telling him that he is waiting to pay his respects and to "congratulate you on the success you have *most deservedly* been blest with"—presumably alluding to Washington's recent success (17 October) at Yorktown (2:1203; my emphasis). Paine's real motive, however, is to complain again of American ingratitude (significantly, he does not refer to Laurens' mission) and to underscore his own disinterested service to the "Cause of America": he has declined "the customary profits which authors are entitled to," assuming that if he dealt "generously and honorably" with

America, America would return the favor. Seeking compensation for his services, Paine is hurt to see America "cold and inattentive to matters which affect her reputation" (that is, her ingratitude to Thomas Paine). Even though he is now impoverished, he does not want "to expose" his economic degradation (so poor "I was obliged to hire myself as a common clerk"), since this would only "serve to entail on [America] the reproach of being ungrateful"—suggesting in the next clause that the embarrassing exposure of his plight "might start an ill opinion of [America's] honor and generosity in other countries, especially as there are pens enough abroad to spread and aggravate it." Indeed, Paine suddenly hints that he will soon be abroad in Europe, since "I cannot experience worse fortune than I have here"—a veiled threat that his presence (and pen) in Europe would "expose" American ingratitude (2:1203–4). He uses the same language of "coldness" and "ingratitude" referring to America that he would use in referring to Washington fifteen years later. It is almost as if in writing Washington, he subconsciously felt he was addressing America. The hint, at any rate, was clear: he wanted Washington, as usual, to do something, and Washington, as usual, did.

In a letter "To a Committee of the Continental Congress" (October 1783), Paine noted that Washington's "friendship" and his high opinion of Paine's "services" to America caused him to become "affectionately interested in the account I gave him" (that is, Paine's financial problems; cf. *CW*, 2:1207). Consequently, Washington "concerted with a friend or two to make my continuance in America convenient to myself until a proper time might offer to do it more permanently" (2:1236). In fact, what Paine alludes to (but does not say) is that Washington (along with Robert Morris and Robert R. Livingston) had arranged it so that Paine would receive eight hundred dollars a year to write for the United States government. The money was being drawn from a secret fund so that Paine would not be accused of being a government hireling.[19]

In contrast, Paine, in the *Letter to Washington,* suppresses Washington's role at Yorktown and erases Washington's military career, demoting his efforts to "that of any other American officer" (*CW*, 2:721). He emerges thematically as the sole self-sung hero of the American Revolution, repossessing the laurels that Washington presumptuously usurped. Moreover, in writing a republican romance of himself as savior of America, Paine resembles Washington in being the "real" hero of Yorktown and hence the personal savior of Washington and his (suppressed) army. There is a contextual connection between the letter (circa May 1780) in which he refers to the lack of supplies distressing Washington's army (describing Washington's distress in the same manner he later refers to his own) and his subsequent representations of himself bringing the crucial supplies that save both Washington and America: both of whom owe Paine the debt of gratitude. In short, having been "saved" by Washington on various occasions, Paine projects onto Washington his own ingratitude, becoming, in effect, the "real" Washington betrayed by traitorous Thomas Paine. Similarly, Washington resembles the real Thomas Paine, who projects onto him the very deceptions and boasting that Paine himself engages in. The figurations in this political, psychological role reversal (masks, doubling, betrayal, and identity) are doubly revealing in context of the "laurels" Paine usurps from Washington. In the *Letter,* the distortions, suppressions, and duplicities—the boasting and ingratitude projected onto Washington are telling signatures of his compulsion to rationalize his resentments and betrayals. The "undisguised language of historical truth" is a disguised language of historical lies, as Paine repeatedly reinvents himself as the author of 1776.

Having asserted that the Laurens-Paine mission helped save America, Paine glowingly highlights his pride in his revolutionary action: "I have had, and still have, as much pride in the American Revolution as any man, or as Mr. Washington has a right to have; but that pride has never made me forgetful whence the great aid came that completed the business" (*CW,* 2:721). In reminding Washington, and the reader, of French aid during the Revolution, Paine is also reminding us of his own aid during the Revolution, which Washington also "forgot" in supposedly acquiescing to Paine's imprisonment.[20] Paine promotes himself as the agent through which French aid saved the Revolution, and he alludes to his own aid in creating the conditions of the Revolution with the publication of *Common Sense* (1776): "Foreign aid (that of France) was calculated upon the commencement of the Revolution. It is one of the subjects treated of in the pamphlet 'Common Sense,' but as a matter that could not be hoped for, unless independence was declared. The aid, however, was greater than could have been expected" (2:721). In saying this, Paine causally connects *Common Sense* with the *Declaration of Independence,* something he repeatedly did from 1779 on. He calls attention to his aid in creating the Revolution and then sustaining it. The Revolution hence begins and ends with Paine, who excels Washington politically and militarily, since he brings the military aid that saves the Revolution while Washington does "nothing."

Paine and France's aid to America is contrasted with Washington's and America's subsequent withholding of aid and hence their ingratitude to both Paine and France. Since the French Revolution had deviated from his optimistic predictions in the *Rights of Man* and other works and since Paine had contended that the Revolution was caused by the American Revolution, which he had authored, Paine writes off any embarrassments (including his imprisonment) by insisting that he had been constant while Washington and other "factions" had not. If the Ur-revolution originates in America, so does the betrayal of its creator.

There is, in addition, another context for Paine's rage. In *Common Sense*, he had celebrated America as an "asylum" for the oppressed (*CW*, 1:31). The "new world hath been the asylum for the persecuted lovers of civil and religious liberty from *every part* of Europe" (19). On 30 November 1781, complaining again of American ingratitude, he wrote Washington "that the country which ought to have been to me a home has scarcely afforded me an asylum" (2:1204). Fourteen years later (20 October 1794), Paine, imprisoned in France, angrily reminded James Monroe that America was obligated to defend him because "the mass of her citizens are composed not of natives only but also of the natives of almost all the countries of Europe who have sought an *asylum* there from the *persecutions* they experienced in their own countries" (2:1371, my emphasis). The themes of asylum and persecution dovetail, I suggest, with those of ingratitude and betrayal, for in withholding aid and "asylum" to Paine, America, Paine believed, was betraying the revolutionary tradition he had commenced in *Common Sense*.

Paine of course personalized betrayal; for him, the real significance and tragedy of the Terror was his ten-month imprisonment in the Luxembourg. The conspiratorial betrayal by the Federalist and Jacobin factions explains the betrayal of both countries' revolutions. Since America is the primary cause of the true French Revolution and Paine is the efficent cause of the true America, he links the Revolution's fall with his own betrayal by Federalist America. In letters to James Monroe and James Madison, he suggests that if he had been able to return to America in 1793, if Washington had not betrayed him, he could have turned American and world public opinion against the Jacobins and somehow saved the French Revolution. Likewise, at the beginning of the Terror, if he had been able to write in French, he "would publicly have exposed" Jacobin "wickedness" (*CW*, 2:1349, 1353). Because the failures of the Revolution are due to the betrayals of Thomas Paine and his principles, he can ignore what he had previously written by returning to a mythic origin that absolves him from the embarrassments of history. Wollstonecraft, as will be seen, appeals to a future that will mysteriously justify the terrorist past; Paine evokes a mythical past to explain present betrayals of the revolutionary tradition he created.

There is a final context to Paine's *Letter*. After he was released from the Luxembourg, Paine began promoting himself as one of the last democratic survivors of the "true" French Revolution (the Revolution up to 1793)—a Revolution betrayed by Robespierre and the Jacobins. When he returned to America in 1802, he, likewise, presented himself as the surviving incarnation of 1776—returning to America to help defeat the Federalist faction—a faction that wanted to reimpose "monarchy" and hence betray the Revolution he had created (see *CW,* 2:909–10, 920, 926, 988, 1125, 1386, 1436, 1488). In the *Letter to George Washington,* Paine was already thematically positioning himself as Washington's revolutionary rival, tearing the mask off the counterrevolutionary betrayer while revealing himself as the principal founder and savior of America: returning at a crucial time in 1802 (just as he had in 1781) to again save a Revolution he had originated. His radical revision of Washington's role in the Revolution was a way of asserting his own origin as the true founder of the Revolution Washington had virtually lost and subsequently betrayed. It was an act of revisionist patricide by which he silenced a rival and rationalized his resentments.

In 1786 David Humphreys, one of Washington's former military aides, started a biography of his commander in chief. Referring to Washington's reproachless reputation, he thought it "remarkable that none of the professional scribblers have presumed to sully the brightness or vilify the grandeur of the Original, by giving (at full length) instead of a just likeness, a monstrous caricature."[21] Humphreys probably could not have imagined that just such a caricature would be forthcoming and that the Original would be sullied and vilified by Washington's former friend and ally, Thomas Paine.

4

From the Beginning: Paine's Obsession with Origins and *The Age of Reason*

I

In *The Letter to George Washington,* Paine had commenced a critique of what had gone wrong in America. There was, not surprisingly, a causal connection between his absence (1787–1801) and "Federalist" deviations from revolutionary principles. Since Paine believed he had established these principles, any betrayal constitutes, for him, a betrayal of America and himself. Even the American Constitution, which he had celebrated in the *Rights of Man,* now seemed to resemble the "British government," that is, Burke's conception of a constitution consisting of both the monarchy and parliament (see *CW,* 2:691–93). Since Paine had been abroad when the Constitution was ratified, he suggests a connection between his absence and all that had gone awry in America. The Federalists, in his republican reading, disguise themselves in revolutionary names; they are "disguised traitors that call themselves Federalists."[1] The "corruption and perfidy" of Washington's Federalist administration explains the betrayal of both the Revolution and Thomas Paine (2:696). Arguing that the Federalists are imitating the British enemy by attempting to institute a hereditary government, that is, monarchy in America (see 2:695–96), he suggestively accuses them of attempting a counterrevolution, à la the counterrevolution in France, by trying imitatively to reestablish the Old Regime.

There was, in addition, another similar historical deviation, for the French Revolution had also been betrayed and hence had not proceeded according to his theory or principles. Indeed, as one of its original founders, Paine had been imprisoned and treated shabbily. His explanation of the French Revolution's betrayal dovetailed with his explanation of the American Revolution's betrayal: both had been betrayed by "factions," and both factions had betrayed Paine.

When he returned to America in 1802, Paine continued formulating a revisionist interpretation of both Revolutions as well as his role in them. In 1795 he had insisted that all "the disorders that have arisen in France during the progress of the Revolution have had their origin" in the violation of the principle of equal rights (*CW,* 2:585; cf. 594). The counterrevolutionary violation of principle explained the betrayal of both Revolutions, and Paine emphasized a thematic link between the Federalist "faction" in America and the Jacobin faction in France.

Paine depicted himself as the aggrieved originator of revolutionary principles. Referring to revolutionary France, he wrote, in 1804, that all that had gone wrong was due to "the possession of power before [the French people] understood principles. They earned liberty in words, but not in fact. The writer of this was in France through the whole of the Revolution, and knows the truth of what he speaks; for after endeavoring to give it principle, he had nearly fallen a victim to its rage" (*CW,* 2:964; cf. 966).

Two weeks after he arrived in America, Paine published the first of eight open letters *To The Citizens of the United States,* noting that when he first arrived in France (1787), the French Revolution "was beginning to germinate," that its principles were sound, since they "were copied from America, and the men who conducted it were honest." The "fury of faction," however, "extinguished" the principles and guillotined the honest men. Hence of all those who began the Revolution, Paine was "almost the only survivor" (*CW,* 2:909). In regard to America, Paine had noticed, around 1789, that "the principles of the Revolution" were also "expiring" and America "was turning its back on its glory"—allusively referring to America's glorious ancestor Thomas Paine—and his betrayal by false, Federalist America. He then refers to his providential return and the relighting of those "expiring" principles he had helped to spark: "But a spark from the altar of *Seventy-six,* unextinguished and unextinguishable through the long night of error, is again lighting up, in every part of the Union, the genuine name of rational liberty" (910). Just as Paine sometimes referred to himself as "Common Sense," he also referred to himself as a "Spark From The Altar Of Seventy-Six" (see, for instance, 2:988), suggesting that he had returned to relight principles he had first established, banishing the Federalist night darkening the land. Just as there was an implicit connection between "expiring" principles and his absence, there was a connection between his providential return and the second salvation of America.

Since the Federalists betrayed America by betraying principles Paine had established, they resembled America's counterrevolutionary enemy—the British monarchy: "They were beginning to contemplate government as a profitable monopoly, and the people as hereditary property." This also explains, for him, Federalist criticism of the *Rights of Man*. Paine, however, assures the American people that there "is too much *common sense* and independence in America to be long the dupe of any faction, foreign or domestic" (*CW*, 2:910; my emphasis). Alluding again to his providential presence in America by the title of his first political pamphlet and the revolutionary signature that highlights "the genuine name of rational liberty" (910), Paine suggests a repetition of revolutionary history: just as he defeated the old Tories, so he will defeat new Tories disguised in republican language.

Similarly, in *First Principles of Government* (1795), he had earlier argued that the Jacobins were reactionaries disguised in republican rhetoric. Using the language of origins, he metaphorically connected Jacobin robbers with the robber barons of England during the Conquest: "Blush aristocracy, to hear your origin, for your progenitors were thieves. They were the Robespierres and the Jacobins of that day. When they committed the robbery, they endeavored to lose the disgrace of it by sinking their real names under fictitious ones" (*CW*, 2:582). In "The True-Born Englishman" (1700), Daniel Defoe had excoriated "conquering William" and his Norman "thieves," relating how they robbed the English nation and then disguised the robbery in artificial titles ("The Rascals thus enriched, he called them *Lords*") and thus "[t]he silent record blushes to reveal / Their undescended dark original" (11.140–69). Paine again was using the myth of the Norman Yoke to reinforce his myth of counterrevolutionary origins. Likewise, he again criticized the usurped linguistic origins of the Jacobins and Federalists. As he had complained that the Jacobins had appropriated the title of "patriot," he also argued, in the second *Letter to the Citizens of the United States* (1802), that the reactionary faction abused the name Federalist; hence, it was necessary "to go back and show the origin of the name, which is now no longer what it originally was" to reveal "the apostasy of those who first called themselves Federalists"—a name now used "as a cloak for treason, a mask for tyranny" (2:915; cf. 949, 1107–8). In letter six he associates the political fall of America with the apostate administration of Washington: "Those who were then at the head of affairs were apostates from the principles of the Revolution" (2:935). In short, Paine was reproducing the political clichés of the Jeffersonian Press: the Federalists attempted to overthrow the "representative system of government" and reintroduce the hereditary system of government; they attempted to overthrow the Revolution and establish a military dictatorship by fabricating "alarms of [a French] invasion" as a pretext to silence the people and usurp their liberties via the notorious Alien and Sedition Acts (see 2:936–37). For Paine, the present struggle is a repetition of 1776: "The plan of the leaders of the faction was to overthrow the liberties of the New World, and place government on the corrupt system of the Old" (Letter 2, 2:917; cf. 1009, 1436). The very "system" that America had fought to overthrow was being treacherously reimposed.

Aside from Washington, who was childless, Paine's principal villain, in his letters *To the Citizens of the United States,* is John Adams, admirer of all things British, whose secret desire is to establish a hereditary dynasty. In London, in 1787, John Trumbull, the American painter, told Paine that since Washington had no children, Adams had proposed that government be made hereditary "in the family of Lund Washington," Washington's cousin.[2] Later, Paine decided that Adams had dynastic pretensions of his own—rewriting his place in the Revolution, just as he had rewritten Washington's. Pusillanimous during the American Revolution, in "the days of the black cockades, John Adams" figuratively "had [a cockade] so enormous and so valiantly large, that he appeared suspended by it" (Letter 8, *CW,* 2:954). Black, of course, was the preeminent counterrevolutionary color: supporters of the ancien régime's return were denominated *noirs,* and black was the "Austrian" color of Marie Antoinette as well as the color of the uniforms supposedly worn by the "blacks," the counterrevolutionary emigrés gathered at Coblenz during the French Revolution. More pertinently, a black cockade was supposedly "the badge of the Federalists," and "the Hanoverian cockade was black."[3] Adams is thus identified with George III and the betrayal of America. Paine's depiction of the fatuous Adams, his mind crazed with "counter revolutionary principles and projects" (*CW,* 2:955), was another effort to discredit a revolutionary founder by making him a counterrevolutionary traitor. The language of denunciation that Paine uses—the references to apostates, traitors, and counterrevolutionary enemies—is also linguistically reminiscent of the Jacobin faction and Robespierre, Paine's primary persecutors in France. His insistence that he "is not persecuting John Adams, nor any other man, nor did I ever persecute any" is ironically overstated (2:956).

In *The Age of Reason,* he had also insisted that "the man does not exist that can say I have persecuted him, or any man, or any set of men, either in the American Revolution or in the French Revolution" (1:594; cf. 2:936, 974).

Persecution, of course, is yet another resemblance Paine sees between the Jacobins and Federalists—they both had persecuted him. In the *Letter to George Washington,* this is underscored in the Robespierre-Washington conspiracy: Washington acquiesced in Paine's imprisonment and hence his persecution, since he was responsible for protecting United States citizens who happened to "fall under any arbitrary persecution abroad" (*CW,* 2:698). Earlier, in 1795, Paine had referred to the Revolution's "persecution" of himself in a speech to the National Convention (2:594). Given this conspiratorial nexus, Paine began insisting on the similarity between the terrorist regime in France and the "terrorist" regime in Federalist America. In letter three *To the Citizens of the United States* (1802), he alludes to the Alien and Sedition Acts, referring to the "Reign of Terror" that "raged in America during the latter end of the Washington Administration, and the whole of that of Adams" (2:918). The conspiratorial connection between both persecuting factions is, of course, their persecution of Paine: "So far as respects myself, I have reason to believe and a right to say that the leaders of the Reign of Terror in America and the leaders of the Reign of Terror in France, during the time of Robespierre, were in character the same sort of men; or how is it to be accounted for, that I was persecuted by both at the same time?" (919). He then refers to Robespierre's memorandum demanding his arrest *"for the interests of America as well as of France"* (920; Paine's emphasis), adding that the "words are in [Robespierre's] own handwriting, and reported to the Convention by the committee appointed to examine his papers, and are printed in their report, with this reflection added to them, '*Why Thomas Paine more than another? Because he contributed to the liberty of both worlds*'" (920; Paine's emphasis).

Even though the last italicized reason for Paine's detention was apparently a notation made by a member of the committee assigned to examine Robespierre's papers, the reader could easily assume that this reason was given by Robespierre "in his own handwriting," following his memorandum on Paine's arrest. Whether or not Paine invented the notation (which, as far as I know, has never been identified),[4] the answer exists as the true reason for Paine's detention, as if Paine himself confirms it: the hero of two worlds was imprisoned for contributing "*to the liberty of both worlds.*" Thus, Paine's conspiratorial linkage of liberty's enemies: "There must have been a coalition in sentiment, if not in fact, between the Terrorists of America and the Terrorists of France, and Robespierre must have known it, or he could not have had the idea of putting America into the bill of accusation against me" (2:920).

This terrorist persecution culminates in Paine's climactic clincher:

> Yet these men, these Terrorists of the New World, who were waiting in the devotion of their hearts for the joyful news of my destruction, are the same banditti who are now bellowing in all the hackneyed language of hackneyed hypocrisy about humanity and piety, and often about something they call infidelity, and they finish with the chorus of *Crucify him, crucify him.* I am become so famous among them, they cannot eat or drink without me. I serve them as a standing dish, and they cannot make up a bill of fare if I am not in it.
>
> (*CW*, 2:920)

The bizarre linkage between terrorism in France and America is allusively in context of Federalist attacks on the "impiety" and "infidelity" of *The Age of Reason.* But by grotesquely comparing himself to Christ who was, of course, also "persecuted" and "betrayed," Paine performs the very sacrilege he mocks. In addition, there is a possible echo of Wollstonecraft's charge, in *The Rights of Men,* that if Burke had been a Jew living at the time of Christ, he too "would have joined in the cry, crucify him—crucify him!" (*Works,* 5:14). Paine's blasphemous joke is extended in the allusion to the Last Supper and the betrayal of the Christly Paine: the Federalist betrayers cannot "eat or drink without" him; he serves "as a standing dish." Their "bill of fare" echoes back to Robespierre's "bill of accusation" (920).

Indeed, Paine continues playing with Scripture, boasting that providence (unlike Moses and the Jews who eventually died) saved and delivered him "in health to the Promised Land" (that is, America). Thus he providentially survived the Terror: of the nine members composing "the first Committee of Constitution" (the nine members assigned to draft the 1793 French Constitution), Paine is the only true survivor—six died, one "[bent] with the times," and one joined Robespierre (*CW,* 2:920). In other words, Paine is the only true revolutionary left: the others were either destroyed or compromised themselves. Paine presents his life in religious terms—persecution and betrayal, deliverance and salvation. If he mocks these terms for others, he appropriates them for himself.

In the fourth and following letter, he tells the American people that he returned to America to rescue her from "some meditated treason against her liberties" and to save his "oppressed" friends—"to take my stand among them, and if other times to *try men's souls* were to arrive, that I might bear my share," even though his initial "efforts to return were ineffectual" (*CW*, 2:926; Paine's emphasis). Paine's "return" is always a return to the American Revolution and hence himself as the Revolution's incarnation. Since there was a new conspiracy, à la the English in 1776, to deprive the American people of their liberties and to reintroduce the British form of government, Paine returns again to liberate America. Alluding to himself in italics as America's deliverer, he quotes the opening lines of the first *American Crisis* essay (1776): "These are the times that try men's souls" (1:50)—a phrase he enjoyed repeating once he returned to America (see *CW*, 2:992, 1460, 1479–80, 1495). To read Paine is to read him reproducing himself endlessly. Since he sees himself perpetuated in revolutions, the second American Crisis is a repetition of his role in the first: Paine returns again to save America.

In America, from 1802 on, he posed as the reincarnation of 1776, the messianic savior returning to confront apostates and to remind a postrevolutionary generation of the revolutionary principles he had fathered. Returning to relight the spark of '76, Paine returned to the land of his mythical origins and to what he believed was his privileged position in a Revolution resurrected and repeated everywhere his luminous words were read. By 1802 he was celebrating himself as the only survivor of both Revolutions. In his letters and publications, he dwells on his imprisonment in France, at a time when his "friends were falling as fast as the guillotine could cut their heads off" and when he anticipated the same result (*CW*, 2:1436). He dwells on the night in July 1793, when 163 people were removed for execution and he had "good reason" to think he was included on the list (2:699). He also dwells on how he miraculously survived, either due to a prostrating illness or, in another version, how an incorrectly marked door fortuitously saved him from the guillotine. Thus, if he was the embodiment of the spirit of '76, he also embodied the spirit of '89. On 6 March 1795 Paine wrote Samuel Adams, telling him that he was "now almost the only survivor of those who began [the French] Revolution" (2:1375; cf. 1125, 1386). In his first letter *To the Citizens of the United States*, he proclaimed that "of those who began [the French Revolution],

I am almost the only survivor, and [have escaped] through a thousand dangers," noting that there was something providential in his protection (2:909).

Likewise, he represented himself as the revolutionary embodiment of '76. Indeed, who was left? Washington and the Federalists were apostate betrayers and the remaining republicans, like Jefferson, were only secondary causes of the Revolution. Paine tacitly asserts the superiority of his own revolutionary credentials by noting that *Common Sense* was prior to the *Declaration of Independence* and hence, in Paine's monomythic vision, the cause of both the proclamation and the establishment of American independence. In the end, Paine emerges as the Revolution's solitary voice. By making himself the "first cause" of the Revolution, he mythically reconceives himself as the Creator who cannot die. In a letter to George Clinton (4 May 1807), he observed that as "a new generation . . . has risen up since the declaration of independence, they know nothing of what the political state of the country was at the time the pamphlet *Common Sense* appeared; and besides this there are but few of the old standers left, and none that I know of in [New York]" (*CW*, 2:1488).

Paine's end is always his beginning. His obsession with his origins appears in metaphors of birth in 1776, repeated in 1789, and resurrected in 1802. Like his friend Lafayette, he becomes the Hero of Two Worlds, fathering the two revolutions he hoped would be reproduced on a worldwide scale. He becomes the metaphoric link between these revolutions, reproducing and repeating himself through words re-creating the mythic possibilities of revolution and self. Creating a privileged position within the revolutionary text he is writing, he endeavors to be the Revolution's authoritative source. This empowerment of himself as the *Ursprung*—the ultimate origin—thematically culminates, as we will now see, in *The Age of Reason* with the erasure of the original Word.

II

In *Paine, Scripture, and Authority,* Edward H. Davidson and William J. Scheick document how Paine, in *The Age of Reason,* incorporates previous biblical criticism (Spinoza and others), as he subversively rereads the Bible. At the same time, Paine becomes complicit with the tradition he confronts, reinscribing oppositional voices and strategies, even as he proclaims his pristine independence. Preoccupied with his own origins and authority, Paine's anxious self-authorizations depend on the authority he displaces and the opposition that is his raison d'être.[5] In this context, I want to expand on Davidson and Scheick's reading by illustrating how Paine contradicts and rewrites the fraudulent Word, while reauthorizing himself as the Logos that sets man free.

The Age of Reason is a quasi-deist tract in which the God of Creation is distantly removed beyond Paine's political cosmos. Since this deist God is "out there," Paine's attack on the "fabricated" biblical Word and words is an endeavor to erase an Ur-source contradicting his original words. His method of discrediting the biblical God's putative Word is the same he uses in discrediting other textual rivals: by exposing the Bible's contradictions and mystifications, Paine emerges as the original source of truth and liberation. In freeing mankind from the false Word, Paine presents himself as the world's primary logos. Thematically, there is a linguistic link between the textual regicide of 1776 (*Common Sense*), the patricide of 1796 (*Letter to Washington*), and the logocide of 1794 (*The Age of Reason*): in each Paine silences a rival source.

In *The Age of Reason,* Paine distinguishes the pristine expression of the true "Deity" from the corrupt words of man. Since the Deity only expresses itself to man in and through the physical creation, it does not use human language as a medium: what man sees is proof of the Deity's creative existence. Because human language is a defective medium, vulnerable to corruption, contradiction, and distortion—the Deity, according to Paine, will never express itself linguistically, since it cannot contradict itself. Hence, the true Deity is in no sense a linguistic rival or source, as is the biblical God who, in Genesis, linguistically creates the cosmos by speaking it into being and then sends the Word to proclaim God's message. In this context, Paine considers the Bible as the ultimate counterrevolutionary text—the erroneous source of mystification and oppression. Used by kings and priests to rationalize despotic power, the Bible, for Paine, is the original source of error. Paine, in essence, reinscribes a traditional Enlightenment critique of the mystified Christian religion.[6] Since God and the Bible, both fabricated, are the fallacious source of the old fallen world, Paine offers his own works as the veritable source of the new revolutionary world. Thus Paine, as has been seen, envisions himself as the Creator—the revolutionary Word overthrowing the counterrevolutionary Logos.

Having removed the remote Deity from the realm of language, Paine thematically silences his primary linguistic rival—Jesus—the reified "Word made flesh." Since the real Deity does not enter human language, Paine insists that Jesus could not have proclaimed God's "word" because Jesus, in a world of multitudinous languages, spoke only Hebrew. As the speaker of an imperfect language, he could not have proclaimed God's "word," since this word would have had to have been translated into other corruptible and contradictory languages.[7] The Jesus who supposedly spoke a human language could not have communicated a permanent truth because all languages are "local and changeable" and "therefore incapable of being used as the means of unchangeable and universal information" (Paine, *CW*, 1:482). In addition, since the spoken words of Jesus were subsequently translated into other written languages, his words became even more corruptible, since no language can be perfectly translated into another.[8] Moreover, since a translation is a removal from an original source (in this case, the spoken words of Jesus), already existing in a corruptible medium, any translation is, *ipso facto,* even more corruptible and defective (*CW*, 1:483). The fact that Jesus spoke and did not write is especially problematic, since spoken language is more perishable and vulnerable to corruption and error. Add to this, Paine insists, the fact that the Old and New Testaments were not only linguistically passed down through a series of corruptible translations, but that the translators themselves deliberately engaged in a series of suppressions and distortions—then it is clear that the Bible's contradictions emanate from human agents rather than a divine source. Paine repeats these points in his first recapitulation ending the first part of *The Age of Reason:* "That the idea or belief of a Word of God existing in print, or in writing, or in speech, is inconsistent in itself for reasons already assigned. These reasons, among many others, are the want of a universal language; the mutability of language; the errors to which translations are subject; the possibility of totally suppressing such a word; the probability of altering it, or of fabricating the whole, and imposing it upon the world" (511–12; cf. 2:749, 788, 793). In essence, Paine plots a series of linguistic removals from a corruptible source to prove that the Ur-Word was an imposed fiction and hence, like the British constitution, nonexistent.

He asserts that there is not only the absence of God and Jesus's original spoken words but the absence of the original written words from the putative authors of the New Testament: Matthew, Mark, Luke, and John. Since there is no evidence, Paine insists, to prove their authorship (and the contradictory accounts of Jesus's life belie any claims to authenticity), the New Testament, like the Old, is also a tissue of fabrications:

There is not the least shadow of evidence of who the persons were that wrote them, nor at what time they were written; and they might as well have been called by the names of any of the other supposed apostles, as by the names they are now called. The originals are not in the possession of any Christian church existing, any more than the two tables of stone written on, they pretend, by the finger of God, upon Mount Sinai, and given to Moses, are in the possession of the Jews. And even if they were, there is no possibility of proving the handwriting in either case.
(*CW*, 1:585)

In addition, the fact that the Bible was written at a time when printing did not exist exposed it to more corruptions, since it had to be copied by hand—thus there were a series of "copies" and yet another series of removals from an unsubstantiated source. That the Bible was originally copied exposed it to suppressions and fabrications, "which any man might make or alter at pleasure, and call them originals" (585).

Paine's critique of biblical tradition through a pejorative vocabulary of "copies" was, in essence, a Platonic critique politicized and derived from earlier Enlightenment critiques of "copied" traditions. In *An Essay Concerning Human Understanding,* Locke had, for instance, attacked the authority of tradition by referring to "a rule observed in the law of England; which is, That though the attested copy of a record be good proof, yet the copy of a copy, ever so well attested, and by ever so credible witnesses, will not be admitted as a proof in judicature." Since "no *probability* can arise higher than its first Original," the "hear-say of an hear-say" is very dubious, "[s]o that in traditional truths, each remove weakens the force of the proof: and the more hands the tradition has successively passed through, the less strength and evidence does it receive from them."[9] In essence, what Locke calls "traditional revelation" must be traced to the "original revelation," and the authority of the former rests on the credibility of the latter.[10] Although Paine claimed he had never read Locke, he was, I suggest, reformulating Locke's critique, albeit radical Levellers and Ranters had also criticized biblical translations and copies during the English Civil War.[11]

Paine had begun *The Age of Reason* by connecting it with the "revolution" begun in *Common Sense* and implicitly continued in the *Rights of Man:* "Soon after I had published the pamphlet 'Common Sense,' . . . I saw the exceeding probability that a revolution in the system of government would be followed by a revolution in the system of religion" (*CW,* 1:465). In his critique of political and religious authorities, he exposes their contradictions and mystifications in order to discredit their sources and origins. His attack on the traditional canon (the Bible, the British constitution, and books like Burke's *Reflections*) sustaining the old, oppressive political and religious order was simultaneously an endeavor to replace this canon with the Trinitarian one of *Common Sense*, the *Rights of Man*, and *The Age of Reason*. But in his critique of "books pretending to be revelation" (*CW*, 2:797), Paine presents his own books as sources of revelation—exposing reactionary errors while revealing linguistic light. Paine's obsession with origins, his hostility to the Word as the original source—an idea permeating Western discourse—reflects his own resemblance to his primary linguistic rival. In presenting himself as the Truth that sets man free, in asserting that "My own mind is my own church" (1:464), in his references to Federalist "apostasy" from the true revolutionary faith, in his fantasies of republics flowing from his prolific words, he unwittingly recreated himself as a mimetic rival, a parodic image of the Ur-counterrevolutionary Word.

Like traditional representations of the biblical Word(s), Paine contended his own words and works were, like the Deist Deity, clear and uncontradictable. He asserted his own linguistic priority by contrasting the Bible's exposed contradictions with his own pristine writings. In an open letter to Thomas Erskine, the London lawyer who, in 1797, conducted the government's prosecution of a man accused of printing a copy of *The Age of Reason*, Paine referred to the Bible's contradictions in order to assert his linguistic superiority:

> The writings of Thomas Paine, even of Thomas Paine, need no commentator to explain, compound, derange, and rearrange their several parts, to render them intelligible; he can relate a fact, or write an essay, without forgetting in one page what he has written in another: certainly then, did the God of all perfection condescend to write or dictate a book, that book would be as perfect as Himself is perfect. The Bible is not so, and it is confessedly not so, by the attempts to amend it.
> (*CW*, 2:732–33)

Since Paine absolves himself of contradiction, the corruptible characteristic of human language in *The Age of Reason*, he implicitly compares himself with "the God of all perfection," who, if he did write a book, would undoubtedly write one that resembles the clear, incontrovertible books of Thomas Paine.

In privileging himself as the original source of linguistic truth, Paine contrasts the contradictory "counterrevolutionary" text with his superior revolutionary bible: "For my own part, my belief in the perfection of the Deity will not permit me to believe that a book so manifestly obscure, disorderly, and contradictory can be His work. I can write a better book myself. This belief in me proceeds from my belief in the Creator" (*CW*, 2:737). Since the true Deity will not reveal itself in corruptible human language, Paine allusively asserts himself as the primary author of the liberated Western world, having already written a "better book." His "belief in me" is a belief in himself as "Creator."

In *The Age of Reason,* after removing the Deity from human history and language, Paine plots a series of removals from an ambiguous "nothing," having no determinable origin or source— no beginning. Having previously disowned the false, royal father and provided Burke corrupt, bastard origins, he proceeds to turn his religious rivals into bastards or orphans. Moses, Jesus, and Mahomet "were of very obscure parentage" (*CW*, 1:478), and "The book of Judges," like the rest of the Bible, "is altogether fatherless" (534).

In contrast, Paine, from the beginning, is the Ur-father, linguistically incarnating himself into history in 1776, producing the American Revolution, which causes the French Revolution and all the other revolutions potentially present in the seeds of his original words. Paine sees himself mysteriously present wherever his procreant words are read. Conceived in a cosmic love affair with himself, his providential existence in print means, for him, that his pure, ubiquitous presence will be forever preserved: ". . . thought when produced, as I now produce the thought I am writing, is capable of becoming immortal, and is the only production of man that has that capacity" (*CW*, 1:591). Not belatedly copied, like the Bible, but reproduced originally, "thought is eternally and identically the same thought in every case"; thus, if "the thing produced has in itself a capacity of being immortal, it is more than a token that the power that produced it, which is the selfsame thing as consciousness of existence, can be immortal also; and that as independently of the matter it was first connected with, as the thought is of the printing or writing it first appeared in" (592).[12] Incarnated into print as the Word made flesh, Paine is ultimately the timeless Word repeated everywhere he is read. In "Extracts from a reply to the Bishop of Llandaff" (1810), he noted that the miracle of print "gives to man a sort of divine attribute. It gives to him mental omnipresence. He can be everywhere and at the same instance; for wherever he is read he is mentally there" (2:786).[13] Although he makes these observations about language and printing in general, they had, for him, a special reflexive significance. In *The Age of Reason,* Paine takes these poetic truths literally, asserting his real presence over the Word he logocidally writes out of existence. Contradicting his thesis that human language is inherently changeable, he valorizes the written immortality of his own pristine thoughts through the exceptional language they exemplify. Since his discussion of his rivals' language is always in terms of contradiction and error, his generalization about the immortal characteristic of written thought is ultimately his own self-exemplary exception.

Paine authorizes both his texts and himself. By continually referring and returning to his pristine mythical origin, he effects his fictional escape from history, freeing himself from responsibility for his words and actions. Traitorous time and counterrevolutionary contradictions are, in the end, causal deviations from the Ur-beginning—the prelapsarian principles he originally published. Obsessed with the etiology of himself, Paine luxuriates in revolutionary self-fashioning. Nostalgically consumed with his mythical creation, he repeatedly returns to a linguistic beginning, pure and impervious to the treacheries of time.

In *Interpreting the French Revolution,* François Furet noted revolutionary historiography's "obsession with origins" and a correspondent myth of origins, in which "1789 became the birth date, the year zero of a new world founded on equality."[14] He documented how this preoccupation with origins and hence "causes" characterizes Jacobin discourse—a discourse mimed by nineteenth-century French historiography of the Revolution.[15] Likewise, Linda Orr has shown how Jules Michelet envisions himself as the "origin" and hence the "author" of "the possibility of all history of the Revolution, really of modern history." Since Michelet works with "original" materials in the central archives, he sees rival revolutionary history as derivative: "Everything else necessarily falls back to the status of the copy, and even the miscopied copy of the already miscopied (*falsified*) copy"—hence Michelet "ends up 'authorizing' his own text."[16] Paine, in this context, initiated a historical writing that characterizes Jacobin historiography—the myth of an original beginning *authorized* by the participators who create it. Paine's history is, in this sense, more mythically Jacobin, since he causally predates the 1789 Revolution. If, as Linda Orr maintains, Jacobin historiography always argues that it constitutes a new, enlightened understanding of history, so that in this "theoretic sense," most modern historians are "Jacobin,"[17] then Thomas Paine was the first.

In the *Rights of Man,* Paine had imagined the citizens of America and France,"a thousand years hence," looking "back with contemplative pride on the origin of their governments" and saying *"this was the work of our glorious ancestors!"* Similarly, within the interstices of Paine's texts, a solitary voice looms out proclaiming, *"I am the origin!"* (*CW,* 1:319).

5

Wollstonecraft and the French Revolution

In September 1792 Mary Wollstonecraft reviewed a book in the *Analytical Review* (volume XIV) that referred to the American Revolution as "the mother-revolution" (*Works,* 7:453). The French Revolution was, however, already replacing the American Revolution as "the mother of us all"—a phrase resonating the Left's strong historical identification with the Revolution over the past two centuries.[1] Indeed, from 1789 on, the Revolution became a mythic entity, the Ur-paradigm for all subsequent "people's revolutions." But the Revolution also disappointed many of its supporters, and hence it also served as a paradigm for "the revolution betrayed"—a claim that both the Girondins and Jacobins would make, as well as its many liberal supporters abroad. The failure of a revolution that was supposed to regenerate both the French nation and humanity resulted in correspondent explications crystallized by the Revolution's admirers. Formulated between 1791 and 1799, these explanations have continued to reappear in various forms as "reasons" for the failure of revolutions in this century as well. The failure or success of a revolution is of course often contingent on the initial expectations that color or define its purposeful meaning. In retrospect, the fact that the Revolution was promoted as a world-regenerative event and that many of the revolutionaries acted on this apocalyptic assumption ironically ensured that the Revolution would contradict the messianic ideology that defined it. The discrepancy between theory and fact hence had to be explained.

In this context, Wollstonecraft helped formulate many of the classic explanations for the failure of a revolution that was supposed to regenerate the world. It is thus illuminating to read her rewriting a revolution that deviated from her idea of what a revolution should be or do. Since enough had gone wrong with the Revolution by 1792, Wollstonecraft was compelled to explain rather than celebrate revolutionary history, even though she was writing about the Revolution's first six months—the Revolution's mythic, pristine moment.

Of her major works, *The French Revolution* (1794) has received only polite, perfunctory attention. Ralph M. Wardle, for instance, considers it her "least original work"; Eleanor Flexner agrees that "it is the least interesting and important of Mary's books"; Margaret Tims observes that the book's "facts are well known, and not in dispute."[2] But Wollstonecraft's book contains many factual errors—errors that are revealing, as the book is—not the least for being written by Wollstonecraft in France during the Terror, four years after the events she narrates had already occurred. Although she provides a cursory overview of French history up to the Revolution and refers to events in 1787 and 1788, Wollstonecraft deals primarily with the first five or six months of the Revolution, roughly from May to October 1789, or approximately the same period of time that Burke deals with in the *Reflections,* although he also refers to events before and after. While Burke was writing almost as these events were unfolding, Wollstonecraft had four years to consider and contemplate the same "facts." She was also closer to her subject, writing the book in revolutionary France, but this had its disadvantages as well.

None of Wollstonecraft's errors are deliberate, but there are conspicuous silences created by the dialectical "times" in which the book is written: she writes about the Revolution's prelapsarian moment (1789) precisely when the Revolution is falling (1793–94). Indeed, the Terror is the book's secret subject.

Wollstonecraft is very conscious of time, and her chronological narrative allows her to determine the Revolution's light and dark moments. Thus it is striking that, referring to events as early as 1788, she is already indicating that there is trouble in paradise. She establishes a prerevolutionary time for "the commencement of those butcheries, which have brought on that devoted country so many dreadful calamities, by teaching the people to avenge themselves with blood!": in response to a riot supposedly provoked by the court and then suppressed by "the hired slaves of despotism," the people (taught by despotism's example) respond the only way they know—with retaliation and vengeance (*Works,* 6:40). This account of the past's pernicious projection into the present contradicts the idea of a revolution purified of the past, a revolution she dates with the fall of the Bastille (118). Since the "past" becomes part and parcel of the Revolution's "inheritance," it is as if the Revolution were genetically flawed from the beginning. In order to see how Wollstonecraft resolves this contradiction, it is necessary to establish a chronology throughout, illustrating how concrete facts continually color her correspondent idea. In this context and as a preface, I want first to consider Wollstonecraft's view of the Revolution up to the writing of *The French Revolution*.[3]

I

From 1789 on, Wollstonecraft thought of herself as an objective reviewer of the French Revolution. But having committed herself to the Revolution in *The Rights of Men* (1790), she expressed presuppositions that were crystallized and honed in her articles in the *Analytical Review* between January 1789 and January 1793. From her reviews of books dealing with prerevolutionary France, she probably derived the idea of the corrupt nature of both the French court and the nobility, as well as the slavish character of the French people—formed by centuries of "oppression" (see, for instance, *Works,* 7:383, 413, 416). With regard to the Revolution, she generally reviews favorably the books and poems that celebrate it, while criticizing those works she considers pejorative (see 7:202, 257, 322–24, 330–31, 341–44, 394–95, 416). Two reviews bear notice.

In December 1789 she commends Richard Price's *Discourse on the Love of Our Country* and cites various passages that subsequently provoked Burke (*Works,* 7:185–87). In one of her last articles (April 1792) before leaving for France, she reviews critically a book titled *An Historical Sketch of the French Revolution, from its Commencement to the Year 1792* (perhaps suggesting the countertitle of her revolutionary history), since the anonymous author "*heartily espouses* the greatest part of Mr. Burke's sentiments" (426). Before exposing the book's "biases," she opens with the following observation:

> The late revolution in France . . . has engaged the attention of all the surrounding nations . . . It is impossible, however, to consider it as an *abstract question* during the present day, for it is immediately connected with the political sentiments of the times, and is apt to take its colouring from the prejudices of the human mind. It will afford a noble subject for the pen of some future historian, and for the contemplation of enlightened posterity.
>
> (425)

Although her comments are pertinent to her own "enlightened" stance, the last sentence indicates that she was already thinking of becoming the Revolution's historian.

We know, for instance, that two months later (June 1792), she was planning a trip with friends to "view the Revolution at first hand," but that it was inexplicably canceled.[4] Later, in a letter (12 November 1792) to her friend William Roscoe, she notes that she is "determined to set out for Paris in the course of a fortnight or three weeks" and urges him "not to mix with the shallow herd who throw an odium on immutable principles, because some of the mere instrument of the revolution were too sharp."[5] Ralph M. Wardle observes that Wollstonecraft "apparently feared lest Roscoe share the general aversion to revolutionary principles that had risen in England because of the overthrow of the monarchy [10 August 1792] in France." Claire Tomalin says that the reference is to the "September massacres" of 1792.[6] Indeed, the imagery ("instrument," "too sharp") even evokes the guillotine, which had been in official operation since April 1792. Two things are notable: on the eve of her voyage to France, Wollstonecraft dismisses concerns about revolutionary excesses, and she formulates one of the classic defenses of revolutionary violence—a revolution necessarily entails the shedding of a little blood before "immutable principles" triumph. This idea, as we will see, is crucial to Wollstonecraft's revolutionary faith.

With a commission from her publisher, Joseph Johnson, to write a series of articles on the Revolution, Wollstonecraft departed from Dover on 8 December 1792 and arrived in Paris soon after. On 26 December she wrote a letter to Johnson dealing with the imminent execution of Louis XVI, indicating that she was perplexed about the Revolution's course.

On 15 February 1793 she wrote another letter to Johnson that was intended to be published as one of her eyewitness accounts of the Revolution, but was instead published posthumously in 1798 as a "Letter on the Present Character of the French Nation." A little more than two months after arriving in Paris, Wollstonecraft is discouraged and pessimistic about what she is witnessing. She writes "rather harshly of a land flowing with milk and honey," doubting her "theory of a more perfect state," fearing that vice or evil "is the grand mobile of action," lamenting the blood being shed and the "frivolous" nature of the French people. Although she hopes for a "fairer day" when immutable principles will presumably triumph, she finds it unnerving to see "men vicious without warmth" and "crimes" secured "which only thoughtlessness could palliate." She ends her gloomy epistle condemning the vanity of unnamed revolutionaries and lamenting "that names, not principles, are changed" (see *Works*, 6:443–46). The letter is a repudiation of everything she had previously written about the Revolution and could have been drafted by Burke.

Indeed, she makes the following points that Burke had made in the *Reflections:* that she fears the replacement of an "aristocracy of birth" with one of "wealth" (*Works,* 6:444; cf. *FR,* 233) and that "names, not principles," are being changed (446; cf. *Reflections,* 248). Referring to the Revolution, Burke had observed that everything "seems out of nature in this strange chaos of levity and ferocity, and all sorts of crimes jumbled together with all sorts of follies" (*Reflections,* 92). Similarly, Wollstonecraft wishes that she could inform Johnson that, "out of the chaos and follies, prejudices and virtues, rudely jumbled together," she "saw the fair form of Liberty slowly rising" (444; cf. *FR,* 143). But she obviously does not see it, and one of her first assessments of the Revolution in France significantly evokes a passage from the *Reflections* that she had applied against Burke in *The Rights of Men* (*Works,* 5:28). She also makes various points that emerge as causal, explanatory theses in *The French Revolution:* the French people's "vanity" (6:443, 446), their effeminacy (443, 445), the influence of the past—old despotism creates modern "misery" (444), the "blood" that "stains" the Revolution (444), and Paris as the locale of these stains—her Girondist thesis. Later, I will examine how these themes impinge on the writing of *The French Revolution.*

Wollstonecraft stayed in Paris from December 1792 to June 1793. She had arrived at a seemingly portentous time. On 1 February 1793 France declared war on Great Britain and the Dutch Republic; even though Wollstonecraft was known as a supporter of the Revolution, she was potentially vulnerable, living in a country where people were becoming increasingly xenophobic. In addition, the struggle between the Jacobins and the Girondins aggravated already existing tensions.

During this time, Wollstonecraft met other fellow travelers (British and American) as well as some of the leading Girondins, including Brissot, Vergniaud, and the Rolands. This is important because her account of the Revolution is tacitly sympathetic to the Girondins, even though they did not politically exist in 1789. It illustrates something fundamental about *The French Revolution:* Wollstonecraft is writing as the Revolution is still unfolding, and hence the "present" impinges on the "past," just as the past affects the present.

In April 1793 Wollstonecraft met and soon fell in love with Gilbert Imlay, an American adventurer. On 31 May the conflict between the Jacobins and Girondins spilled over into the streets when eighty thousand radical supporters surrounded the National Convention, caused the city barriers to be closed (1 June), and forced, on 2 June, the expulsion of twenty-two Girondin deputies from the Convention. As a citizen of a neutral but sympathetic country, Gilbert Imlay was able to acquire an American passport for Wollstonecraft, and when the city's barriers were reopened after the June insurrection, she moved to an isolated cottage in the woods at Neuilly, a little village three miles from Paris—then relatively remote.[7]

In a letter to her sister, Eliza W. Bishop (13 June 1793), Wollstonecraft notes that she has moved and is "writing a great book."[8] She had, in effect, started her history at the very beginning of the Terror.

This was her one blissful interlude (June–August 1793). In mid-August, she moved back to Paris and set up house with Imlay; in mid-January 1794 she moved to Le Havre to join Imlay again and to escape "the growing cruelties of Robespierre."[9] By March she finished her book (including proofreading) and subsequently moved back to the outskirts of Paris, sometime between late August and mid-September. On 9 April 1795 she returned to London (departing from Le Havre), having spent two years and four months in revolutionary France. With this chronology, we can now turn to the book itself.

II

The complete title of Wollstonecraft's history is *An Historical and Moral View of the Origin and Progress of the French Revolution; and the Effect it has produced in Europe.* The title conveys the idea of a chronological survey of an ongoing revolution that is both progressing and bringing "progress" (a favorite word of hers— that is, the "progress" of "enlightened" ideas and principles) to Europe. The Revolution is a "cause" producing an "effect" on the European world. Since Wollstonecraft's perspective is "moral" as well as historical, there is the implied promise of revealing the Revolution's true, inner significance.

In the preface, Wollstonecraft opens with the "contrast" the Revolution presents "between the narrow opinions of superstition, and the enlightened sentiments of masculine and improved philosophy" (*FR,* 6). This contrast commences a series of Manichean readings of the Revolution; in Book two, chapter one, for instance, Wollstonecraft indicts the prerevolutionary clergy *in toto:* "France maintained two hundred thousand priests, united in the same spirit of licentiousness; who indulged themselves in all the depraved pleasures of cloaked immorality, at the same time they embruted the people by sanctifying the most diabolical prejudices" (50–51; cf. the "French nobility," 75). Although Wollstonecraft often engages in such melodramatic generalizations, her demonization of the Old Regime is related to her explication of revolutionary problems.

In the preface she alerts us to these problems—the "rapid changes, the violent, the base, and nefarious assassinations" which "cloud" our "perspective," lead to an erroneous understanding of the Revolution, unless, of course, the reasonable historian directs "us to a favourable or just conclusion" (*FR,* 6). The adjective *favorable* seems premature, as if the objective historian has already prejudged the Revolution, so the forthcoming *just* seems more neutral, although it also suggests that a favorable conclusion may also be just. Returning to the language of "judgement" used in *The Rights of Men,* she notes that despite "the calamitous horrours produced by desperate and enraged factions," the "cool eye of . . . judgement" will see that "it is the uncontaminated mass of the French nation whose minds begin to grasp the sentiments of freedom," in spite of the madness and horror produced by "depraved manners, the concomitant of that servility and voluptuousness," which has long "embruted the higher orders of this celebrated nation" (6).

The sentence illustrates her rhetorical strategy throughout: she will balance horrors with goodness, atrocities with provocations. Her point that all the horrors of the Revolution flow from the influential past (the "servility and voluptuousness" of the "higher orders") is one of the persistent themes of the book: the oppressive presence of the past is a "cause" of revolutionary problems. Although she will later indict "the uncontaminated mass of the French nation" (that is, the Third Estate), she concludes with her triumphant thesis of the Revolution: the French Revolution was not produced by "the abilities or intrigues of a few individuals"— not tied to transient circumstances—it is ever ongoing, "the natural consequence of intellectual improvement, gradually proceeding to perfection," with "principles" seemingly "hastening the overthrow of the tremendous empire of superstition and hypocrisy, erected upon the ruins of gothic brutality and ignorance" (*FR,* 6–7).

Writing in Neuilly during the first flush of love, Wollstonecraft exorcises her letter of 15 February with the book's principal thesis: the Enlightenment caused the Revolution that proceeds progressively and gradually through people's minds, freeing them (through knowledge) psychologically, so they can be politically liberated. It is a thesis she will bring forward whenever her faith in the Revolution wavers and with which she will conclude her book.

Chapter one showcases this thesis. It encapsulates the Enlightenment's view of itself, tracing the slow progress of reason and knowledge into the eighteenth century, albeit resisted futilely by the dark forces of despotism and superstition, which fade reluctantly before the light of reason. This was already a cultural cliché by the time Wollstonecraft reworked it into her book, and the corollary that the Enlightenment contributed to or "caused" the French Revolution was not only a "right-wing" thesis (popularized by Burke) but was insisted on and popularized by the "left wing" as well. Wollstonecraft's contribution to the thesis was her contention that the Enlightenment and the Revolution were not separate events—the Revolution was an extension, a continuation of the Enlightenment, expressed and incarnated in a more militant form. For Wollstonecraft, the Revolution expresses history's progressive logic.

She notes that on the "eve of the American war," there was a "revolution in opinion, which perhaps alone can overturn the empire of tyranny" (FR, 19). She is referring to "public opinion"—a new power that was changing the way people thought about themselves and the world—a power that was creating the social conditions for political change in Europe (cf. 23, 37, 52, 56, 70, 77, 85, 105, 113, 161, 192, 212, 229). She had first noted this revolution in opinion in A Vindication of the Rights of Woman (1792), observing that "men of abilities scatter seeds that grow up and have great influence on the forming opinion; and when once the public opinion preponderates, through the exertion of reason, the overthrow of arbitrary power is not very distant" (Works, 5:87, n. 5). For Wollstonecraft, the change from traditional to "progressive" thinking is a natural and inevitable result of "enlightenment." In this context, she saw that "public opinion" was a new power filling a vacuum created by the ideological default of the Old Order.[10] For revolutionary writers (1789–1799), the importance of public opinion was an established commonplace.

In The French Revolution, Wollstonecraft's enlightenment thesis makes change inevitable, albeit gradual, and hence present problems can be dismissed as transitory impediments. Throughout the book, Wollstonecraft contends that the regeneration of the human race will happen in the future; thus she hails "the glorious day from afar!" (FR, 21). The argument of paradise deferred is a classic explanation for revolutions that inexplicably fail to follow theory and has been repeatedly used for the past two centuries. Wollstonecraft's contribution was her vision of the Enlightenment as a kind of expanding energy consummating itself in the future.

Since she is writing about an ideological revolution, she highlights her thesis by framing her book around it: she opens (Book 1, chapter 1) with an overview of the Enlightenment's progress, and then she presents two other overviews (same thesis, only different people and forces)—Book 2, chapter 4; and Book 5, chapter 4, the book's concluding chapter. By framing the thesis structurally in a beginning, middle, and end, she emphasizes its thematic importance.

The thesis also allows her to insist that the Revolution is not sustained by people, inevitably disappointing, but by Truth Triumphant (knowledge, reason, enlightenment)—an idea ultimately untainted by the temporal defects of human beings and their agents. Her idea of the Revolution thus possesses a kind of timeless purity momentarily "stained" by temporal impurity. This transitory impurity explains why the French people seem to resist the Revolution's true significance. First, there is the past, an efficient cause of both the privileged classes' as well as the common people's corruption: oppressed for centuries, the people respond the only way they know, following the models and examples of their former oppressors. This is one of Wollstonecraft's explanations of the Revolution's violence. Wollstonecraft was not the first to formulate classic explanations of revolutionary violence, but she was among the first to refine them. In addition to the explanations the French themselves were offering, English supporters of the Revolution had, from the beginning, crystallized some of the central themes Wollstonecraft later developed. The thesis that old oppression causes revolutionary violence had already been advanced by Thomas Paine, Arthur Young, Thomas Christie, James Mackintosh, and, as we will see, Helen Maria Williams.[11]

Another cause Wollstonecraft advances to explain revolutionary contradiction is the "effeminate" character of the French people. Using the conventional language of the seventeenth-century Commonwealthmen's concern over the effeminacy of men degraded by antirepublican institutions, Wollstonecraft argues that the French are consequently vain, capricious, superficial, and emotional, explaining why enlightened ideas are not sustained. This also relates thematically to the past, since the "effeminate" or "emasculated" (*FR*, 73) court either (in the past) beguiled "the awe-struck populace" (19) or (in the present) conspires to destroy the Revolution by confusing the people. She usually denominates these "courtiers" as "the cabal" or "the cabinet." But she also characterizes the entire French nation as "effeminate" (25, 121–22, 213, 225, 230), suggesting that not much could be expected from such weak people. Her usage is pejorative, as she returns to the republican language of *The Rights of Men.*

The effeminate character of the French people accords with another motif—their theatrical nature. (In the book's final chapter, she even suggests that the "rhetorical" nature of the French language contributes to their theatrical proclivities, *FR,* 228.) This also becomes all encompassing, since both the courtiers and revolutionaries represent themselves in ostentatious theatrical terms— in exhibitionistic displays and dramatic poses, similar to the "aristocratic" theater of Corneille and Racine (24–25, 112–13, 124, 133, 144, 156, 169, 195, 228). In *The Rights of Men,* Wollstonecraft had presented Burke in the same pejorative terms, but her repeated references to revolutionary "theater" suggest the theatrical nature of the Revolution itself, reinforced by all the "illusions" she documents, blurring the distinction between human "actors" and the Revolution as Truth Triumphant. Thus, despite her denigration of political theater, Wollstonecraft dramatizes many of her historical scenes and herself as well, presenting the Revolution, in the end, as a Shakespearean tragedy. In the preface, however, she refers to the progress of reason, shining "on the grand theater of political changes" (6).

These unacknowledged contradictions illustrate her ambivalence toward the Revolution's concrete realities. After alluding again to the French people's theatricality, she refers to "ranting sentiments, which, with mock dignity, like party-coloured rags on the tree of liberty, stuck up in every village, are displayed as something very grand and significant" (*FR,* 26). Her contemptuous reference to the liberty tree, one of the Revolution's principal symbols, is apparently an attack on a theatrical part of the Revolution she disdains. But there is more to it than this.

In France she undoubtedly had the opportunity to see many liberty trees "stuck up in every village," since by 1792, there were already sixty thousand, and they were emblematically reproduced on "posters, crockery, letterheads, and bookbindings." On 18 February 1794 (30 Pluviôse, year 2), the National Convention "decreed that a Liberty Tree be planted in each town and placed under the care of good citizens."[12] While Wollstonecraft may be simply attacking an ostentatious symbol, she had to know that it was a symbol directly associated with the Revolution and that people in

France could be beaten or arrested for desecrating it.[13] In Paris, during the Terror, twelve people were guillotined for desecrating liberty trees—a "counterrevolutionary" act for which one could be indicted. Indeed, hostility toward the Revolution was often expressed in attacks on liberty trees.[14] Later, Wollstonecraft writes straightforwardly about the events of 1 October 1789 and the people's indignation after learning that the national cockade had been trampled during a reception at Versailles for the Flanders Regiment. She quotes an indignant Mirabeau: "The National cockade . . . that emblem of the defenders of liberty, has been torn to pieces, and stamped under foot; and another ensign put in its place" (*FR*, 195). In the same chapter, dealing with the market women's march to Versailles (5 October 1789), she notes that the "national troops were eager to convince the mob, that they were equally offended at the disrespect paid to the emblem of liberty" (202).

In her treatment of the liberty tree, Wollstonecraft, in effect, linguistically "disrespects" a revolutionary "emblem" celebrated by "patriots." The desecrated liberty tree "stuck up in every village" ominously suggests the revolutionary pikes affixed ostentatiously with "aristocratic" heads—an association reinforced ironically by the Phrygian bonnet or "liberty cap" that usually topped the trees. In addition, the "party-coloured" rags (an adjective meaning "diversity of colors," see Samuel Johnson, 1755 *Dictionary, SV*) refer to the tricolor ribbons that were also affixed to the trees, but perhaps she is also punning pejoratively on *party,* often associated with division or faction in the eighteenth century (see *FR*, 211, for instance). Moreover, the "rags" (another insult to *la patrie*) adorning "the shrivelled branches of the tree of liberty" certainly suggest that liberty is dying.[15] In short, by "insulting" a national symbol of the Revolution, Wollstonecraft performs the metaphoric equivalent of desecrating the cockade, revealing early in the book (Book one, chapter one) her latent ambivalence to the Revolution she is witnessing.

Her idea of a progressive ideological revolution continually bumps up against the realities of the concrete, flesh-and-blood Revolution, accounting for many of the book's tensive ironies. For instance, while Wollstonecraft sometimes insists that the Revolution constitutes a radical break from the past, she continually introduces evidence suggesting that the Revolution reproduces the past. Even her contrasts between the past and present reinforce this sense of repetition. In Book one (chapter one), she offers a critique of "the most celebrated nations" of antiquity to illustrate precisely what the Revolution is not:

> During the period they had to combat against oppression, and rear an infant state, what instances of heroism do not the annals of Greece and Rome display! But it was merely the blaze of passion . . . for after vanquishing their enemies, and making the most astonishing sacrifices to the glory of their country, they became civil tyrants, and preyed on the very society, for whose welfare it was easier to die, than to practice the sober duties of life, which insinuate through it the contentment that is rather felt than seen.
>
> (*FR*, 21)

Writing in the summer of 1793 and having already suggested that the past mars the Revolution, turning the oppressed into oppressors, Wollstonecraft seems strangely oblivious that the passage can be read ironically to apply to contemporary France, since her description arguably mirrors what is currently happening. Throughout the eighteenth century, writers commonly referred to ancient empires, like Sparta or Rome, or Eastern despotisms, such as Turkey, when they were really alluding to the situation at home and wanted to evade official censorship. The reader knew how to transpose Rome for London or Paris. If Wollstonecraft's procedure were less clear, one might suspect she was secretly criticizing the revolutionary regime during a dangerous time for writers and practically everyone else in France. Although she appears not to do this, she does have enough private doubts that are reflected in her linguistic subversions of the Revolution.

The example of Rome is illustrative, since she later (anticipating Marx) refers critically to the revolutionary "mania of imitating the Romans"; indeed, this "mania" had become a kind of revolutionary cult, "producing instances of false magnanimity, that always arise from imitation" (*FR*, 131). As an example of this "false magnanimity," she refers to French women, "not to be outdone by the [R]oman dames," theatrically sacrificing "their ornaments for the good of their country," and "the lively applauses of the assembly were reiterated with great gallantry" (169; cf. 144, 219). This example pejoratively reinforces her initial reference to Rome (21), just as her reference to imitation reinforces the idea of repetition, a point she remakes later when she remarks that "all sudden revolutions have been as suddenly overturned and things thrown back below their former state" (183).

The contradiction between a revolution that is progressive and linear and one that is repetitious and cyclical underscores the tension between her idea of the Revolution and the Revolution as she actually experiences it. Sometimes she inscribes this contradiction into the text that says precisely what she denies. Thus, in arguing that civilization is advancing, she reminds us of the past and the "atrocious vices and gigantic crimes, that sullied the polish of ancient manners," and then switches to the present and asks a rhetorical question to illustrate that "a civilization founded on reason and morality is, in fact, taking place in the world": "What nobleman, even in the states where they have the power of life and death, after giving an elegant entertainment, would now attract the detestation of his company, by ordering a domestic to be thrown into a pond to fatten the fish?" (*FR,* 111).

She means to say, of course, that a contemporary nobleman could not "now" do or get away with such an atrocious act without attracting "detestation," but the sentence says that no modern nobleman would now "attract the detestation" of his callous or intimidated company—just like the past. Moreover, the reader would be reminded of contemporary noblemen in France being arrested or guillotined, albeit not fed to fish, and this would suggest, again, that the oppressors and the oppressed had merely changed places. Because Wollstonecraft is seemingly oblivious to the reading with which she undermines her thesis, her attempt to escape history's vicious circle evokes a subversive reading relevant to Marx's well-known opening comments in *The Eighteenth Brumaire of Louis Bonaparte* (1852). Wollstonecraft, however, suggests that the Revolution is repeating "feudal" rather than revolutionary history, and she presents the Terror as a repetitive dramatic tragedy. Thus, as we will now see, she emplots the French tragedy as her revisionist version of *Macbeth.*

6

Wollstonecraft, *Macbeth,* and the Death of Louis XVI

VARIOUS persons and events illustrate the tensions involved in Wollstonecraft's revision of history. Her treatment of Louis XVI is especially significant, since his execution haunts some of her most memorable passages. Her depiction of the king illustrates her own ambivalence towards the Revolution, for there are two Louis. First, there is the Louis who lacks resolution and who is manipulated and governed by the court and Marie Antoinette. This Louis is effetely effeminate, without a "character" (*FR,* 71, 171), like Alexander Pope's misogynistic characterization of "most women" in "Epistle II. To a Lady" (11.1–2). It is this Louis who is weak and wavering, existing only as a "cipher." This particular representation of the king was a standard one in the 1790s. The other Louis, however, is radically different.

He is disgustingly repulsive—a glutton who had a "total disregard of delicacy, and even decency in his apartments," a husband who had a "devouring passion" for the queen, yet treated her "with great brutality, till she acquired sufficient finesse to subjugate him" (*FR,* 73). Although she found his embraces "abhorrent" (73), Marie Antoinette sexually manipulated him and, "managing the disgust she had for his person, she made him pay a kingly price for her favours" (74). Since the queen is "a complete actress," Wollstonecraft suggests this was her greatest role, enabling her to gain "unbounded sway" over the lust-crazed king (74). Indeed, the decadent past again repeats itself: the mistresses of Louis XV had manipulated him and "fought to forget his nauseous embraces in the arms of knaves" (28)—precisely as Marie Antoinette supposedly reacted to his grandson.[1]

Wollstonecraft, in short, adopts a current sexual interpretation (dating from the 1770s), illustrating the Bourbons' disgusting depravity, but her demonization of Louis extends to a demented Louis (*FR,* 74) who amuses himself by having animals tortured (much to the queen's repressed disgust), a Louis who, like other French kings, is a "sensual bigot" fond "of those religious systems, which, like a sponge, wipe out the crimes that haunt the terrified imaginations of unsound minds" (74). Indeed, after sanctioning the "demands" of the queen and the Comte d' Artois (his reactionary brother), who draw concessions by encouraging his "bestiality" during "moments of revelry, prolonged to the most disgusting excess of gluttony and intoxication," the bestial Louis retires to "his confessor to erase from his tender conscience the remembrance of the vices he resolved to indulge, and to reconcile the meanest dissimulation with a servile fear of the Being whose first attribute is truth" (188).

This demeaningly demonized Louis bears no resemblance to any credible historiography then or now. In fact, this grotesque caricature contradicted his image in France, where his supposed impotence had been, for years, the source of ribald jokes.[2] Wollstonecraft undoubtedly acquired her unrecognizable caricature from revolutionary sources with a vested interest in justifying his execution. The linguistic degradation of the queen's image and body are of course well known, but the correspondent assault on the king's image and body, recorded by Wollstonecraft, suggests a lost revolutionary version of the king's character and life.[3] While Wollstonecraft's two dialectic depictions of Louis (weakly effeminate versus sexually and religiously depraved) can probably be reconciled—the weak and dissipated Louis dominated by both his manipulative wife and his own morbid mind—what interests me is why Wollstonecraft needs to demonize the king. The answer is, I think, that his European reputation as a mild monarch coupled with his execution on 21 January (1793) dramatically turned European opinion against the Revolution. As a person struggling to believe in the Revolution, Wollstonecraft needed to believe his death was warranted, since disapproval of the execution constituted an implicit condemnation of the French Revolution. Consequently, Wollstonecraft deals with Louis' death (and her own ambivalence) theatrically, since the unspoken "guilt" she allusively evokes makes the king's (and France's) tragedy both ephemeral and explainable—the Terror becomes the event that paradoxically produces the comedic future—the happy ending that will wash the Revolution's guilty blood away.

It is this context that explains the power of Wollstonecraft's Versailles apostrophe, arguably the most memorable scene in her book.[4] The passage is preceded by an allusive comparison of Marie Antoinette with Lady Macbeth: the former's heart is hardened, and tenderness is banished "from the female bosom" (*FR*, 84)—alluding to Lady Macbeth's claim that having "given suck" to "the babe that milks me," she could have "dash'd the brains out" (*Macbeth*, 1.7.55–60)—a sentiment prefigured by her "unsex me" soliloquy: "Come to my woman's breasts, / And take my milk for gall, you murd'ring ministers" (see 1.5.41–54). This speech reverberates against her previous comment that Macbeth's nature "is too full o' th' milk of human kindness" (16–17), and which Wollstonecraft had earlier alluded to when she referred to (only to question) Louis' "milkiness of heart" (*FR*, 74; cf. Louis' "timid humanity" and his "desire to prevent the shedding of blood," 122). With these initial echoes of *Macbeth*, I want to show how Wollstonecraft envisions the king's tragedy and the monarchy's end within the theatrical terms of Shakespeare's play.

She begins the first paragraph of the Versailles apostrophe dramatically:

> How silent is now Versailles! The solitary foot, that mounts the sumptuous stair-case, rests on each landing-place, whilst the eye traverses the void, almost expecting to see the strong images of fancy burst into life. The train of the Louises, like the posterity of the Banquoes, pass in solemn sadness, pointing at the nothingness of grandeur, fading away on the cold canvass, which covers the nakedness of the spacious walls—whilst the gloominess of the atmosphere gives a deeper shade to the gigantic figures, that seem to be sinking into the embraces of death.
>
> (*FR*, 84)

Since the previous paragraph dealt with an incident that supposedly occurred 12 July 1789, there is an eerie transition to Versailles' silence—a silence the reader would relate to the "October Days" of 1789—when the royal family was forcibly removed from Versailles to Paris.

In addition, both the reader and Wollstonecraft would be reminded of other events impinging on Versailles' silence—the storming of the Tuileries on 10 August 1792 (the effective end of the monarchy) and the imprisonment of the royal family in the Temple (a revolutionary "repetition" of the October Days). But it is the execution of Louis on 21 January 1793 that provides the haunting context of Versailles' silence—an execution Wollstonecraft feared in letters written to her sister, Everina Wollstonecraft, and Joseph Johnson (December 24, 26, 1792). Since her chronological narrative, in *The French Revolution,* deals primarily with the Revolution's first six months, this chronological fiction absolves her from having to name the king's death directly, even though she evokes it by referring to Versailles' "silence."

In the apostrophe, her vision of the Louis is directly related to Macbeth's vision of "the posterity of the Banquoes" (see *Macbeth,* 4.1.112–24): she allusively positions herself in the place of Macbeth—the murderer of both the king and Banquo. Since "the posterity of the Banquoes" is likened to the "train of Louises," Wollstonecraft becomes the metaphoric murderer of the monarchy. In addition, her "strong images of fancy" echo the "strange images of death" that Ross says Macbeth "didst make" (*Macbeth,* 1.3.96–97) and that prefigure other images of death as well. But Wollstonecraft strongly misreads or rewrites the text she is evoking, since she suggests the monarchy's definitive end, while in Shakespeare's tragedy, Macbeth's vision of Banquo's "line"—a line that seems to "stretch out to th' crack of doom" (4.1.117)—establishes both its duration and legitimacy. Wollstonecraft's allusion, in fact, can be read as actually legitimizing the Bourbon line, which would eventually prevail despite Louis' (Duncan/Banquo's) death.[5] Similarly, the "train of Louises . . . pointing at the nothingness of grandeur" (*FR,* 84) subverts or is subverted allusively by Macbeth's lament that "the blood-battered Banquo smiles" and "points" (at the royal line), acknowledging "them for his" (4.1.123–24). Wollstonecraft's "nothingness of grandeur" is, in *Macbeth,* the promise of a long regal line. Her allusions to *Macbeth* evoke the authoritative text(s) that haunt her revisionist drama.

For instance, the ghostly images that seem to be fading as the paragraph ends reappear in the next paragraph:

> Warily entering the endless apartments, half shut up, the fleeting shadow of the pensive wanderer, reflected in long glasses, that vainly gleam in every direction, slacken the nerves, without appalling the heart; though lascivious pictures, in which grace varnishes voluptuousness, no longer seductive, strikes continually home to the bosom the melancholy moral, that anticipates the frozen lesson of experience. The very air is chill, seeming to clog the breath; and the wasting dampness of destruction appears to be stealing into the vast pile, on every side.
>
> (*FR,* 84–85)

Who is entering the "endless apartments" but the synecdochic "solitary foot" that initially mounted "the sumptuous stair-case" and reached the top at the end of the previous paragraph. Like its predecessor, the passage is haunted by ghostly presences as Wollstonecraft imaginatively watches herself in the third person, additionally distancing and disguising herself through half revealed "parts"—a "solitary foot," an "eye" that "traverses," or a "shadow" reflected in long mirrors. This distancing is modified by the present tense, which paradoxically intensifies her closeness to the ghostly past.[6]

Moreover, Wollstonecraft is linguistically retracing the steps of the last intruders—the revolutionary "ruffians" who invaded the palace, mounted the "grand stair-case" and then broke into the "different apartments" (FR, 204) on 6 October 1789—the day the royal family was forced to return to Paris. Wollstonecraft returns to the scene of a crime she believes "stained" the Revolution (see FR, 204–6, 209) and guiltily retraces its "steps." She even resembles the ghostly presences that seem to haunt Versailles—suddenly she is a "fleeting shadow," fleeing from and or reflected in the long glasses that distort and magnify her. In Macbeth, Banquo's ghost is the "horrible shadow" frightening Macbeth (3.4.107), so it is not clear whether Wollstonecraft is seeing only an image of herself or the Bourbon phantoms as well. The "long glasses" also conjure, again, Macbeth's vision of Banquo's line. The eighth king, we will remember, holds up a "glass" reflecting "many more" kings, and it is at this point that the blood-spattered Banquo smiles and enjoys his silent triumph over Macbeth (4.1.119–24). There is a strange nexus between the murdered monarchy and the haunted image Wollstonecraft sees reflected in this wilderness of textual mirrors.

In addition, the effect of the passage contradicts her "fearlessness" (the heart is not "appalled"), as she makes her way down the stairs with a "melancholy moral" probably related to "the nothingness of grandeur" of the vanquished Bourbons, but that comes across like so much whistling in the dark. Trying to convince herself that the past is dead, she closes the paragraph with "lascivious pictures" that are "no longer seductive," just as in the previous paragraph the "train of the Louises" fades "away on the cold canvass."

This effort to exorcise the ghostly past fails again in the subsequent paragraph, where it is clear that she has fled the palace to seek relief in the garden below:

> The oppressed heart seeks for relief in the garden; but even there the same images glide along the wide neglected walks—all is fearfully still; and if a little rill creeping through the gathering moss down the cascade, over which it used to rush, bring to mind the description of the grand water works, it is only to excite a languid smile at the futile attempt to equal nature.

> (FR, 85)

Synecdochically distancing herself again, the "oppressed heart" seeks immediate relief from the presence of the past, since that is what is obviously oppressing it. In the previous paragraph, the heart was not "appalled" by shadowy images, but here it seeks relief from the "images" it now finds haunting—"the same images [that] glide along the wild neglected walks"—the "strong images" of "the Louises" mentioned in the first paragraph. For a moment, "all is *fearfully* still" (my emphasis), like the silence that haunts Versailles or the ghostly Louis haunting Wollstonecraft. The "languid smile" ending the paragraph is ostensibly Wollstonecraft calming herself with the smiling reflection that the artificial pomp of Versailles—the *water works,* a "contrivance for producing a pleasing spectacle by means of water in motion; an ornamental fountain or cascade" (*OED*, def. no. 3), and perhaps the suggestive "tears" (no. 3b) shed for the monarchy—cannot equal nature. But the "languid smile" also evokes Banquo's triumphant smile or perhaps the collective smile of the ghostly images rebuking her "futile attempt to equal nature" or Shakespeare, for the echoes of *Macbeth,* like the knocking at the door (*Macbeth*, 2.3.1–20), are too loud to be ignored.[7] Oppressed by the past, Wollstonecraft simultaneously exorcises and evokes it.

There is even more smiling in the next paragraph, as she continues resisting the past:

> Lo! this was the palace of the great king!—the abode of magnificence! Who has broken the charm? Why does it now inspire only pity? Why; because nature, smiling around, presents to the imagination materials to build farms, and hospitable mansions, where, without raising idle admiration, that gladness will reign, which opens the heart to benevolence, and that industry, which renders innocent pleasure sweet.
>
> (*FR,* 85)

The series of rhetorical questions deflates the majestic ruins that no longer awe or inspire, since it is the Terror that has "broken the charm" with the death of Louis XVI and hence the death of the monarchy—the "great king"[8] perhaps reminding her additionally of Louis XIV and the other dead kings who seem to haunt the palace "like the posterity of the Banquoes."

But Wollstonecraft has also broken the ghostly charm of the past by breaking off precisely at this point and making the death of kings, which she previously framed in terms of *Macbeth,* a matter of "pity" rather than tragedy. This allows her to turn from the past to the future—the ambiguous "languid smile" now becomes the approving smile of nature sanctifying the "life" that will be born out of the monarchy's death. Walking through the ci-devant royal garden, she imagines the "materials" of the murdered monarchy providing the farms and mansions where "gladness will reign," in a pastoral utopia projected in the future. Working with previous "materials," it is within this context that her regicide paradox emerges: out of the murdered monarchy's ruins, the utopian future will spring (cf. *Rights of Men, Works,* 5:56 [par. one, 1.11], 57 [par. two, 11.1–4]).

But having seemingly just exorcised the murdered monarchy with a vision of the smiling future, she again breaks "the charm" and abruptly begins "weeping":

> Weeping—scarcely conscious that I weep, O France! over the vestiges of thy former oppression; which, separating man from man with a fence of iron, sophisticated all, and made many completely wretched; I tremble, lest I should meet some unfortunate being, fleeing from the despotism of licentious freedom, hearing the snap of the *guillotine* at his heels; merely because he was once noble, or has afforded an asylum to those, whose only crime is their name—and, if my pen almost bound with eagerness to record the day, that levelled the Bastille with the dust, making the towers of despair tremble to their base; the recollection that still the abbey is appropriated to hold the victims of revenge and suspicion, palsies the hand that would fain do justice to the assault, which tumbled into heaps of ruins walls that seemed to mock the resistless force of time. Down fell the temple of despotism; but despotism has not been buried in its ruins! Unhappy country!—When will thy children cease to tear thy bosom? When will a change of opinion, producing a change of morals, render thee truly free? When will truth give life to real magnanimity, and justice place equality on a stable seat? When will thy sons trust, because they deserve to be trusted; and private virtue become the guarantee of patriotism? Ah!—when will thy government become the most perfect, because thy citizens are the most virtuous!
>
> (*FR,* 85)

In this apostrophe to France, the exorcised past is again being evoked.

Wollstonecraft's weeping remembrance of France's former oppression actually links it with the present oppression of the Terror. For it is surely the Terror that causes her to tremble "lest she meet some unfortunate being, fleeing from the despotism of licentious freedom, hearing the snap of the *guillotine* at his heels; merely because he was once noble" (*FR,* 85). Although the vague victim could be any noble or citizen, this "unfortunate being" with the "*guillotine* at his heels" resembles evocatively Louis XVI, "this

unfortunate man" (189) who, before he was executed, was warn-
ingly made to "look around . . . when *danger was at his heels*"
(128; my emphasis). In Wollstonecraft's regicide drama, there is
no catharsis, since "pity" is now refigured as "terror." The past
that she has seemingly exorcised and escaped suddenly reproduces
itself before her weeping eyes, in the form of the revolutionary
"present."

Although she seems to project the suppressed theme of guilt,
evoked in the previous allusions to *Macbeth,* on to the bloodied
Revolution, there is also a sense of personal responsibility, since
she hesitates "to record the day" the Bastille fell—a fall from which
she dates the Revolution's birth (*FR,* 118). It is almost as if she
feels that by linguistically opening the Bastille, she will be legitimizing the revolutionary terror and the "past" it seemingly
reproduces.

For instance, her reference to "the abbey" that is still "appropriated to hold the victims of revenge and suspicion" (*FR,* 85)
underscores the repetition, since the Abbaye, the prison attached
to the abbey at Saint-Germaine, was used by the Old Regime for
disciplining members of the Gardes françaises and for debtors of
high social status. During the Revolution, it was reused as a prison
for soldiers and political prisoners. It was also the scene of the
first of the September Massacres.[9] Moreover, it was the prison
where Wollstonecraft's friend, Madame Roland, was incarcerated
(31 May–8 November 1793) before she was guillotined (8 November), so there may be a personal basis to the allusion as well.

As the old site of monarchic oppression becomes the new locus
for revolutionary oppression, Wollstonecraft reverts to her thesis
that the oppressive past influences the revolutionary present:
"Down fell the temple of despotism; but despotism has not been
buried in its ruins!" The "ruins" of "despotism" (the Bastille) are
reminiscent of the ruins of Versailles and the dead past that "lives"
incarnated in the same repetitive forms (the Abbaye). For even as
the Bastille falls—that "temple of despotism"—Wollstonecraft, I
suggest, punningly alludes to another "Temple"—the prison where
the royal family was imprisoned after the storming of the Tuileries
(their first prison) and the fall of the monarchy (10 August 1792).

Having evoked the king's death, the Terror, and the revolutionary prisons that replicate the past as a hesitant prelude to the next
chapter, in which she will "record" the Bastille's fall, Wollstonecraft recovers her faith in the Revolution and escapes the doubts
and qualifications by a series of evasive rhetorical questions that
defer the regeneration of France and the Revolution's eventual con-

summation in the "future"—a mythical cause-and-effect time when the French people will be spiritually transformed and their government becomes "the most perfect, because thy citizens are the most virtuous!" (*FR*, 85). Present revolutionary violence will somehow be mysteriously justified by a fantasied future.

It is a classic revolutionary response to present problems, allowing her to write her way out of the restrictive complications the Revolution seemingly reproduces. But since, as I suggest, the repressed subject of the Versailles apostrophe is the king's death, I want to focus now on the letter she wrote to Joseph Johnson (26 December 1792) and show how it impinges on the apostrophe, recollecting that the letter precedes the apostrophe by at least six months.

Both passages are arguably the most memorable of her revolutionary texts, and both deal with the king's death. Shortly after arriving in Paris, Wollstonecraft wrote her sister, Everina, a letter (24 December 1792), noting that the "day after tomorrow I expect to see the king at the bar—and the consequences that will follow I am almost afraid to anticipate."[10] The reference is to the king's trial for treason, and although Wollstonecraft seems to think, mistakenly, that he will be executed on the 26th, her apprehension is reinforced in her letter to Joseph Johnson, which she postponed to the same night (the 26th), so that she could tell him "that this day was not stained by blood."

The pertinent parts are as follows:

> About nine o'clock this morning, the king passed by my window, moving silently along (excepting now and then a few strokes on the drum, which rendered the stillness more awful) through empty streets, surrounded by the national guards, who, clustering round the carriage, seemed to deserve their name. . . . I can scarcely tell you why, but an association of ideas made the tears flow insensibly from my eyes, when I saw Louis sitting, with more dignity than I expected from his character, in a hackney coach going to meet death, where so many of his race have triumphed. My fancy instantly brought Louis XIV before me, entering the capital with all his pomp, after one of the victories most flattering to his pride, only to see the sunshine of prosperity overshadowed by the sublime gloom of misery. I have been alone ever since; and, though my mind is calm, I cannot dismiss the lively images that have filled my imagination all the day. Nay, do not smile, but pity me; for, once or twice, lifting my eyes from the paper, I have seen eyes glare through a glass-door opposite my chair, and bloody hands shook at me. Not the distant sound of a footstep can I hear. My apartments are remote from those of the servants, the only persons who sleep with

me in an immense hotel, one folding door opening after another.—I wish I had even kept the cat with me!—I want to see something alive; death in so many frightful shapes has taken hold of my fancy.—I am going to bed—and, for the first time in my life, I cannot put out the candle.[11]

There are many similarities between this letter and the apostrophe.

Like her Versailles script, Wollstonecraft notices the "stillness," whether in the silence of the streets or her own remote apartments. The king "moving silently along" resembles the "train of the Louises" that "pass in solemn sadness" (*FR*, 84) or the royal ghosts gliding "along the wide neglected walks," where "all is fearfully still" (*FR*, 85). There is the same sense of desertion and remoteness, whether in Versailles, where Wollstonecraft warily enters "the endless apartments" (*FR*, 84), or in her own remote "apartments" in Paris, "one folding door opening after another" (cf. *Macbeth*, 2.2.5 and *FR*, where ruffians break into the royal "apartments" at Versailles on 6 October 1789 [*Works*, 6:204]).

Similarly, her vision of the "train of Louises" at Versailles "sinking into the embraces of death" (*FR*, 84) resembles her vision of Louis XIV "overshadowed by the sublime gloom of misery"—both passages are triggered by the last of the Bourbon kings. In addition, just as her "fancy" conjures up Louis XIV in Paris, so "strong images of fancy" evoke the "train of the Louises" (*FR*, 84), and the "lively images" filling her imagination in Paris are like those "strong images of fancy" she expects to see "burst into life"—the "same images" gliding along the "neglected walks" at Versailles (*FR*, 84–85). Moreover, the "strong images of fancy" which I suggested allusively evoke "the strange images of death" in *Macbeth* (1.3.97) are prefigured in her desire "to see something alive; death in so many frightful shapes has taken hold of my fancy."[12]

The similarities continue. Her rhetorical address to Johnson—"Nay, do not smile, but pity me"—evokes the "languid smile" over Versailles' "broken charm"—a Versailles that now inspires "only pity" because "nature, smiling around, presents to the imagination" future "materials" (*FR*, 85). But it also evokes Banquo's silent smile, and the "tears" flowing "insensibly from" Wollstonecraft's eyes in Paris prefigure her "weeping" over the tragedy of France at Versailles (*FR*, 85).

In Paris, Wollstonecraft also imagines ghostly visitors: "once or twice, lifting my eyes from the paper, I have seen eyes glare through a glass-door . . . and bloody hands shook at me."[13] Since the entire letter is about the king's impending death, the glaring eyes are connected in her mind with Banquo's ghostly eyes, glaring at the guilty Macbeth:

> Avaunt and quit my sight! Let the earth hide thee!
> Thy bones are marrowless, thy blood is cold;
> Thou hast no speculation in those eyes
> Which thou dost glare with.
>
> *(Macbeth,* 3.4.94–97)

Not surprisingly, given all the Macbethean echolalia, the "bloody hands" that "shook" at her also conjure up the banquet scene, where the terrified Macbeth tells the ghostly Banquo, "Thou canst not say I did it. Never shake / Thy gory locks at me" (3.4.50–51).

Noting this "echo . . . of Macbeth's cry to Banquo's ghost," Margaret Tims wonders whether Wollstonecraft was "feeling a twinge of guilt at her tacit complicity in the Revolution."[14] Although Tims decides that Wollstonecraft was probably spooked by the solitude, her original suggestion is more compelling, since Wollstonecraft allusively becomes Macbeth in both passages—passages connected by the king's death. Wollstonecraft, in effect, reworked the imagery and associations in her letter to Johnson into the Versailles apostrophe—an apostrophe whose secret subject is regicide and guilt.

What then is the nature of Wollstonecraft's "tacit guilt"? Since 1789, she had helped legitimize the Revolution abroad and, despite mounting evidence that something had gone wrong, she continued to do so in her subsequent works. Before leaving for France, she had written to William Roscoe (12 November 1792), cavalierly dismissing squeamish complaints that "some of the mere instrument of the revolution were too sharp."[15] Then arriving in France, she was suddenly confronted with the reality of the king's execution and "the mere instrument of the revolution" that would chop off his head. Wollstonecraft's dilemma was the now-familiar one of the intellectual who has enthusiastically supported a revolution suddenly gone bad. While she condemns some of the revolutionary excesses and acknowledges tacitly feelings of guilt by allusively equating herself with the regicidal Macbeth, she also provides strong misreadings and displaces or projects her "guilt" onto other things (the past, the capricious French, unnamed Jacobins). Wollstonecraft could not ultimately renounce her faith in the idea of the regenerative French Revolution—a revolution she feared could be stained with innocent blood—blood that also seemed to be on her own hands. The two previous passages (Versailles and Paris) are ritualistically written around exorcism and confession, but it is precisely when she accuses herself that she blindly "looks away," seemingly unaware of the incriminatory implications.

In the letter to Johnson, for instance, she sympathizes with the vulnerable Louis and fears that the day might have metaphorically been "stained with blood," just as the letter itself or the "pages" she is apparently writing about the Revolution.[16] The ghostly visitor who shakes his hands at her reveals her ambivalence toward the "real" Revolution, since the visitor either represents the revolutionary terrorist seeking another innocent victim (Wollstonecraft herself) or, more likely, a victim of the Revolution, like the king who accusingly shakes "bloody hands" at her.

Confronted by his ghostly condemner accusingly shaking his "gory locks," Macbeth protests his innocence—"Thou canst not say I did it" (*Macbeth,* 3.4.50–51). Macbeth is, of course, technically correct on two accounts—he did not directly participate in Banquo's murder, even though he arranged it, and the ghostly Banquo cannot say literally he "did it" but can only silently reproach him. The same process of rationalization seems to transpire in the letter. The angry eyes that glare at her "through a glass-door"[17] also suggest a mirror (like the "mirrors" at Versailles) or a reflection, in which Wollstonecraft sees herself accusingly, since she imaginatively conjures up the threatening specter, synecdochically seen as "eyes" and "hands"—the same way she sees herself in the Versailles apostrophe.

Moreover, the "bloody hands" certainly suggest Macbeth's gory hands and the royal blood that stains them (*Macbeth,* 2.2.58–61)— a scene repeated when Lady Macbeth tries obsessively to wash the blood from her hands, just as Wollstonecraft is ritualistically writing "out" her sense of guilt over the king's spilled blood— blood that she fears, in her letter to Johnson, will metaphorically "stain" the pages she writes.[18] Having identified herself with the regicide Macbeth, she also, as we will see, puts herself in the place of Lady Macbeth—the woman who also has innocent blood on her hands.

In *The French Revolution,* Wollstonecraft continues to write out the book's secret subject. After commenting that "the sex, called the tender, commit the most flagrant acts of barbarity when irritated" (*FR,* 125–26), she refers to revolutionary violence and "transactions, over which, for the honour of human nature, it were to be wished oblivion could draw the winding-sheet, that has often enwrapped a heart, whose benevolence has been felt, but not known" (126). The imagery expresses her wish to forget or cover

up and bury the revolutionary violence that stains the Revolution
and "the honour of human nature." It is followed by two revealing sentences:

> But, if it be impossible to erase from memory these foul deeds, which,
> like the stains of deepest dye revived by remorse in the conscience,
> can never be rubbed out—why dwell circumstantially on the excesses
> that revolt humanity, and dim the lustre of the picture, on which the
> eye has gazed with rapture, often obliged to look up to heaven to
> forget the misery endured on earth? Since, however, we cannot 'out
> the damned spot,' it becomes necessary to observe, that, whilst despot-
> ism and superstition exist, the convulsions, which the regeneration of
> man occasions, will always bring forward the vices they have engen-
> dered, to devour their parents.
>
> (*FR,* 126)

Wollstonecraft's comment on the impossible endeavor "to erase
from the memory these foul deeds . . . revived by remorse in the
conscience" is approximately the same language she uses to criticize Louis XVI, who "employed his confessor to erase from his
tender conscience the remembrance of the vices he resolved to
indulge" (*FR,* 188). Louis, we will remember, was "particularly
fond of those religious systems, which like a sponge, wipe out the
crimes that haunt the terrified imagination of unsound minds" (74).
Even though there is an implicit distinction between the "crimes"
that Louis believes are "wiped out" by his "confession" and Wollstonecraft's realization that it may not be possible "to erase" the
"foul deeds" from revolutionary memory, the result is similar, since
Wollstonecraft chooses to "look away" from revolutionary crimes
and then rationalize them away by blaming the past. The fact that
she uses a confessional language linking her to Louis suggests that
his murder is one of the "foul deeds" and "excesses" staining
("stains of deepest dye") her conscience.

There are also suggestive echoes of Lady Macbeth's guilty conscience, a conscience Macbeth wishes erased or cleansed:

> Canst thou not minister to a mind diseas'd
> Pluck from the memory a rooted sorrow,
> Raze out the written troubles of the brain,
> And with some sweet oblivious antidote
> Cleanse the stuff'd bosom of that perilous stuff
> Which weighs upon the heart?
>
> (*Macbeth,* 5.3.41–45).

The "perilous stuff" (the regicidal murder) that "weighs upon the heart" is reminiscent of Wollstonecraft's "oppressed heart," which seeks "relief" in the Versailles apostrophe (*FR,* 85). By alluding to blood that she reinscribes into the text ("stains of deepest dye" that cannot be "rubbed out") and identifying with Lady Macbeth, who also cannot "out the damned spot," Wollstonecraft again implicates herself allusively with the king's murder. (In *The Female Reader* [1789], she quotes the famous sleepwalking scene, including Lady Macbeth's guilty words; see *Works,* 4:213.)

After alluding to this blood and just before her direct identification with Lady Macbeth, Wollstonecraft had tried to look away: "why dwell circumstantially on the excesses that revolt humanity, and dim the lustre of the picture, on which the eye has gazed with rapture, often obliged to look up to heaven to forget the misery endured on earth" (*FR,* 126). These circumstantial "excesses" are, of course, the concrete atrocities that "dim" her ideological "picture" of the Revolution. Indeed, the metaphors reveal the discrepancy between the Revolution's reality and her imaginative idea of the Revolution—for her "painting" does not imitate or replicate reality—it encapsulates her vision of a "spotless" revolution that "the eye has gazed with rapture." This is certainly preferable to the hostile eyes that had glared at her in her letter to Johnson, and she reinforces her revolutionary illusion by looking "up" (and away) to "heaven," forgetting "the misery endured on earth," once the "picture" is stained by real excesses.

Her stained revolutionary "painting" is, in fact, like the painting of the "Louises" she sees at Versailles, "fading away on the cold canvass" or the "lascivious pictures . . . no longer seductive" or enchanting (*FR,* 84–85). But her exercise in revolutionary repression, embodied in her endeavor to look away, is also illusory, since "we cannot 'out the damned spot.'" Consequently, she rationalizes the revolutionary spot away with the consoling idea that the existence of "despotism and superstition" causes the temporal "convulsions" that will disappear when man is regenerated and the past is erased (*FR,* 126). But this is just another looking off into an ideological future where the pleasing "picture" will be mysteriously restored.

Wollstonecraft again suggests that the past will continue to be reproduced until it is erased and that "despotism and superstition . . . will always bring forward the vices they have engendered, to devour their parents" (*FR,* 126). The familial metaphor umbilically connects the oppressive past with the revolutionary present, and while the parents (despotism and superstition) reproduce ("engender") the vices ("foul deeds," "excesses," "spots," "convulsions") that cannibalistically devour the parents, their close relation suggests a genetic reproduction and hence a repetition of the past, ending only when man is regenerated in the future. The eventual erasure of the metaphors—the biological relation destroyed by the "convulsions" or birth pains of regenerated man—reexpress the role of ideology in Wollstonecraft's history.

The imagery of revolutionary offspring devouring their parents is reminiscent of Sin being "devoured" by her incestuous offspring in *Paradise Lost* and the various gods devoured by their children in the Greek myths. In addition, Wollstonecraft is apparently alluding to and reversing Vergniaud's comment (13 March 1793) that "the Revolution, like Saturn, successively devouring its children, will engender, finally, only despotism with the calamities that accompany it."[19] Wollstonecraft had met Vergniaud in the winter of 1793 and may have written the passage after his death (he was guillotined 31 October 1793), in which case, the saying becomes doubly ironic, since Vergniaud had presided over the king's trial and had voted for his death, pronouncing the death sentence in January 1793.

All of this brings us back to her statement that "we cannot 'out the damn spot,'" since the collective "we" encompasses the collective guilt of all supporters of the Revolution, but it retrospectively includes the Revolution's opponents as well, since they "cause" the "excesses." For instance, in the next paragraph, she refers to revolutionary terrorists as "a spurious race of men, a set of cannibals, who have gloried in their crimes," but she palliates the Revolution's "blood" by quoting Mirabeau: "But if the anger of the people be terrible . . . it is the sang froid of despotism, that is atrocious; those systematic cruelties, which have made more wretches in a day than the popular insurrections have immolated in a course of years!" (*FR,* 126). Suddenly, it is "the sang froid of despotism" that is not only more "cold-blooded," but more bloodthirsty as well. Mirabeau continues comparing despotism with the Revolution in Wollstonecraft's footnote (n. 2): "Let us compare . . . the number of innocents sacrificed by mistake, by the sanguinary maxims of the courts of criminal judicature, and the ministerial vengeance exercised secretly in the dungeons of Vincennes, and in the cells of the Bastille, with the sudden and impetuous vengeance of the multitude, and then decide on which side barbarity appears" (*FR,* 126).

As Wollstonecraft approvingly quotes Mirabeau's selective balancing of revolutionary excesses that are "terrible" with despotism's "atrocious" systematic cruelties, or, in the footnote, the public revolutionary trials of "innocents sacrificed by mistake" with the "ministerial vengeance" exercised secretly in despotism's dungeons, she sanctions another classic rationalization of revolutionary violence: the oppressive violence of the past exceeds revolutionary excesses. Washing a revolution clean with the Brobdingnagian blood of its opposition, the argument makes the opposition the efficient cause of both the "excesses" as well as its own merited death. All this bears on Wollstonecraft's preoccupation with the blood that stains the Revolution and herself as well. She ends the chapter (Book 3, chapter 1) noting that French soldiers swore "not to stain their hands with the blood of their fellow citizens" (*FR,* 127), but it is the guillotine's "blood," of course, that "stains" both the Revolution (216) and Wollstonecraft's conscience. Towards the book's end, the Parisians (the perpetrators of the bloody Revolution) are "covered" with "foul stains" (198).

Now we need to turn again to the letter to Johnson. Just before going to bed, Wollstonecraft lifts her eyes "from the paper"—the confessional letter she is writing to Johnson—and then sees hostile eyes glaring at her as well as the "bloody hands" that shake at her ominously. Unnerved by "so many frightful shapes" of death possessing her "fancy," her own hands presumably shake as she finishes the letter with the trembling statement that "for the first time in my life, I cannot put out the candle."[20]

It is appropriate that she also concludes the letter with additional echoes from *Macbeth.* Macbeth, himself, sees many frightful shapes, including his ghostly accuser, and in act five, Lady Macbeth, "troubled with thick-coming fancies" (5.3.38), writes on paper, reads it, and then seals it before returning to bed (5:1.4–9). The paper is presumably a confession of her guilt, which she writes out and then seals, just as Wollstonecraft presumably seals her letter before going to bed with light. In the sleepwalking scene, Lady Macbeth carries a taper, and the gentlewoman informs the doctor that "she has light by her continually. 'Tis her command" (*Macbeth,* 5.1.24–25)—a passage Wollstonecraft included earlier in *The Female Reader* (*Works,* 4:213).

In this intertextual interstice, *The French Revolution* and the letter to Joseph Johnson conflate, as Wollstonecraft frames the king's death and the Revolution's blood in the theatrical terms of *Macbeth.* Since the Revolution's tragedy is also her own, her ingenuous dismissal of the "tragedies" of the ancients (because they teach no "moral" lesson) is contextually significant: Oedipus, for instance, "though perfectly *innocent* . . . is fearfully punished

. . . for a *crime* in which *his will had no part*" (*FR*, 112; my emphasis).[21] Wollstonecraft writes "out" the spot, the stain, the ghostly presence of the guillotined king—the collective blood of the Revolution's victims. This "writing out" is simultaneously an exposure of her own ambivalent feelings as well as a crossing out or erasure—an expiatory exorcism of the incriminatory blood she feels to be on her hands.

In "'That Great Stage Where Senators Perform': *Macbeth* and the Politics of Romantic Theatre," Mary Jacobus argues that regicide in *Macbeth* was associated in Romantic theater with the French Revolution.[22] Wollstonecraft, as we have seen, established an earlier context for revising the Revolution through the paradigms of *Macbeth*. The fact that other pro-revolutionary writers such as Helen Maria Williams also used *Macbeth* to write "out" their personal tragedy as well as France's public tragedy suggests that Shakespeare's drama provided them the terms to articulate, to act out, and to resolve the crisis in representation. In *The French Revolution,* Wollstonecraft projects guilty blood onto the past and the unnamed Jacobins ("branded with an indelible stigma," 6:144) who "stain" the Revolution—a Revolution inevitably purified by the future that will finally redeem it.

In retrospect, Wollstonecraft's emplotment of the French Revolution as a Shakespearean tragedy corresponded with the narrative strategies of other writers who were recreating their own versions of history, for history is a story that invariably involves the genres and strategies of fiction. By framing the Revolution in terms of *Macbeth,* Wollstonecraft suggested that all that was contradictory, confusing, and ambiguous could be resolved in an intelligible form and that ultimately the French Revolution made sense. The Revolution stained with innocent blood, the Revolution transformed into an alien event was reconceived as the recognizable, "tragic" repetition of the past, ineluctably purified by the redemptive future. The deferral and consummation of the "real" French Revolution in a mythic future meant that the French tragedy could be resolved and eventually rewritten as comedy—an ironic return to the happy ending that the Revolution's advocates had predicted in 1789. The future resolution of France's tragedy was a way of resolving the crisis in prior representation. *Macbeth* made it possible for Wollstonecraft to explain the Revolution's betrayal by casting France's public tragedy as her own private tragedy as well. It allowed her to explain the prelapsarian revolution's "fall" and to exorcise private doubts by revising the Revolution's theatrical plot. The rewriting of the Revolution also entailed the rewriting of *Macbeth* and the refiguration of difference as well as similarity. While it may be that her strong reading of Shakespeare also enabled her to rationalize and project guilty blood onto a counterrevolutionary "other" or that revolutionary drama trivializes the Terror by making its blood theatrically "unreal," it may also be that an event as complexly variegated as the French Revolution paradoxically attains its protean, historical shapes through the supreme fictions of the human imagination. Wollstonecraft's achievement, in *The French Revolution,* was to recreate one such luminous form.

7

The Bastille's Blood: The October Days,
Barriers, and Marie Antoinette

I

In her version of *Macbeth,* Wollstonecraft writes "out" the Terror, and her account of the storming of the Bastille reillustrates how she reconciles tensions within her revolutionary history, since it impinges again on her preoccupation with the Revolution's "blood." In Wollstonecraft's writings, the Bastille is the monstrous symbol of royal despotism, as it was for most of enlightened Europe, and the publicity generated by prison literature such as Linguet's *Memoirs of the Bastille* and Latude's *Memoirs of Vengeance* contributed to what we now know was a ubiquitous cultural myth.

Wollstonecraft's narrative is from the crowd's point of view. This allows her to re-create the event as it was happening, and it exonerates her from any errors (writing four years after the event), since she is simply recounting the vanquishers' version. She is aware that the Bastille's fall had been exaggerated; hence she refers repeatedly to "rumors" and "exaggerations" inflaming the people's "imaginations." This is a strategy she employs throughout (see *FR, Works,* 6:82, 93, 97, 127, 129, 164, 195, 203). But while she qualifies her narrative by acknowledging that events may have been exaggerated, the revolutionary version becomes her official history, since the crowd's viewpoint dominates her account.

Similarly, she moderates acts of revolutionary violence, here and throughout, by using assorted emotional words in their different grammatical forms: *intoxication* (*FR,* 27, 119, 123, 176, 218), *inebriation* (29, 55, 155), *enthusiasm* (123, 140), *effusions* (213), *giddiness* (133, 143, 210), *excesses* (60, 126, 129, 150), and *effervescence* (56, 79, 95, 99, 127, 151, 192, 222). The effect is to suggest unfortunate but understandable emotional excitement extenuated by the circumstantial pressures of the moment—rumors, provocations, and misunderstandings. In her letter to Joseph Johnson (15 February 1793), Wollstonecraft had criticized the palliation of revolutionary violence (*Works,* 6:445), but in her history she often comes across as doing just that, as when she laments that sometimes it is necessary "to give the soft name of enthusiasm to cruelty" (198; cf. 129). In *Preface to M. Brissot's Address to His Constituents* (1794), Burke had noted that revolutionaries use "the whole compass of language" to find "synonymes and circumlocutions for massacres and murder. Things are never called by their common names. Massacre is sometimes *agitation,* sometimes *effervescence,* sometimes *excess;* sometimes too continued an exercise of *revolutionary power.*" But antirevolutionaries also had their own palliative vocabulary.

The primary difference between Wollstonecraft's delicate treatment of the "crowd" that takes the Bastille and her severe condemnation of the "mob" that invades Versailles (October 5 and 6, 1789) is that the former event constitutes, for her, the mythic origin of the Revolution (*FR,* 118), while the latter is yet another "stain" on the Revolution's good name.

But since Wollstonecraft was writing about the Bastille's fall during the Terror, she was already noting revolutionary contradictions and hence recording her own ambivalence about the Revolution's mythic beginning. For instance, the royal troops gathered in Paris just before the Bastille's fall are a provocative cause for the "premature" birth of "liberty": "From the presence of these troops, and their abortive attempt to crush liberty in the egg, the shell was prematurely broken, and the enthusiasm of Frenchmen excited before their judgement was in any considerable degree formed" (*FR,* 123). Looking back on the Revolution's origin, she implies that its birth was prematurely forced, precipitating the "enthusiasm" and "excesses" that continue to stain it.

In the same chapter (Book 3, chapter 1) following (two chapters earlier) her account of the Bastille's fall, she stops to consider whether the Revolution was worth all the excesses—that is, the Terror. If the National Assembly had "been allowed quietly to have made some reforms, paving the way for more, the Bastille, though tottering on its dungeons, might yet have stood erect. And, if it had, the sum of human misery could scarcely have been increased" (*FR,* 123). There are two initial ways of reading the first sentence: the National Assembly's hypothetical "reforms" would have allowed the structure of despotism, though damaged, to remain intact; or, these reforms would have prevented the premature release of violent liberty and rendered the Bastille a powerless "form." The second sentence, however, supports the second reading, suggesting that if the Bastille had not fallen, "the sum of human misery could scarcely have been increased," since the Terror has created at least as much misery as the old despotism. Although there is seemingly a quantitative equivalence of the misery produced by both, Wollstonecraft implicitly questions the Revolution by connecting the Bastille's fall to the Terror's "misery."

This is reinforced in the subsequent sentences: "For the *guillotine* not finding its way to the splendid square it has polluted, streams of innocent blood would not have flowed, to obliterate the remembrance of false imprisonment, and drown the groans of solitary grief in the loud cry of agony—when, the thread of life quickly cut in twain, the quivering light of hope is instantly dashed out—and the billows suddenly closing, the silence of death is felt! This tale is soon told" (*FR*, 123).

The passage reflects Wollstonecraft's ambivalence, in which she seems confused or unclear as to whether the Bastille's fall was worth the guillotine's blood. The implicit subjunctive ("For [if] the guillotine [had] not found its way") is balanced by the guillotine's real presence in the "splendid square it has polluted"—the *place de la Révolution* (formerly the place de Louis XV), where it first "found" its way on 21 January 1793, for the execution of Louis XVI. The "innocent blood" of its victims is balanced by the "remembrance" of the Bastille's victims, a "remembrance" that is obliterated or washed away by the guillotine's blood, since one crime cancels another. It is almost as if this blood is expiatory— the price paid for the Old Order's crimes.[1] But it is also as if all the Revolution's "stains"—the blood, the guillotines, and the Terror escape and flow from the Bastille's "opening."

There are other ambiguities. The contrast between the public executions and the secret imprisonments—the blood drowning the "groans of solitary grief [the Bastille's prisoners] in the loud cry of agony" (the "public" guillotine) insinuates a distinction between imprisoned "life" and revolutionary "death." Wollstonecraft emphasizes this by closing the sentence with the sharp finality of death ("the thread of life quickly cut in twain") and the drowning "billows" that return us to the imagery of "innocent blood" drowning the "groans" of the Bastille's prisoners.

The reference to "innocent blood" washing the remembrance of former crimes again evokes *Macbeth*, as does "the quivering light . . . instantly dashed out . . ." when the "tale is soon told." Being informed of his wife's death, Macbeth refers to life as a "brief candle" he wishes "out"—"a tale told by an idiot, full of sound and fury, signifying nothing" (5.5.23, 26–28). The significance of Wollstonecraft's twice-told tale is more difficult to determine, since she proceeds to qualify the guillotine's finality: "We hear not of years languished away in misery, whilst dissolution by inches palsies the frame, or disturbs the reason: yet who can estimate the sum of comfort blasted; or tell how many survivors pine the prey of an imagination distracted by sorrow?" (FR, 123).

The opening sentence seems to say that everyone talks of the Revolution's "blood" but not about the victims of despotism—victims who languished for years in cells, wasting away or driven mad—confined to experience a living death worse than death itself. This is reinforced by the second clause, suggesting that despotism's secret crimes may have incalculably affected its as-yet-unknown survivors, maddened by "sorrow." The "sum of comfort blasted" refers to "the sum of human misery" (FR, 123), and yet "comfort" does not seem as severe as "misery." Despite Wollstonecraft's suggestion that despotism's crimes and victims are so extensive as to be yet unknown, her language again betrays her ambivalence, since the conjunction "yet" can also be read as a transitional "nevertheless" or "despite this" ("yet who can estimate the sum of comfort blasted; or tell how many survivors pine the prey of an imagination distracted by sorrow?"). Indeed, the "imagination distracted by sorrow" is equally applicable to the Revolution's victims, wasting in prisons already alluded to in the Versailles apostrophe (85), as well as to people grieving for guillotined friends or families.

In addition, her ambivalence about the Bastille's significance causes her to qualify the people's heroism with the recurrent thesis that the past has corrupted their character: "The character of the [F]rench, indeed, had been so depraved by the inveterate despotism of ages, that even amidst the heroism which distinguished the taking of the Bastille, we are forced to see that suspicious temper, and that vain ambition of dazzling, which have generated all the succeeding follies and crimes." In fact, the past's pernicious presence generates those cause-and-effect relationships that underpin her history: "The morals of the whole nation were destroyed by the manners formed by the [old] government" (FR, 123).

Conscious of the contradiction that the Revolution is again merely reproducing the past, Wollstonecraft suggests that although the French people were not prepared for liberty, the immense "natural" forces "aroused" by the Revolution paradoxically created the poison that would eventually cure and regenerate them: when the "depraved" French "changed their [political] system, liberty, as it was called, was only the acme of tyranny—merely with this difference, that, all the force of nature being roused, the magnitude of the evil promised, by some mighty concussion, to effect its own cure" (*FR*, 123; cf. 228–29, 235). Although the "acme" of revolutionary "tyranny" surpasses despotism's "tyranny," the Revolution contains its own curative future.

This way of thinking about history and her narration of the Bastille's fall (Book 2, chapter 3) illustrate how facts and events are vehicles for the thesis that propels them. After emphasizing the silent and secret dungeons of despotism, covertly submerged and concealed, and the unheard "groans" of its victims, after focusing on the Bastille's "towers of despair" (*FR*, 85) and making it the symbol of Gothic oppression ("the strongest and most terrific prison in Europe, or perhaps the world," 97), Wollstonecraft reinscribes her own silences and suppressions in her account of the Bastille's fall.

The Bastille represents what it contains: despotism's suppressed prisoners. Since she dates the Revolution with "the taking of the Bastille" (*FR*, 118), she equates the death of the Old Order with both the liberation of the Revolution's forces as well as despotism's prisoners: "The destruction of the Bastille—that fortress of tyranny! which for two centuries had been the shame and terrour of the metropolis, was the sentence of death of the old constitution" (104).

But when it comes to the climactic moment when all of despotism's silent victims are to be liberated, Wollstonecraft is confronted with an embarrassing detail, which she submerges in an initially defensive footnote (n. 7) at the bottom of the page:

> In the Bastille, it is true, were found but seven prisoners. Yet, it ought to be remarked, that three of them had lost their reason—that, when the secrets of the prison-house were laid open, men started with horrour from their inspection of instruments of torture, that appeared to be almost worn out by the exercise of tyranny—and that citizens were afraid even for a moment to enter the noisome dungeons, in which their fellow-citizens had been confined for years.
>
> (*FR*, 104)

Having linguistically reopened the Bastille and discovered an awkward absence ("but seven prisoners"), she suggests that there were probably more prisoners who had been hidden, removed, or executed, since only seven were "found." She then focuses on the three madmen as tacit evidence that they were probably driven insane by the "instruments of torture" that shocked and startled the horrified citizenry once "the secrets of the prison-house were laid open."

The reference to torture reappears later in a footnote (n. 2) quoting Mirabeau on the Bastille's secret cells: "At the moment when the hell created by tyranny for the torment of its victims opens itself to the public eye; at the moment when all the citizens have been permitted to descend into those gloomy caves, to poize the chains of their friends . . ." (FR, 126). Mirabeau himself had been imprisoned in the Bastille and after its fall had taken a tour of the *cachots,* dramatically knocking out the first stone of its edifice to thunderous applause. Unlike Wollstonecraft, he merely alludes to tyranny's dark secret—repressive torture and madness. We now know that torture, including its "instruments," took on an exaggerated afterlife in the sensational accounts following the Bastille's fall.[2] Wollstonecraft was simply reproducing what most of Paris believed, although her quotation from Mirabeau contradicts her own contention that people had been afraid "even for a moment to enter the noisome dungeons, in which their fellow-creatures had been confined for years" (FR, 104). In fact, from its initial "opening," visiting the Bastille was the rage of Paris, a kind of revolutionary slumming so popular that guided tours were given and people "locked themselves in overnight so that they could claim in the morning to have slept with rats, spiders, and toads that had been the companions of Latude."[3]

What is interesting, however, are not the errors or exaggerations in Wollstonecraft's account, but how the entire metaphoric structure of her indictment stands as a silent statement of what she herself conceals. The Bastille's dark, suppressive cells conceal the shocking secret "opened" and revealed by the Revolution—instruments of torture explaining both the disclosed "madness" and the conspicuous absence of prisoners. But her selective focus on the "three" mad prisoners suppresses the presence of the other four prisoners, who are acknowledged, in her account, yet absent. Simon Schama notes that "[o]f the seven prisoners, four were forgers who had been tried by regular process of law. The Comte de Solanges . . . had been incarcerated at the request of his family for libertinism and was happy enough to be released. . . . The remaining two prisoners were lunatics, and both returned in fairly short order to Charenton."[4]

Despite the absence of the four forgers and the ironical return of the two lunatics to "imprisonment" (Charenton was an insane asylum), it is the unmentionable Comte de Solanges who represents the Revolution's suppressed secret: the Bastille had been, among other things, the prison preferred by aristocratic patriarchs who had their recalcitrant or unruly sons, of whom Mirabeau is a classic example, imprisoned by force of the infamous *lettres de cachet* (cf. *FR,* 75). While Wollstonecraft and other revolutionary historians openly reveal the Bastille's dirty "secrets" and linguistically participate in the liberation of the Old Order's victims, they simultaneously suppress a contradiction covertly contained within despotism's bastion: the presence of the Revolution's class enemy.

Wollstonecraft sees the Revolution through tropes of liberation and imprisonment. They express her hopes and fears and crystallize her confusion and ambivalence. She dates the Revolution's birth with the fall of the Bastille, yet she fears the replication of similar oppressive structures. Toward the end of the book, the radicalized Parisians decide that liberty cannot be "secured" unless "the court and the [national] assembly were brought within the walls of the capital" (*FR,* 210).

Wollstonecraft's words display the Revolution's contradiction: "liberty" is "secured" through imprisonment, for the "walls of the capital" refer to the "barriers of the capital," within which the people also demand that the king "be obliged to reside" (*FR,* 211). These "barriers" are the "tollgates" in the city wall of Paris, where the Old Regime formerly collected customs and that were subsequently assaulted by revolutionary mobs on various *journées.* Later, she refers to these barriers as "impediments" to freedom and industry under the Old Regime: people could not "travel from one place to another without being stopped at the barriers" (226), but these old barriers are also converted by radical revolutionaries into barriers that literally confine their vulnerable victims.

In Book 5 (chapter 3), Wollstonecraft narrates how the National Assembly returned with the royal family to Paris on 6 October 1789—a return she sees as a strategic error, since the Assembly would be intimidated or controlled "by the intrigues or folly of any desperate or factious leader of the multitude—suffering themselves to be environed by its wall, shut in by its barriers—in a word—choosing to live in a capacious prison; for men forced, or drawn into any such situation, are in reality slaves or prisoners" (*FR,* 215). Understanding why the king was compelled to do this but astonished that the National Assembly's members would, in effect, make themselves prisoners, she does not seem to notice how she has linked the king's imprisonment (now in the Tuileries) with the Assembly's capitulation (see, for instance, 214).

Two paragraphs later, she is describing the magnificent "entrance into Paris, by the Tuileries" and then focuses on the "barriers . . .

stately edifices, that tower with grandeur, rendering the view, as the city is approached, truly picturesque" (*FR*, 215).

Even though the "barriers" have previously appeared as "prisons," her pictorial preface prepares us for a picturesque view that is abruptly undermined:

> But—these various barriers, built by Calonne, who liked to have Paris compared with Athens, excite the most melancholy reflections. They were first erected by despotism to secure the payment of an oppressive tax, and since have fatally assisted to render anarchy more violent by concentration, cutting off the possibility of innocent victims escaping from the fury, or the mistake, of the moment. Thus miscreants have had sufficient influence to guard these barriers, and caging the objects of their fear or vengeance, have slaughtered them; or, violating the purity of justice, have coolly wrested laws hastily formed to serve sinister designs—changing its sacred sword into a dagger, and terming the assassin's stab the stroke of justice, because given with the mock ceremonials of equity, which only rendered the crime more atrocious. The tyrant, who, bounding over all restraint, braves the eternal law he tramples on, is not half so detestable as the reptile who crawls under the shelter of the principles he violates. Such has been the effect of the enclosure of Paris: and the reflections of wounded humanity disenchanting the senses, the elegant structures, which served as gates to this great prison, no longer appear magnificent porticoes.
>
> (*FR*, 216)

Her perspective is again framed by the past.

The comparison of Paris with Athens by Calonne, the Old Regime's controller general and (now) detested counterrevolutionary (see *FR*, 34), suggests again that the French are doomed to repeat or imitate the past. Similarly, the Old Regime's hated tax barriers (cf. 226) are now barriers that imprison or facilitate murder; consequently, the Revolution's "anarchy" is "more violent by concentration." The "innocent victims" trying to escape "fury" resemble the "unfortunate being, fleeing from the despotism of licentious freedom" in the Versailles apostrophe (85). As the perversion of justice results in the perversion of language, revolutionaries term "the assassin's stab the stroke of justice," and as justice's "sword" is turned into the assassin's "dagger," Wollstonecraft allusively distinguishes between the Macbethean "tyrant" who, "bounding over all restraint, braves the eternal law he tramples on" (cf. *Macbeth*, 1.7.27) and the revolutionary "reptile who crawls under the shelter of the principles he violates," resembling, in another context, "Milton's devil" who pays "homage, in spite of himself, to the eternal justice he violates under the pretext of self-preservation" (54).

But who are these unnamed "miscreants," these revolutionary assassins and reptiles? Her perspective of Paris as a vast prison reveals that they are Jacobins, since she is referring to the present ("Such has been the effect of the enclosure of Paris") and since she herself experienced this "enclosure" when the city barriers were closed during the June insurrection (1793), which ended with the Girondins' defeat.

The next paragraph marks a strange transition, since she describes Parisians tripping "along the charming boulevard," amidst beautiful buildings and "clustering flowers" (FR, 216). As "the heavens too smile," the passage is similar to the Versailles apostrophe, where after fleeing the haunted palace, Wollstonecraft emerges to find "nature, smiling around," before "weeping" over France's tragedy (85).

Something like this happens again in the "barrier" passage, since, in the subsequent paragraph, Wollstonecraft is suddenly saddened again:

> Why starts the tear of anguish to mingle with recollections that sentiment fosters—even in obedience to reason? For it is wise to be happy! . . . But how quickly vanishes this prospect of delights! . . . The cavalcade of death moves along, shedding mildew over the beauties of the scene, and blasting every joy! The elegance of the palaces and buildings is revolting, when they are viewed as prisons, and the sprightliness of the people disgusting, when they are hastening to view the operations of the guillotine, or carelessly passing over the earth stained with blood. Exasperated humanity then, with bitterness of soul, devotes the city to destruction; whilst turning from such a nest of crimes, it seeks for consolation only in the conviction, that, as the world is growing wiser, it must become happier; and that, as the cultivation of the soil meliorates a climate, the improvement of the understanding will prevent those baneful excesses of passion which poison the heart.
>
> (FR, 216)

Like the Versailles apostrophe, the smiling scene turns into a scene of death.

"The cavalcade of death" that moves along alludes to the public guillotine that had been moved to different public places as the Revolution progressed—an allusion reinforced by the reference to the "operations of the guillotine" staining the earth. Referring to the hardened Parisians who hasten to view the guillotine's operations or pass "over the earth stained with blood," Wollstonecraft is probably remembering the day (summer of 1793) when she saw "the blood of the guillotine fresh upon the pavement" and exclaimed against it.[5] She is, in effect, returning to the blood that stains the Revolution and the Parisians who now appear "disgusting."

As Paris becomes the locus of the Revolution's stain and an exasperated Wollstonecraft wishes to see it destroyed, she is perhaps thinking of other cities "destroyed" by Paris, such as Lyon in the 1793 federalist revolts. "Exasperated humanity" devoting "the city to destruction" also evokes Girondist threats to annihilate Paris[6] or, in a more subversive counterrevolutionary context, the infamous Brunswick Manifesto (25 July 1792). Since Paris was also the locus of the Revolution's birth, there is again a portentous sense of repetition, since she sees the city as an immense prison— the ancient palaces and buildings turned into revolutionary prisons.

The clash between revolutionary reality and her ideological perspective of the Revolution causes her to do something we have seen before, most memorably in the allusive "out the damned spot" passage (*FR,* 126): she turns her eyes and averts the "scene." Turning from the blood of Paris and its "nest of crimes," she "seeks for consolation" (in the Versailles apostrophe, the "oppressed heart seeks for relief in the garden," 85) in the idealistic "conviction, that, as the world is growing wiser, it must become happier"—even though the evidence of the passage contradicts this questionable assertion. It is this strange ideological blindness to what she is actually seeing that allows her to preserve her revolutionary faith.

II

The book's silent suppressions are the metaphoric equivalence of this blindness or "looking away." Wollstonecraft's treatment of Marie Antoinette is illustrative. Her portrayal of the queen relies on popular depictions of her as the manipulative Austrian "whore," interested only in enjoying her personal pleasures and in maintaining her privileged position. Consequently, the queen emerges as one of the self-interested promoters of the monarchy, a shameless bitch conspiring with the corrupt court to overturn the Revolution.[7]

In *The Rights of Men,* Wollstonecraft had already recorded her hostility to Marie Antoinette, rejecting Burke's romantic portrayal in the *Reflections* (see *Works,* 5:18, 25). In her French history, she is much more severe with the queen than with Louis, whose murder reverberates through the book—perhaps because the queen still represented, for her, that frivolous "beauty" celebrated by the Old Order. But Marie Antoinette had also been guillotined (11 October 1793) nine months after her husband and four months after Wollstonecraft had started her history. Although one might expect that her death would also be a haunting presence, there is a strange silence (broken by only one footnote), undoubtedly because Wollstonecraft felt her death was warranted.

When Wollstonecraft first introduces the queen (Book 1, chapter 2), she is the "young and beautiful *dauphine*," albeit already corrupted by the court's "voluptuous atmosphere" (*FR*, 29). She is compared to a prostitute (30), and her depraved sexual nature is emphasized: she participates in "messalinian feasts"—the adjective smears her with orgiastic associations commonly attributed to the notorious Roman queen (see also 73). The comparison between both queens was a commonplace in revolutionary discourse. In fact, the only concession Wollstonecraft makes is to the queen's "bewitching manners" and a beautiful face that rendered her a "flattered beauty" with "fascinating smiles" (72)—a beautiful woman dazzling "the eyes even of superior men" (74)—an allusion to Burke's vision of the queen in the *Reflections*. But it is paradoxically the queen's sexual nature that also makes her less than a woman. Thus, in a coy allusion to sensationalist accounts of the queen's "lesbianism,"[8] Wollstonecraft notes that "madame Polignac fled to Basle" after the Bastille's fall: "Thus went into exile an amiable woman" who had "great favour with the queen"—a queen "whose strange predilection for handsome women blighted the reputation of every one, whom she distinguished" (124).

There is an additional allusion pertinent to Wollstonecraft's demonization of the queen. After depicting her as an archetypal castrator (with "sufficient finesse" she sexually "subjugate[s]" the king—her "empty mind" discovers "pleasures" that emasculate her "circean court"), Wollstonecraft formulates her major indictment:

Lost then in the most luxurious pleasures, or managing court intrigues, the queen became a profound dissembler; and her heart hardened by sensual enjoyments to such a degree, that when her family and favourites stood on the brink of ruin, her little portion of mind was employed only to preserve herself from danger. As a proof of the justness of this assertion, it is only necessary to observe, that, in the general wreck, not a scrap of her writing has been found to criminate her; neither has she suffered a word to escape her to exasperate the people, even when burning with rage, and contempt. The effect that adversity may have on her choked understanding time will show; but during her prosperity, the moments of languor, that glide into the interstices of enjoyment, were passed in the most childish manner; without the appearance of any vigour of mind, to palliate the wanderings of the imagination.

(*FR*, 73)

Wollstonecraft, in effect, accuses the queen of cowardice (see also 68) and her "proof" is that "in the general wreck, not a scrap of writing has been found to criminate her."

To unlock this enigmatic comment, it is necessary to know that Wollstonecraft is alluding to the *armoire de fer*—the secret cabinet Louis XVI had constructed (in early 1792) to safeguard his private correspondence (containing, inter alia, incriminating evidence that he detested the national Constitution and had privately attempted to contravene many of his public oaths and promises).

In November 1792, when the National Convention was preparing to bring Louis to trial, the *armoire*'s existence was revealed by the locksmith who had helped Louis construct it. Since the *armoire* was instrumental in the Convention's case against Louis, Wollstonecraft suggests that because no additional evidence was found that also incriminated the queen, she was, ipso facto, a coward who probably had the evidence of her own treasonous activities destroyed or suppressed—"her little portion of mind was employed only to preserve herself from danger."

Although not known at the time, the queen had, in fact, been conspiring against the Revolution, sending military information to France's enemies. But even though the *armoire* was unconnected to the queen's treasonous activities, containing only Louis' private correspondence, Wollstonecraft makes its unspoken existence and the "silence" or absence "within" conspicuous "proof" of the queen's cowardice—her disloyalty to her family and the monarchy "in the general wreck." Wollstonecraft wrote this passage when the most hated woman in France was imprisoned and would soon be tried for treason, a time during which the queen's life and the lives of those associated with her (including her immediate family) depended on her public behavior. Thus her additional comment that the queen was also a coward because she did not let "a word to escape her to exasperate the people" is rather smug coming from a woman who was comparatively privileged, living under the protection of an American passport.[9]

But it is her own silences and suppressions that are thematically telling, for in the box to which she evasively alludes, other incriminating evidence was found: the discovery that Mirabeau had been secretly paid by the court to help restore the king's prestige and authority. Indeed, this revelation led to Mirabeau's posthumous disgrace (he had died on 2 April 1791), when the Convention ordered that his remains be removed from the Panthéon and tossed into a common grave. Although Wollstonecraft, at times, criticizes Mirabeau for his vanity and theatrical posturing, he was, in addition to being one of the central documentary sources for her history, also one of the few revolutionaries she admired. Writing to Gilbert Imlay in August 1793, she teasingly threatens to "make love to the *shade* of Mirabeau, to whom my heart continually turned," adding defensively that she does not think "Mirabeau devoid of principles"—precisely what was being said about him after the *armoire* was opened.[10]

Although it can be argued that Wollstonecraft does not mention either the *armoire* or Mirabeau because she is dealing with the Revolution's first six months, this is not convincing since she dispenses with this chronological fiction whenever she pleases and because she silently acknowledges the *armoire*'s existence in her obscure allusion—an allusion that would be recognized only by those familiar with the Revolution's history, in a passage that makes sense only in context of the allusion and the king's incriminatory writing. Why allude to something that might confuse the general reader? One could, of course, also argue that it makes no sense to mention Mirabeau, since he is not pertinent to what Wollstonecraft is discussing—the queen's cowardice. But this is precisely what Wollstonecraft consistently does: she "writes out" (in the simultaneous sense of exposure and erasure) what she is writing against—in this case, the "cowardice" illustrated by the absent evidence that confirms it. If the passage depends on the unlocking of the allusion for its contextual sense, the allusive absence of the *armoire* is a kind of apprehensive suppression of the "key," since a direct mention of the box might lead a curious reader to discover other incriminatory evidence: Mirabeau's presence and the fact that he had planned for the king's escape to the eastern frontier, where he would declare the abolition of the National Assembly and the establishment of a friendly legislative body.

In Wollstonecraft's treatment of the queen, the footnote (n. 3) following her comment that the "effect that adversity [that is, the king's death and her own imprisonment] may have on her choked understanding time will show" notes that the paragraph "was written some months before the death of the queen" (*FR*, 73) and hence acknowledges that Wollstonecraft was rereading it after the queen's death. She thus makes a point of refusing to revise or amend her harsh opinion (including what even the queen's enemies conceded—that in "adversity" the queen had conducted herself with admirable dignity). The note illustrates that even the queen's execution could not make Wollstonecraft compromise her critical convictions. But while the queen's posthumous presence does not permeate *The French Revolution* as the king's does, her execution does, I think, impinge on Wollstonecraft's narration of the October Days of 1789.

III

Many readers have found her account perplexing, since she had previously criticized Burke's account of the October Days, in *The Rights of Men,* as "most exaggerated" (*Works,* 5:26). While hers is longer because she lingers on the march to Versailles (5 October), whereas Burke moves immediately to the events of 6 October, she, in effect, both confirms Burke's account and surpasses it in the number of condemnatory details she adds.

Her description of the market women who first gathered in Paris (5 October) is just as pejorative as Burke's description of the same women accompanying the captive royal family to Paris on 6 October. Here is Burke's account: The "royal captives . . . were slowly moved along, amidst the horrid yells, and shrilling screams, and frantic dances, and infamous contumelies, and all the unutterable abominations of the furies of hell, in the abused shape of the vilest of women" (*Reflections,* 165). In *The Rights of Men,* Wollstonecraft had quoted this passage and then dismissed it with a backhanded slap at Marie Antoinette: "Probably you mean women who gained a livelihood by selling vegetables or fish, who never had any advantages of education; or their vices might have lost part of their abominable deformity, by losing part of their grossness" (*Works,* 5:30; the last clause alludes to *Reflections,* 170).

But in *The French Revolution,* these lower-class women begin to resemble Burke's furies: "The concourse, at first, consisted mostly of market women, and the lowest refuse of the streets, women who had thrown off the virtues of one sex without having power to assume more than the vices of the other" (*FR,* 6:196–97). Moira Ferguson and Janet Todd note that "here . . . [Wollstonecraft] sounds closer to Burke than to her former self." Joan Landes observes that "Wollstonecraft dismisses the march on Versailles in an almost Burkean fashion." Eleanor Flexner comments that the "reader is reminded of Mary's old antagonist Edmund Burke—and may legitimately wonder which of them wrote some of its passages."[11]

In addition, Wollstonecraft's other repulsive women also resemble Burke's. Referring to mob intimidation of the National Assembly, Burke writes of "women lost to shame" (*Reflections,* 161). Referring to the prostitutes in the Palais Royale who, she suggests, were paid by the duc d'Orléans and composed part of "the singular army of the females" who marched on Versailles, Wollstonecraft writes of "the most shameless girls" and "the vilest of women" (*FR,* 207)—the last words repeating Burke's description of the market women in the *Reflections* (165). Moreover, Burke's "furies of hell, in the abused shape of the vilest of women" (*Reflections,* 165) appear, again, in Wollstonecraft's description of the market women, "with the appearance of furies" (*FR,* 197). But Wollstonecraft's pejorative description is stronger: her market women only appear to be furies, whereas Burke's are actually furies "in the abused shape of the vilest of women."

There are other Burkean echoes in the account of 6 October, when the royal palace was invaded by the revolutionary mob. In the *Reflections,* both the king and queen "lay down . . . to indulge nature in a few hours of respite, and troubled melancholy repose" (164). In *The French Revolution,* "the harassed king and queen were prevailed on to seek the repose they needed" (204). It is at this point that both narratives record the revolutionary mob's violation of the palace. In the *Reflections,* the queen is startled out of her sleep by the voice of a sentinel warning her "to save herself by flight":

> that this was the last proof of fidelity he could give—that they were upon him, and he was dead. A band of cruel ruffians and assassins, reeking with his blood, rushed into the chamber of the queen, and pierced with an hundred strokes of bayonets and poniards the bed, from whence this persecuted woman had but just time to fly almost naked, and through ways unknown to the murders had escaped to seek refuge at the feet of a king and husband, not secure of his own life for a moment.
>
> (164)

In contrast, Wollstonecraft begins her account with the mob invading the palace from the outside.

First, a "gang of ruffians, rushed towards the palace," killed a palace guard and then (after entering) murdered another guard at the top of the stairs they had mounted (*FR,* 204–5). Apparently Burke's account is still playing in her mind, since she uses the same word, *ruffians,* to characterize the mob which "rushed toward the palace," just, as in Burke's version, the mob "rushed into the chamber of the queen."

The violation of the queen's chamber is also similar: "The most desperate found their way to the queen's chamber, and left for dead the man who courageously disputed their entrance. But she had been alarmed by the tumult, though the miscreants were not long in making their way good, and, throwing a wrapping-gown around her, ran, by a private passage, to the king's apartment" (*FR*, 205). Both passages convey a sense of sexual suspense and danger, as the queen is forced to flee *en déshabillé*, although Burke's account is more dramatic, since the revolutionary "rapists" pierce the queen's bed with a series of murderous, phallic stabs.[12]

Both accounts are arguably similar because both Burke and Wollstonecraft are dealing with the same "facts," but many of these had been disputed from the beginning. It is these disputed facts, however, with which both Burke and Wollstonecraft agree. For instance, both Burke and Wollstonecraft agree that a guard or "sentinel" was attacked by the mob outside the queen's chamber, although Burke believes he was killed, while Wollstonecraft suggests that he was wounded but "left for dead" by the frenzied mob.[13] But Burke's opponents pounced upon this detail, insisting that the guard's death was a fabrication. Various twentieth-century scholars have reiterated this criticism. J. T. Boulton, for instance, says that it "is noteworthy that Burke never deleted the reference to the death of the guard, though, even if not at the time of writing, certainly before many editions were out, he must have known it was false. Several of his opponents in the subsequent controversy informed him of it."[14]

Since this was a disputed fact, it is equally noteworthy that Wollstonecraft accepts Burke's version. Modern historians agree that two guards were either attacked or killed (Burke deals with only one). William Doyle, for instance, writes that "an enraged mob poured into the palace, massacred two guardsmen, and almost broke into the queen's apartments." D. M. G. Sutherland notes that "two bodyguards were killed," as does John Hardman: "In the early hours of 6 October, a portion of the crowd broke into the Palace, made for the Queen's apartments and outside the doors hacked down two of her Bodyguards whose resistance had nevertheless enabled her to reach the King along [a] secret passage constructed in 1775."[15] Simon Schama provides some Burkean specifics: "A guard fired on the onrushing crowd; a man fell and the soldier was then killed on the spot. Miomandre de Sainte-Marie, a

second guard posted outside the Queen's apartments, attempted
to reason with them and, failing, shouted to those within that the
Queen's life was in danger. He too was struck down, but his warning had come just in time."[16] Miomandre de Sainte-Marie apparently survived the attack, even though he was initially believed to
be dead. In *Vindiciae Gallicae* (1791), James Mackintosh, a vigor-
ous supporter of the French Revolution, criticized Burke's "frivolous and puerile adversaries" for "convicting" him of "some minute
errors": "Mons. *Miomandre,* the [s]entinel at the Queen's-gate, it
is true, survives, but it is no less true, that he was left for dead by
his assassins."[17]

But aside from questions of historical accuracy, by placing a
guard outside the queen's chamber, Wollstonecraft, like Burke, emphasizes the danger the queen is exposed to once the guard is
murdered and the mob "violates" her chamber. Indeed, while both
Burke and Wollstonecraft agree that "ruffians" entered the queen's
chamber (albeit Wollstonecraft's more subdued "miscreants" who
"were not long in making their way good"), many modern historians contend that the mob was actually stopped, at the last minute,
by members of the National Guard (a point that has never been
definitively resolved). But the entrance of the mob, in both Burke's
and Wollstonecraft's accounts, suggests the sexual hostility the
queen is exposed to.

Wollstonecraft, for instance, refers to "the singularly ferocious
appearance of the mob" and the "brutal violation of the apartment
of the queen" (*FR,* 206). Burke's "pierced" bed (*Reflections,* 164)
and Wollstonecraft's "violated" apartment are symbols of the
queen's violated honor, metaphoric embodiments of the mob's
transferred aggression. Gary Kelly notes, with surprise, that
"[Wollstonecraft's] account of the attack on Versailles resembles
Burke's and even echoes its language and rhythm."[18] Indeed, her
vivid narrative of the October Days resembles what she had previously called Burke's "most exaggerated description" (*Rights of
Men, Works,* 5:26) in the *Reflections.*

To understand what is happening here, we need to turn to her
final assessment of the October Days and her final reference to the
queen: "The laws had been trampled on by a gang of banditti the
most desperate. . . . The sanctuary of repose, the asylum of care
and fatigue, the chaste temple of a woman, I consider the queen
only as one, the apartment where she consigns her senses to the
bosom of sleep, folded in its arms forgetful of the world, was violated with murderous fury" (*FR,* 209). Wollstonecraft alludes to
the official *Châtelet* report on the October days presented to the

National Assembly which James Mackintosh had cited in *Vindiciae Gallicae* (1791): *"that the asylum of beauty and Majesty was not profaned."*[19] She rejects this account by insisting that Marie Antoinette's "asylum" was indeed "violated" and profaned. In the end, Wollstonecraft sympathizes with Marie Antoinette as a woman, dignifying her with images of protected purity (*sanctuary, asylum, chaste temple*), almost as if she is restoring the woman's honor— her virginal womanhood, which had been violated and stained, not only by the degrading albeit frustrated physical attack, but by the voluminous pornographic attacks on her "body." In the end, she turns the sexual monster—the manipulative whore, the insatiable nymphomaniac, the orgiastic lesbian—back into a flesh-and-blood woman who has been outrageously wronged. In doing this, Wollstonecraft restores posthumously to Marie Antoinette (unnatural and unhuman) her appropriated humanity, for she herself had participated in the sexual demonization of the queen.

Her comment that she considers the queen "only as" a woman (*FR*, 209) points back to the *Reflections* and Burke's complaint that revolutionary ideology reduces a queen to a woman and a woman to an animal (171)—a complaint she replied to in *The Rights of Men*, ironically agreeing, "All true, Sir; if she is not more attentive to the duties of humanity than queens and fashionable ladies in general are" (*Works*, 5:25). In *The French Revolution,* she finally makes peace with the queen's ghost, probably having written the passage after her execution (16 October 1793), and possibly as a reaction to her degrading trial (she was accused, among other things, of sleeping with her young son and encouraging him to masturbate).

Indignant that the "ruffians" escaped justice and that the October Days had stained the Revolution, she complains that members of the National Assembly "ought to have stood up as one man in support of insulted justice" (*FR*, 209), just as Burke had disappointedly observed that he would have thought "ten thousand swords must have leaped from their scabbards to avenge even a look that threatened [the queen] with insult" (*Reflections*, 170). Wollstonecraft had mocked Burke's phrase earlier when she noted that "admirers of the old system" would undoubtedly come to the rescue of their beleaguered monarchy, "for it was not to be supposed, that the chivalrous spirit of France would be destroyed in an instant, though *swords had ceased to leap out of their scabbards* when beauty was not deified" (*FR*, 189). Although the only chivalrous swords drawn in the queen's behalf appear in her account of the "chivalrous scene" of 1 October, when the "half-drunken multitude" erupts into exclamations of "*vive le roi, vive la reine*" and "royal healths were drunk over drawn swords" (*FR*, 194), Wollstonecraft belatedly draws her own chivalric pen, restoring both the queen's honor and humanity. Her revisionist account reflects, in the end, another Burkean resemblance, as she rewrites her previous account of the October Days and the pristine French Revolution.

8

The Inevitability of Progress: A Revolution Within, Happier Far

I

GIVEN all the contradictions and ambiguities in *The French Revolution,* I want to return to the ideas that ground Wollstonecraft's history and demonstrate how they resolve the contradictions that confront her. Early in her narrative (Book 1, chapter 4), she refers to the events of June 1789 and the two options that confronted the French people. They could have waited patiently for the "general dissemination of truth and knowledge" to meliorate prejudices and governments and by not insisting on "premature reforms," the Old Order would gradually and naturally have passed away (*FR, Works,* 6:45). This is the argument she uses later in her discussion of the monarchy and Second Estate (61, 159, 219).

The second option is more radical and is, like the first, formulated in the collective voice of the people: if the Old Order is constitutionally incapable of remedy or reform, if it will not pass peacefully out of history, then a "radical cure" is necessary. The people "are justified in having recourse to coercion, to repel coercion." A revolution is justified if the Old Order's oppression is greater than the "convulsions" produced by such a revolution, in which case, it is better to regenerate the country by rooting out the "deleterious plants" that poison it. Thus, since the rich have oppressed the people, it follows that when the people come to power, they will oppress their oppressors, who have taught "them how to act when possessed of power" (*FR,* 46).

Wollstonecraft's point is that the French chose the second option ("they seemed determined to strike at the root of all their misery at once," *FR,* 45) and hence precipitated all the convulsions and disasters that followed. She locates the Revolution's repetitive contradictions at the very beginning, concluding reluctantly that "Europe will probably be, for some years to come, in a state of anarchy" (*FR*, 46).

But this "anarchy" is qualified by the subsequent clause, "till a change of sentiments, gradually undermining the strongholds of custom, alters the manners" of a corrupt people (*FR*, 46). In other words, no matter what people do, revolutionary principles will eventually change them internally so that the correspondent external changes can also take place. This is her triumphant thesis, and it allows Wollstonecraft to conclude her chapter optimistically: despite several "acts of ferocious folly" that have stained the "grand revolution," she is confident "that people are essentially good, and that knowledge is rapidly advancing" (46). She warns against inferring "that the spirit of the moment [that is, the transitory violence] will not evaporate, and leave the disturbed water more clear for the fermentation" (47). In her letter to Joseph Johnson (15 February 1793), she had similarly noted that she could "look beyond the evils of the moment, and do not expect muddied water to become clear before it has had time to stand" (*Works*, 6:445). Since time will eventually justify her revolutionary belief, this paradigmatic looking beyond or "away" from the transitory "evils of the moment" allows her to focus on the revolutionary Idea—the triumphant knowledge, principles, and "light" that will eventually regenerate the world.

Wollstonecraft is, nevertheless, disturbed that the progressive logic of history is opposed by nefarious groups, whether the courtiers and tyrants of the Old Order or "false patriots" who have led the people, "in their ardour for reform, to the commission of actions the most cruel and unjust" (*FR*, 68). Although she never names these false patriots, it becomes clear that she is referring to the Jacobins, and her reluctance to name them is understandable, given that she was writing during the Terror.

It is also notable that the evil without (counterrevolution) is located within as well, and that these Manichean divisions proliferate like amoebae, so that the Revolution becomes divided against itself. The logical corollary is the "cure" that makes the Revolution "pure": the simultaneous eradication of evil (counterrevolutionary opposition) and the creation of virtue. Although there is an immense difference between the regeneration of France as Wollstonecraft envisions it and the Republic of Virtue envisioned by Robespierre and Saint-Just, revolutionary vanguards characteristically scrutinize individuals for defects, deviations, or digressions from a revolutionary "idea"—the "purity" residing within the true revolutionary (for example, the Jacobin *scrutin épuratoire*). In this context, a revolution "within" must be consummated before a revolution without can be completed, or, as Wollstonecraft puts it, "public happiness" was not to be attained or expected "before an alteration in the national character seconded the new system of government" (*FR,* 196). Her argument throughout is that the French were not prepared ideologically for "the new system of government."

But since the triumph of the revolutionary ideal is inevitable, this allows her to criticize liberals ("many of the admirers of the revolution, in its infancy") for criticizing the Revolution once it deviates from what they thought it was going to be (*FR,* 146). Concentrating only on the ephemeral "stains," they miss the big picture (cf. 235).

Another characteristic of revolutionary thought—engendered by the example of the French Revolution—is that the "revolution" is never a local affair. It is a world-transforming event, an inevitable historical force that changes the course of history. Although Europe is the "world" for Wollstonecraft, this idea allows her to deflect her disappointment from the French people, since "this revolution did not interest [F]renchmen alone; for its influence extending throughout the continent, all the passions and prejudices of Europe were instantly set afloat" (*FR,* 146).

For Wollstonecraft, even though the Revolution is ultimately realized in and through people, the revolutionary idea itself is never wrong—it is the people who fail to live up to it or, more appropriately, live it. The closest she comes to criticizing a revolutionary idea is when she mocks the vainglorious French for trying to implement a radical idea too rapidly. Thus, in distinguishing between the American and French Revolutions, she notes that the French ignored a practical revolutionary model ("the example of the Thirteen states of America"). Driven by national vanity, the French rejected revolutionary precedent and insisted on regenerating the whole human race: "But, no; the regeneration of France must lead to the regeneration of the whole globe. The political system of Frenchmen must serve as a model for all the free states in the universe! *Vive la liberté* was the only cry . . . whilst the whole nation, wild with joy, was hailing the commencement of the golden age" (*FR,* 169; cf. *Rights of Men, Works,* 5:33).

Here Wollstonecraft sounds as contemptuous as Burke, but it is not the idea she is criticizing, for she also believes in the "regeneration of the whole globe," albeit "gradually" (see *FR,* 160, 166, 183, 212). Although she sarcastically refers to the "commencement of the golden age," she had also expected this quick regeneration until concrete realities convinced her that regeneration would take place in the future. Two months after arriving in France (15 February 1793), she had written her gloomy letter to Joseph Johnson, lamenting that "the perspective of the golden age . . . almost eludes my sight," causing her to lose "in part my theory of a more perfect state" (*Works*, 6:444–45). But it is her "theory" that ultimately survives all the unpleasant realities the Revolution seems to produce. She merely slows it down.

Throughout her history, she insists that individuals in the Revolution are not important because individuals, like the French people, are invariably disappointing: Mirabeau secretly trucks with the monarchy, Tallyrand and Mournier leave, Lafayette flees, and the Jacobins guillotine the Girondins. The only thing left is her revolutionary theory, the one thing she cannot critically examine.

It is this theory that allows her to work out the apparent contradictions of the Revolution and to become reconciled with stubborn facts that are ultimately, for her, transitory or illusory. Thus, if the Revolution seems to be repeating the past, it is because all "sudden revolutions have been as suddenly overturned, and things thrown back below their former state" (*FR*, 183). In other words, sudden "revolutions" cause things to regress because they are not true "progressive" revolutions. In the first sense, Wollstonecraft uses the old meaning of *revolution* as a "return" to a former point in time. But since the true Revolution is progressively inevitable, albeit gradual, even the defects of both its supporters and opponents cannot ultimately stop it—"The vanity and weakness of men have continually tended to retard this progress of things: still it is going forward; and though the fatal presumption of the headstrong French, and the more destructive ambition of their foreign enemies, have given it a check, we may contemplate with complacent serenity the approximation of the glorious era, when the appellations of fool and tyrant will be synonymous" (183–84).

In the end, she reconciles temporal reality with ideological idealism, even as the French people become the flawed vehicle for her ideological tenor: "But, from the commencement of the revolution, the misery of France has originated from the folly or art of men, who have spurred the people on too fast; tearing up prejudices by the root, which they should have permitted to die gradually away" (*FR*, 159). Since rapidity makes the Revolution regress, she transforms the imagery of "light"—the triumphant "knowledge" (celebrated by Enlightenment and revolutionary writers) that obliterates the past's obscurant darkness—into "blindness": "Such mistakes . . . prove the necessity of gradual reform; lest light, suddenly breaking-in on a benighted people, should overpower the understanding it ought to direct" (183). Later, members of the National Assembly "suffered themselves to be hurried forward by a multitude, on whom political light had too suddenly flashed" (*FR*, 210). Extreme revolutionary light resembles past darkness. In Wollstonecraft's metaphoric formulation, too much revolutionary light results ironically in a return to the blindness and "darkness" of the past.

Since she suggests that the French people were not prepared to see the light, she also suggests that gradual streaks of rays will restore their sight—the revolutionary vision they have lost sight of. This emphasis on a gradual revolution that is inevitably progressing despite momentary lurches complements the thesis that the Revolution is to be consummated in the future. It allows revolutionary sympathizers to look away or to explain present contradictions as temporary, illusory, aberrant, or even "necessary" for the moment. But more importantly it allows the apparent contradiction between revolutionary ideology and revolutionary reality to be resolved, since critics mistakenly blame revolutionary "errors" on revolutionary "theory," when, in fact, the errors are due to the imperfect implementation of the theory (see *FR*, 219).

The last chapter of *The French Revolution* illustrates this. Since this constitutes Wollstonecraft's conclusive statement on the Revolution, it is significant, I think, that she returns to the great question-begging thesis—the inevitable progress of knowledge and reform beginning with the Enlightenment and now spreading like "centrifugal rays" through Europe (*FR*, 224). She also reiterates previous theses, the effeminate nature of the French (230) and the idea that old oppression causes new oppression (234), but it is her final vision of revolutionary principles resolving contradictions that preoccupies her. Throughout her history, Wollstonecraft has, at times, contradicted herself or sounded like Burke, whom she also opposes at various points. Referring to revolutionary mobs, Burke had written that "Rage and phrenzy will pull down more in half an hour, than prudence, deliberation, and foresight can build up in a hundred years" (*Reflections*, 279–80). Referring to the revolutionary French, Wollstonecraft notes that "it was a much easier task to pull down than to build up" (*FR*, 226; cf. *FR*, 2nd par., 235, and *Reflections*, last sentence, 247).

Wollstonecraft recognizes the contradictions within the Revolution, and she resolves them by turning again to their source—the French people who are staining revolutionary theory. Positing the conventional, sentimental distinction between superior primitive societies and corrupt European "civilization," she traces "the contradictions in the French character" to the corrupting influence of the European past (*FR*, 232). The contradictions in the French character presumably account for the contradictions in the Revolution and in Wollstonecraft's history as well. But the contradictions paradoxically provide the resolution to the problem: for if it is "internal" character defects that distort revolutionary principles, the solution is to change the French character with revolutionary principles.

Sounding at times like Marx writing about prerevolutionary Russia ("the [F]rench were in some respects the most unqualified of any people in Europe to undertake the important work in which they are embarked," *FR*, 230), Wollstonecraft imagines a future change in the French character, once the appropriate ideological education effects the external political change: "As a change also of the system of education and domestic manners will be a natural consequence of the revolution, the [F]rench will insensibly rise to a dignity of character far above the present race; and then the fruit of their liberty, ripening gradually, will have a relish not to be expected during its crude and forced state" (231). The real Revolution is thus deferred to the future and to a grateful posterity finally worthy of the revolutionary idea. Although she reverses Marx's thesis that material changes transform the ideological superstructure, she formulates an idea that subsequent revolutionary writers found appealing: a revolution "within" that precedes the external, political revolution. Ironically, Robespierre and the Jacobins, the implicit villains of her history, were also obsessed with this idea.

Probably writing near the height of the Terror as she concluded her final chapter,[1] the Revolution becomes increasingly more unreal as she imagines future Parisians leaving the corrupt capital and regenerating themselves in the rural countryside (*FR*, 229, 231). This pastoral fantasy of regeneration coincides with the last two paragraphs, in which she asserts her idea of "principles of policy" leading to a "political system" that would check "follies" and cure the French body politic, regenerated through the disease that poisoned it (235). Thus, while superficial observers will see only "the excrementitious humours exuding from the contaminated body," the philosophical eye "will be able to discern the cause, which has produced so many dreadful effects"—both the cause-and-effect reasons for the "dreadful" revolutionary past as well as the purified future. Reaffirming her principal thesis, it is an idea through which she religiously keeps her revolutionary faith.

II

Wollstonecraft wrote one more book bearing on her re-vision of the French Revolution—*Letters Written During a Short Residence in Sweden, Norway, and Denmark* (1796).[2] Ostensibly an epistolary journal of her travels in these countries, the book also touches on the Revolution and is relevant to her previous characterization of the French people. In this context, I want to trace briefly her view of the Revolution from the time she published her history (1794) through the *Letters Written in Sweden*.

Considering that Wollstonecraft was living and writing in France during the Terror, there is strikingly little about the Revolution in her correspondence, undoubtedly because it was a dangerous time and place to be writing. In a letter to her sister, Eliza W. Bishop (13 June 1793), she notes that she writes her letters "with *reserve* because all letters are opened." In a subsequent letter to Eliza (24 June), she warns her not to "touch on politics."[3] The fact that she knew that letters were being opened probably accounts for her paraphrase of Mirabeau's denunciation of letter opening and her own critical comments in *The French Revolution* (*Works,* 6:130–31). In a letter to Everina Wollstonecraft (10 March 1794), she writes that she has "just sent off" a large part of her manuscript, even though her friend Helen Maria Williams (recently released from prison) has warned her to burn it. Commenting that it is impossible for her to convey any idea of "the sad scenes" that have affected her, she adds that "death and misery, in every shape of *terrour* [my emphasis], haunts this devoted country." She is, however, glad that she "came to France because [she] never could have had a just opinion of the most extraordinary event that has ever been recorded" (cf. *Reflections,* 92).[4] Having just sent off her manuscript and "recorded" some of the extraordinary events of the Revolution, the complimentary "just opinion" most likely alludes to her own book. She also notes that she has "met with some uncommon instances of friendship" that she will "call to mind when the remembrance is keen of the anguish it has endured for its fellow creatures, at large—for the unfortunate beings cut off around me—and the still more unfortunate survivors." The imagery evokes the Terror, for the "unfortunate beings cut off" evokes the guillotine, especially when we remember that she had used a similar image in *The French Revolution*—"when, the thread of life [is] quickly cut in twain" (*FR,* 123). Even though she seems to want to balance the bad memories ("unfortunate beings cut off" and "the more unfortunate survivors") with good memories ("uncommon instances of friendship"), this calling "to mind" seems more a way of forgetting or suppressing the "unfortunate" memories, just as in the passage (just quoted) about the guillotine, "innocent blood" (the lesser evil) obliterates "the remembrance of false imprisonment" (the greater evil, *FR*, 123).

In a letter to Ruth Barlow (8 July 1794), she seems to think that the Revolution will eventually triumph, even though the "blood" sickens her: "The French will carry all before them—but, my God, how many victims fall beneath the sword and the Guillotine! My blood runs cold, and I sicken at thoughts of a Revolution which costs so much blood and bitter tears."[5]

The Terror ended with the overthrow of Robespierre and his associates on 27 July 1794. In a letter to Gilbert Imlay (23 September 1794), Wollstonecraft observes that the French "write now with great freedom and truth, and this liberty of the press will overthrow the Jacobins, I plainly perceive."[6]

In another letter to Imlay (1 October 1794), she follows up on this observation: "The liberty of the press will produce a great effect here—the *cry of blood will not be in vain!* Some more monsters will perish—and the Jacobins are conquered. Yet I almost fear the last flap of the tail of the beast."[7] The imagery of crying blood was first used in her posthumously published letter to Joseph Johnson (15 February 1793): "I am grieved . . . when I think of the blood that has stained the cause of freedom at Paris; but I also hear the same live stream cry aloud from the highways, through which the retreating armies passed with famine and death in their rear" (*Works*, 6:444). Although the transitional "but" ("but I also hear") seems to balance the blood shed by retreating foreign armies with the blood that stains the Revolution, the image reappears thematically focused in *The French Revolution,* where the "innocent blood" spilled by the guillotine drowns out the "memory" of the Bastille's prisoners in "the loud cry" of the guillotine's victims (*FR*, 123).

On 10 February 1795 she writes Imlay, telling him that she wishes "one moment that I had never heard of the cruelties that have been practiced here, and the next envy the mothers who have been killed with their children." But in her subsequent letter (19 February 1795), she resists returning to England—"a country, that has not merely lost all charms for me, but for which I feel a repugnance that almost amounts to horror"—adding, astonishingly, "why is it so necessary that I should return?—brought up here, my girl [her daughter Fanny] would be freer."[8] Although it would appear that Wollstonecraft's republican sympathies were reviving, it is more likely that she feared that by moving back to London her tenuous link with Imlay would finally be broken. She did, however, return to London, and Imlay persuaded her (in 1795) to act as his business agent in seeking compensation for a treasure ship that he owned. This was the catalyst for her journey to Scandinavia as well as her *Letters Written in Sweden,* which I now consider.

Wollstonecraft's book constitutes a revision of various theses she had advanced in *The French Revolution,* and I will lead into a consideration of the significance of this revision by discussing the book's French dimension in chronologic order. *Letters Written in Sweden* starts initially with contradictory emphases. In letter 1, for instance, she writes of the beautiful Swedish landscape, a pastoral scene, which makes her forget "the horrors" she "had witnessed in France" (*Works,* 6:247). But in letter 3, she mentions the Revolution's positive effects: "Besides the [F]rench revolution has not only rendered all the crowned heads more cautious, but has so decreased everywhere (excepting amongst themselves) a respect for nobility, that the peasantry have not only lost their blind reverence for the seigniors, but complain, in a manly style, of oppressions which before they did not think of denominating such, because they were taught to consider themselves as a different order of beings" (255). Here, indeed, is Burke's dreaded "revolution in manners" (*Reflections,* 175) and despite the execrable, albeit presumably unwitting, pun that the French Revolution had "rendered all the crowned heads more cautious"—given the fate of Louis XVI—Wollstonecraft's support of the Revolution seemed to get stronger the further she was from France.

In letter 7 she believes the Revolution will eventually cause the Norwegians to begin to transcend the narrow circle of their families, since politics, as a "subject of discussion, enlarges the heart by opening the understanding" (*Works,* 6:274).

In Letter 13 the Norwegians "wish well to the republican cause; and follow, with the most lively interest, the successes of the [F]rench arms. So determined were they, in fact, to excuse every thing, disgracing the struggle of freedom, by admitting the tyrant's plea necessity [see *Paradise Lost* 4.394–95], that I could hardly persuade them that Robespierre was a monster" (*Works,* 6:302). We have seen this argument before—Robespierre (or the Jacobins) stain the Revolution, causing it to deviate from its destined course. Robespierre is an aberration within the Revolution. This suggests, however, that some individuals or monsters are important.

In letter 19 she criticizes capital punishment (cf. *FR,* 53–54) and public executions, which harden "the heart" of the spectator and the "common people" who flock to see them "in all countries" (*Works,* 6:323). One assumes this includes France, since she had criticized the Parisians who hasten "to view the operations of the guillotine or carelessly" pass "over the earth stained with blood" (*FR,* 216). Letter 19, however, marks a dialectical turn of thought for her. Seeing herself as an objective historian providing "a dispassionate view of men," and hence not pretending "to sketch a national character" (precisely what she did in *The French Revolution*), she will merely "note the present state of morals and manners, as I trace the progress of the world's improvement" (*Works,* 6:326). This last clause alludes to the title of her revolutionary history and the thesis that propels it. Having previously sketched the French national character (vain, frivolous, benighted), she begins her turn: "I believe I should have been less severe in the remarks I have made on the vanity and depravity of the [F]rench, had I travelled towards the north before I visited France."

Her repudiation of her former criticisms continues:

> The interesting picture frequently drawn of the virtues of a rising people, has, I fear, been fallacious, excepting the accounts of the enthusiasm which various public struggles have produced. We talk of the depravity of the [F]rench, and lay stress on the old age of the nation; yet where has more virtuous enthusiasm been displayed than during the last two years, by the common people of France, and in their armies? I am obliged sometimes to recollect the numberless instances which I have either witnessed, or heard well authenticated, to balance the account of horrours, alas! but too true. I am, therefore, inclined to believe that the gross vices which I have always seen allied with simplicity of manners, are the concomitants of ignorance.
>
> (*Works,* 6:326)

Although she had earlier traced the vices rather than the "virtues" of the French, several things stand out. First, she absolves the French from mob "enthusiasm," the word she used previously to soften revolutionary "excesses," for instead of signifying the people's violent sentiments and imagination, *enthusiasm* now suggests spontaneous and generous patriotic emotions and endeavors.

Second, she seems to suggest that the French people are not depraved because of their cursed history ("the old age of the nation"). This reversal is significant, since her thesis that old despotism engendered new terror was a crucial component in her understanding of the Revolution's contradictions.

Third, she typically balances the good against the bad ("number-less instances" of "virtuous enthusiasm" which balance or cross out "the account of horrours"), and this leads to her conclusion that what she previously took for "depravity" was only the effect of ignorance. In other words, having traveled to Scandinavia and discovered that Nordic people have the same character flaws as the French, she exonerates the French for her "severe" remarks, since, given the fact of universal ignorance, the Revolution would have played out the same way in any other country. Since she had already given up her belief in the sudden regeneration of the world, she can patiently expect the gradual replacement of ignorance with knowledge. Like the Revolution itself, her thesis is gradually progressive.

In the subsequent letter (20), she makes her last pertinent remarks about France. Wollstonecraft opens the letter with another retraction exonerating French character:

> I have formerly censured the [F]rench for their extreme attachment to theatrical exhibitions, because I thought that they tended to render them vain and unnatural characters. But I must acknowledge, especially as women of the town never appear in the [P]arisian, as at our theaters, that the little saving of the week is more usefully expended there, every [S]unday, than in porter or brandy, to intoxicate or stupify the mind. The common people of France have a great superiority over that class in every other country on this very score.
>
> (*Works*, 6:327)

At this point, she negates another of her previous theses: the theatrical nature of the French people.

But it is interesting that her proof resides in the French women, presumably of the "common people." (A couple of sentences later, purity also resides in the "abstemious" English and Scandinavian women in contrast to their "intoxicated" men.) The sentence is, however, confusing, apparently distinguishing between the French women who do not visit "the Parisian" theaters and the English women who do visit London theaters. But the last clause seems to clash against this reading: "that the little saving of the week is more usefully expended there, every Sunday, than in porter or brandy, to intoxicate or stupify the mind." Where is this ambiguous "there"—but presumably in the theaters where the French women's money is better spent than the money their English counterparts waste on liquor. Wollstonecraft frequently gets tied up with what she is trying to say, but it is clear that the real distinction is between French "sobriety" and European "intoxication."

This is borne out in the remainder of the paragraph:

It is merely the sobriety of the [P]arisians which renders their fêtes more interesting, their gaiety never becoming disgusting or dangerous; as is always the case when liquor circulates. Intoxication is the pleasure of savages, and of all of those whose employments rather exhaust their animal spirits, than exercise their faculties. Is not this, in fact, the vice, both in England and the northern states of Europe, which appears to be the greatest impediment to general improvement? Drinking is here the principal relaxation of the men, . . . but the women are very abstemious, though they have no public amusements as a substitute. I ought to except one theater, which appears more than is necessary; for when I was there, it was not half full; and neither the ladies nor actresses displayed much fancy in their dress.

(Works, 6:327–28)

Although she previously wrote that the French people increase their "gaiety" by "the moderate quantity of weak wine, which they drink at their meals" *(FR,* 227), she devotes too much time, in the passage above, to what seems to be a banal sociological observation. What is happening here?

We will remember in the previous letter (19), she linguistically meliorated *enthusiasm*—an explanatory word in *The French Revolution* for revolutionary excesses. Something similar happens in letter 20. Metaphorically, the French people are absolved of "intoxication"—a word she uses in *The French Revolution,* along with *inebriation,* to stress the causal physical and emotional "excesses" that momentarily overcome the people. Even the violently "inebriated" Parisians are now associated with "sobriety," especially in connection with their *fêtes.*

The reference to these sober revolutionary festivals is not gratuitous, for as Mona Ozouf has shown in her study of the *la fête révolutionnaire,* both antirevolutionary and anti-Jacobin writers (they are not always synonymous) in France and abroad represented the revolutionary festivals as "masquerades stained with wine and blood"—festivals of intoxicating, orgiastic violence.[9] In contrast, the "patriots" stressed the solemn, dignified nature of these festivals in order to sacralize the Revolution. In fact, the official organized Parisian festivals were stylized and "sober," while the unofficial festivals in the provinces tended to be more unruly, although they never approached the exaggerated caricatures of antirevolutionary criticism.

Living in Paris, as she did, Wollstonecraft would have been exposed to the most carefully choreographed revolutionary festivals and would have undoubtedly known of the critical counterrevolutionary representations. In a letter to Gilbert Imlay (22 September

1794), she mentions attending a Parisian *fête*.[10] Indeed, her emphasis on the Parisian festival is a silent rejection of the violence and hence the "inebriation" attributed to the Revolution by its enemies. In this context, Wollstonecraft linguistically performs what Ozouf says was one of the fundamental purposes of the festivals—to create a sense of harmony camouflaging the contradictions and divisions within revolutionary France—to negate violence "by denying it in a world in which it must not even be named."[11]

Wollstonecraft projects this unnamed violence (the Revolution's "inebriation" and savagery) onto the Revolution's enemies (England) and the other Northern European peoples where she has discovered flaws she formerly attributed uniquely to the French. The "other" Europe is suddenly associated with "savages": that is, the supposedly civilized world confronting or resisting the wild barbaric Revolution is metaphorically identified as the real source of drunken savagery, while France is revealed to be sober and hence "rational."

In this context, it is important to remember that metaphors of intoxication were frequently used by antirevolutionary writers, as Burke does throughout the *Reflections,* to stigmatize the Revolution. All this metaphoric and symbolic freight bears on Wollstonecraft's references to drunkenness and sobriety and her reversal of the counterrevolutionary metaphors—metaphors she had used herself to characterize revolutionary excesses—and hence the "terms" of counterrevolutionary criticism. Although it is impossible to determine her conscious intent in passages like this, her reversed metaphors do make a silent metaphoric case that would have been difficult to maintain publicly in the period following the Terror: the moderate sobriety of the French (even the Parisians!) versus the savage "intoxication" of the rest of Europe.

In *Letters Written in Sweden,* Wollstonecraft modifies or revises criticisms she had made in *The French Revolution.* Believing that the Jacobin beast had given the last flap of its tail and died, she finally makes peace with the French people. Since progress is inevitable and the French are found, in retrospect, not to be that bad, her vision of the Revolution in the subsequent book is more sanguine than the troubled vision of her French history. *Letters Written in Sweden* was, in essence, Wollstonecraft's final rewriting of a revolution that had, by turn, inspired and disappointed her. In the end, her revision of *The French Revolution* reinforced her belief that principles are ultimately more important than people and that the Revolution would work out its own self-fulfilling logic in the bright, progressive future.

For Wollstonecraft and other radical writers, the question they continually reposed was where, when, and what was the real French Revolution? Whether it was the storming of the Bastille or the period encompassing the Festival of Federation (14 July 1790), radical writers were consumed with the Revolution's true origin and its tragic digression: when did the Revolution begin and at what point was it betrayed? Wollstonecraft and others answered the question in a variety of similar ways. But it was Helen Maria Williams who, as we will see, repeatedly made the question her own personal fiction.

9

Helen Maria Williams and the French Revolution

In March 1787 William Wordsworth published his first poem, a sonnet titled "On Seeing Miss Helen Maria Williams Weep at a Tale of Distress." Wordsworth's poem was, however, a poetic fiction, since he never saw or met Williams until 1820 in France.[1] The sonnet, however, illustrates that Williams was, albeit largely forgotten now, a prominent public figure in the 1780s and that her feminine sensibility was a celebrated part of her public persona.

Born in 1761, Williams was educated at home in Berwick-on-Tweed but moved to London in 1781 with her mother and two sisters (her immediate family) and began acquiring fame after Dr. Andrew Kippis, a prominent Dissenter and an old family friend, helped publish her first poem and introduced her to London literary society. As a poet, Williams was instantly popular. Her house became a literary salon, and she met or communicated with literary luminaries, including Robert Burns and Samuel Johnson. In 1784 she published *Peru,* a poem that treats tangentially the Spanish exploitation of South America and, after a collection of poems in 1786, she published a poem dealing with the slave trade (1788), through which she solidified her reputation as a progressive poet, concerned with enlightened issues and causes. Friends and admirers celebrated her in a series of poems. She was also known for her poetic, "feminine" sensibility. An anonymous poem in the *European Magazine* (1787) praises her for portraying "the softer feelings of the heart."[2] By 1789 Williams was known as a young, attractive poet, identified with progressive political positions and a generous feminine sensibility. In 1790 she published a sentimental novel, *Julia,* dealing with social manners and mores, interspersed with poems, including (*de rigueur*) one on the Bastille.

Several years before, in 1785, Williams had befriended Monique Coquerel, the wife of Augustin Thomas Du Fossé, a French emigrant who had angered his aristocratic, Norman father by marrying

153

the socially inferior Monique. Augustin, consequently, had been forced to flee to England, where he was lured back to France by his father's false promises of reconciliation, and imprisoned for two years, before escaping again. When his father died in 1787, he returned to France and renounced his inheritance as eldest son, entitling him to most of his father's fortune. Despite this generous act, his younger brothers conspired against him, causing him to flee again to England. He finally returned with his wife to France on 15 July, the day after the Bastille fell, and in 1790 invited Williams and her family to visit them and to attend the famous *Fête de la Fédération* (14 July 1790) in Paris. Williams enthusiastically accepted, for the French Revolution had become her new passion. On 25 June 1790 she wrote to a friend, informing him that she would momentarily give up her pleasant *soirees* for "the sublimer delights of the French Revolution."[3]

She arrived in Paris on 13 July and the next day witnessed the celebrated *Fête*—one of the great spectacles of the Revolution. Her famous description, published four months later, conveys the electrical excitement of a Revolution inspiring the generous emotions and hopes of many people who believed, in the jubilant summer of 1790, that the Revolution would regenerate the world. After traveling through various regions and making new friends, Williams returned to England in the first days of September a true believer, enamored with the Revolution's magical possibilities. She was, however, irritated that the Revolution had been misrepresented in English newspapers—misrepresentations contradicting her sense of the Revolution she had just experienced personally. She angrily read Burke's *Reflections* but was later satisfied that Paine had demonstrated his errors and distortions.[4]

Soon after her return, she published the first volume of *Letters from France,* which included her celebratory account of the *Fête*.[5] The publication established her as a supporter of the Revolution and involved her in the acrimonious political debate that was beginning to explode. Her book was generally reviewed favorably and was credited with influencing nascent public opinion. In 1791 Williams persuaded her family to return to France for two years, and they arrived, according to her biographer, in the middle of July, the month after the French royal family's disastrous flight to Varennes.[6] Williams' friends disapproved of her political pilgrimage, fearing for her safety in a country that suddenly seemed volatile and unstable. Her friend Anna Seward feared Williams would nevertheless remain in France: she would charm patriot hearts and, in turn, be charmed.[7] Fluent in French and undaunted, Williams immersed herself in the Revolution.

In Paris, between winter 1791 and spring 1792, Williams met prominent revolutionaries, including Robespierre, Vergniaud, and Madame Roland, who became a personal friend. Williams was as popular in France as she had been in England, but, like Paine, she associated and identified with the Girondins—something that would also cause her future problems. At the end of April 1792, she returned for the last time to England and was back in Paris shortly before 10 August—the *journeé* in which a revolutionary mob invaded the Tuileries and effectively ended the fiction of the French monarchy. From her hotel, Williams witnessed the attack and provided a drink to one of the harried Swiss guards, who, after requesting it, died. Taking a walk the next day, she was frightened and fled when she saw the mutilated corpses of the guards who had been massacred.[8] In England, however, Williams was suddenly an example of an English woman corrupted by the Revolution. Ray M. Adams notes that "the account of this experience [the 10 August *journée*] passed with great exaggeration to England," where she was represented as slumming in the Tuileries, walking indifferently through the corpses of the massacred Swiss guards.[9] In the second edition of his *Life of Johnson,* an indignant James Boswell deleted the word "amiable"—an adjective he had previously applied to Williams, referring to her amicable meeting with Johnson in 1784. In *Letters on the Female Mind* (1793), Laetitia Matilda Hawkins, the conservative antirevolutionary writer, apparently refers to the exaggerated account of Williams' walk of 10 August, quoting an extract of a recently published trip: "I might have been shocked had I seen but one dead body, but seeing such heaps, I did not feel concerned."[10] Williams of course never wrote these words, suggesting that a fabricated account was attributed to her and was apparently believed by many in England, including Hawkins. In 1798 the *Gentleman's Magazine* was still referring to the fabricated event, reporting that Williams had "walked without horror, over the ground . . . when it was strewn with the naked bodies of the faithful Swiss guards."[11] Likewise, the *Anti-Jacobin* (30 April 1798) provided this additional distortion: Williams ". . . danced, with all the fury of a drunken Bacchante, round the mangled bodies of the faithful Swiss," handling "their scorched and gory limbs with brutal curiosity."[12]

After the September Massacres (2–6 September 1792), Williams rented an apartment on the Rue Hélvetius and never returned again to England, where she was now socially *persona non grata*. Many of her friends and admirers abandoned her as a woman lost and infected with the "French disease." The controversial nature of the Revolution had made her a controversial figure, and she was demonized as a woman who had unsexed herself by participating in degrading revolutionary politics. In *Letters on the Female Mind* (addressed specifically to Williams), Laetitia Matilda Hawkins warned her that she might not be welcomed in England, even by her former friends, unless she recanted her previous revolutionary sentiments.[13]

Williams' unorthodox relationship with John Hurford Stone added to her notoriety. Stone was a wealthy English coal merchant (married) who was also an enthusiastic believer in the Revolution. In France, he established various factories producing wallpaper, cotton, and silk; in the early 1790s he was shuttling between Paris and London, trying to position himself for a financial killing once the Revolution triumphed. He was a republican capitalist who saw the Revolution as a wonderful way to maximize profits. In Paris he was a member of the British Club—the group of British citizens engaged in varying degrees of espionage, between 1792 and 1793. Through his brother William, in England, Stone was sounding out various liberal and radical Whigs, trying to determine whether the conditions for a French invasion were propitious and whether they would react favorably to such a possibility. In a letter to the Committee of Public Safety (18 November 1794), Stone promised to provide a report on the opinions of Lansdowne, Stanhope, Lauderdale, and Fox.[14] In 1796 Stone's letters to his brother William were quoted extensively in the latter's trial for treason in London. Although William Stone was acquitted on the technicality that he had discouraged an invasion (when he had actually reported that conditions were not yet ripe), the stigma of treason tainted John, often referred to by antirevolutionary Britons as "the traitor Stone." Sex and politics were inextricably intertwined in the revolutionary period, and since Williams' relationship with Stone was considered adulterously "republican," she seemed a woman who was both treasonous and "fallen."

Whether or not, as some have surmised, Williams and Stone were, at some point, secretly married, they were close companions until his death in 1818. Williams regularly signed or initialed her name with Stone's surname and was buried next to him nine years later. In 1937 a letter from Williams to Ruth Barlow, the wife of Joel Barlow, was published for the first time. In the letter (dated by the editors circa April 6–16, 1794), Williams worries whether she will ever experience "that most exalted of all happiness . . . I mean conjugal felicity," referring to a "Mr. S____," and adding that if it were her fate "to live in future a state of celibacy," she "would not have a word with him on that subject—my own wants are very circumscribed," a phrase the editors believe means that "if she is not to be married she does not expect any financial assistance from [Stone]."[15] Stone was divorced from his wife two months later, in June 1794.

Since Stone was a member of the British Club, some readers today may assume that Williams was also engaged in treason against England. She may have been, as David Erdman suggests, at a meeting of the Club (November 1792) when a toast was proposed to British women who had written in behalf of the Revolution.[16] But although she often criticized her country, irritating many English readers, she was, I believe, constitutionally incapable of treason. Stone probably did not inform her of his own quasi-treasonous activities. In the *Letters,* she self-consciously refrains from mentioning his name, even when she is referring to him, probably because of the controversial nature of their relationship as well as the controversial nature of the Revolution. We know, for instance, that Stone wrote five anonymous letters (2–6) dealing with French military affairs, letters that Williams incorporated into her own *Letters* (1:3.30–241).[17] Williams prefaces these letters by noting that for "particular reasons" she cannot name the anonymous contributor, although the informed reader will be able "to determine from what quarter they proceed" (1:3, "Advertisement"). Later, in what I take as an evasive allusion to Stone (2:3.53–54), she suggests that he had advised the French against invading England, which may or may not indicate that she was aware of his correspondence with his brother, William.

This raises a related point. From 1792 and in subsequent years, Williams entertained, often lavishly, at her home on the Rue Helvétius, every Sunday evening, although she suspended these *soirées* during the Terror and the Empire (1802–1815). Given her modest income from her writings, some critics have wondered how she could have afforded these entertainments and have suggested that she was secretly subsidized by the British government to report on the British in Paris.[18] In contrast, both the Jacobin and Napoleonic governments suspected that she might be spying for England and, consequently, had her under surveillance at various times. In the paranoid politics of the revolutionary era, anything seemed possible. Stone, for instance, was arrested by French authorities (12 March 1795) for supposedly revealing French plans to invade the Cape of Good Hope by passing information, via his brother, to

William Pitt. Even though he was soon acquitted by the Directory, it was not the last time he was arrested.[19] Rather than suppose that one or both were double agents, an obvious explanation for Williams' capacity to entertain is Stone's wealth. It is true that, circa 1812, Stone's "business speculations led to the loss of his fortune."[20] In the latter part of her life, especially after Stone's death, Williams lived in relative poverty, subsisting on a pension from a nephew, even though she endeavored to keep up appearances and somehow mysteriously succeeded. There is no evidence, however, that she ever spied for either England or France, although the psychic tensions resulting from her dual allegiance were undoubtedly immense.

From 1790 through the Terror and the subsequent establishment of the Directory, Williams continued publishing her sequential *Letters from France*. The second volume of her *Letters* dealt with the period of late 1791 to April 1792. Williams wrote the third and fourth volumes during the first four months following Louis XVI's execution in January 1793. Although the contradictory course of the Revolution disturbed her, the fourth volume (letter 5, 1:4.155–271) concluded with a series of causal explanations of why the Revolution was not progressing, ending with an optimistic prediction that in seven years (ca. 1800), the Revolution will have been judged a success. This letter was written by Thomas Christie and had apparently been requested by Williams in order to explicate the Revolution's contradictions.[21]

After June 1793, when the National Convention was surrounded and the Girondist deputies arrested, Williams' friendship and identification with the Girondins made her suspect to hostile Jacobins, and the ongoing war with Britain made her vulnerable to arrest. She later recalled that a private letter written to friends during the incipient Terror, in which she had described the "tyrant" Robespierre, had been imprudently published as extracts in a London newspaper and that, consequently, the Committee of Public Safety (having translated the extracts) considered her a security risk. During this period, Williams was forced to burn a compromising book she had written just before her apartment was searched by French authorities—something she was compelled to do on various other occasions.[22] Later, in 1794, she advised Wollstonecraft to burn her own manuscript on the French Revolution.

In her *Letters*, Williams says that in spring 1792 Bertrand de Barère (member of the National Convention, later a member of the Committee of Public Safety) and assorted Girondist deputies spent their evenings at her home and that they all knew she was writing "some letters . . . since . . . published in England, in which I had drawn the portrait of the tyrant [Robespierre] in those dark shades of colouring that belonged to his hideous nature" (*Letters,* 2:1.171). She suggests that the cowardly, opportunistic Barère (who had made compromising pro-Girondist statements in her apartment) subsequently became a Jacobin and contrived her arrest in October 1793. She notes that after May 1793, the Committee of Public Safety was translating letters of hers appearing in English newspapers and "the work [was] mentioned as mine" (173), that is, the "letters" dealing with the "tyrant" Robespierre (171). The "work" is, of course, her *Letters from France,* the third and fourth series of which were published anonymously in 1793. Although Williams exaggerates her critical treatment of Robespierre (she, in fact, does not spend that much time on him), this was sufficiently enough to endanger her life, since in the first letter of the third series (1:3.1–29) and subsequently in the fourth series, she severely criticizes the Jacobins *in toto.*

In a letter (31 October 1793) to an acquaintance, Anna Seward, Williams' friend, refers to the anonymous edition, observing that it, in effect, "puts [Williams'] head on the guillotine."[23] In an open letter to the *Gentleman's Magazine* of February 1793, Seward observed that Williams "has sent out this work as her palinode and harbinger, to smooth her reception here, and apologize for the too-confident triumph of her former volumes."[24] In *A Tour in Switzerland* (1798), Williams says that she was forced to flee France in 1794 because "I had written a work, published in England, in which I had traced, without reserve, the characters of our oppressors."[25] In a letter written after Robespierre's fall, Williams suggests that in August 1793 she and the remaining English who had not yet been arrested were hoping to be expelled from France, since "all passports to leave the country were [being] refused" (*Letters,* 2:1.4–5). Indeed, both the purge of the Girondins and Williams' precarious position support Seward's comment that the 1793 book was an indirect recantation and that Williams was planning to somehow return to England. In her own *Letters,* Williams refers to two surreptitious copies of "the work" smuggled in from London and her correspondent apprehension (having requested that one copy be destroyed) that "the other might, by means of those domiciliary visits which were so often repeated, have been thrown into the hands of revolutionary commissaries" (2:1.174). In allowing the anonymous 1793 edition to be published, Williams demonstrated extraordinary courage (and probably desperation). This would also suggest that she was, as Anna Seward surmised, trying to return to England and "smooth" her subsequent reception, but that her plans somehow went awry. Williams had also demonstrated courage by twice visiting Madame Roland, who had been imprisoned since 31 May 1793—when any association with Girondins was dangerously compromising.

After a revolutionary decree mandating the detention of foreigners (9 October 1793), Williams and her family were finally arrested at 2 A.M., 12 October, interrogated, and imprisoned hours later in a detention center, before being moved to the Luxembourg prison. (Stone was arrested on 10 October and released at the end of the month.) On 26 October Williams and her family were moved to the English Conceptionist Convent in Paris but were allowed to return briefly to their apartment to collect some personal belongings. Williams later recalled that the guard, showing some chivalrous delicacy, turned his back, allowing her to burn some incriminating correspondence, including a letter from Madame Roland.[26] In the *Letters,* she mentions "being permitted" to return to the apartment but says nothing about the burned correspondence (2:1.181–82), suggesting that she may perhaps have subsequently embellished the event. Through the efforts of a personal friend, Williams and her family were released sometime in November or December. Woodward could not ascertain the date but speculates it was in the second week of December; Ray M. Adams says it was "during the last days of November."[27] In her *Letters,* Williams says the imprisonment lasted two months (2:1.204–5), making the mid-December date probable; but she then mentions that her release preceded by a "few weeks" (208) the execution of Rabaut Saint-Etienne (5 December 1793), placing the release in November. (While Woodward's dated biography is useful—the only full biography published in the past two hundred years—a new thorough one is needed.) At any rate, Williams and her family quickly moved to "the most remote part of the fauxbourg Germain," where they tried to lay low and avoid police surveillance (*Letters,* 2:2.2) On 5 April 1794 Williams saw Danton being transported to the guillotine, one day after a law had been passed ordering foreigners and ci-devant nobles to leave Paris within ten days. She and her family, consequently, had to move near Marlay, a village close to Versailles; but with the help of a local revolutionary committee, they were soon permitted to return to Paris. In June, fearing that her prior association with the Girondins and the publication of the 1793 book endangered her, Williams obtained a passport from generous friends and escaped to Switzerland, traveling with Stone and Benjamin Vaughan, another English fellow traveler. Ray M. Adams believes she stayed for six months, composing more of the *Letters* before returning to Paris.[28]

In 1798 she published *A Tour in Switzerland* in two volumes. She excoriates Robespierre and the Jacobins (happily fallen), but she seems content about the possibility of an invasion of Switzerland by French forces, poised to liberate its "oppressed" people. Chris Jones notes that Williams, in the *Tour,* discredits the myth of Swiss "democracy"—an eighteenth-century cultural commonplace.[29] In 1786 Williams had praised Switzerland in her "Epistle to Dr. Moore," as "a land where Freedom rears her humble home."[30] Her subsequent revisionist critique, in *A Tour in Switzerland,* makes an explicit case for a liberating French invasion, even though she generally opposed foreign intervention. Like so many of her contemporaries, she is especially impressed with Napoleon, liberator of Italy and admirer of Ossian.[31]

After she had returned to France, Williams continued her prolific publishing, exposing the Terror and dealing with the events of the Directory and the subsequent Consulate. She had initially admired Napoleon, who flattered her as he had other foreign writers whom he had tried to cultivate (he told Paine that he slept with *Rights of Man* under his pillow and that gold statues should be erected to him in every city of the world). Williams, however, soon became disillusioned. In 1802 she irritated Napoleon by publishing a poem on the Peace of Amiens. According to her, Napoleon resented that his name had not been mentioned and that she had extolled the British navy. Consequently, he had Williams and her family arrested and detained for one day.[32]

For the rest of her life, Williams remained a controversial figure. In England she was denounced as a radical republican; in France she was accused of being a political opportunist, switching sides whenever it was politically convenient. Neither caricature was true. Williams was a liberal supporter of the pre-1793 Revolution; she denounced the Terror, but she never renounced her emotional faith in the Revolution. Like Wollstonecraft, she also never disowned her idea of the Revolution—an idea that, unlike Wollstonecraft's, is primarily an emotional one. In 1800 she still saw the Revolution as history's most glorious event, insisting that she could pardon those who accused her of defending the Revolution (that is, her English compatriots) but could never forgive those who accused her of betraying it (her French critics). In 1815 she looked back with sad irony on her naive revolutionary enthusiasm, but she continued defending her *consistent* emotional response. She reiterated the conventional argument that the Old Order had caused the Revolution's excesses—a Revolution whose crimes stemmed from ignorance rather than cruelty.[33]

From 1803 to 1815, Williams struggled. Napoleon's hostility made her wary of publishing. She closed her salon and did little entertaining until 1816. She subsequently continued writing on French political subjects, but there was little interest in England, where people were tired of anything French and where she no longer had an admiring audience. Although she and Stone periodically planned to emigrate to America, they were still in Paris when Stone died in 1818. Emotionally and economically exhausted, Williams was invited to live in Amsterdam with her nephew, A. L. C. Coquerel, the son of her sister, Cecile, whom she had helped raise after the latter's death in 1798. She was, however, unhappy in Holland and returned to live in Paris on the modest pension her nephew provided her. Largely forgotten and unread in England, she was a revolutionary ghost for those occasional curious, albeit admiring, visitors like William Wordsworth, who stopped to see her in 1820. She died on 14 December 1827 and was buried beside Stone in *Père Lachaise*.

Among her many publications, Williams devoted thirteen volumes to France, spanning thirty turbulent years of French history. Eight of these deal with the revolutionary period, starting with the Festival of Federation (14 July 1790) and ending with the establishment of the Directory (3 November 1795). I will concentrate on these eight volumes, the *Letters from France,* and will begin by contrasting Williams and Wollstonecraft before considering Williams' revolutionary history.

10

Comedy, Tragedy, and Romance in Williams' *Letters from France*

I

In many ways Helen Maria Williams is the antithesis of Mary Wollstonecraft, even though they both have a Girondist view of the Revolution. Wollstonecraft emphasizes reason and judgement, while Williams stresses emotion and the heart. Williams' "political creed is entirely an affair of the heart," which she opposes to her "head" (*Letters,* 1:1.66). She notes that political arguments are often confusing, but once "a proposition is addressed" to her heart, then she has "quickness of perception" and can "decide, in one moment, points upon which philosophers and legislators have differed in all ages" (1:1.195–96). By emphasizing "quickness of perception," she emphasizes her *sensibility* (see Samuel Johnson, 1755 *Dictionary,* def. no. 2), especially the "feminine" sensibility that Wollstonecraft excoriates in *A Vindication of the Rights of Woman* (1792). In 1777 Hannah More reproduced a common sexual stereotype, noting that "women have generally quicker perceptions."[1] In Rouen (September 1791), Williams observed that "to feel the general good" one only needs "to possess the sensibility of a woman."[2] Williams was, in effect, arguing that her feminine, emotional response to the Revolution was superior to "masculine" ratiocination. Whereas Wollstonecraft, in both of her *Vindications,* opposed sexual distinctions and stressed genderless virtues common to both sexes, Williams defined herself within the conventional categories of feminine response. In doing this, she continued a mode of self-definition for which she had been celebrated in the 1780s. Gary Kelly notes that "Williams' tactics were to write in an acceptably feminine mode, the familiar letter; to write as a woman of feeling; and to employ many topics and devices of the literature of Sensibility—a literature, that is, of self-authentication and a literature already feminised to some extent."[3] In addition, by dramatizing her heartfelt emotional response to the Revolution, Williams establishes a suggestive link between the Revolution and Romanticism, a nexus of interest to current criticism. Since "love is computed in the arithmetic of the heart" (*Letters,* 1:1.163), Williams loves the Revolution because it is a "system of politics . . . by which those I love are made happy" (1:1.196). Since it is "far more amiable to give way to the impulse of the heart" (1:2.97), she argues that the Revolution is an apocalyptic emotional event and that her feminine response is hence truer than a "cold," intellectual analysis. By insisting on a feminine reading of the Revolution, Williams implicitly challenged the conventional meaning of gendered discourse and ensured that her feminine response would become an issue to those who envisioned the Revolution as a political event outside the perimeters of "proper" feminine discourse.

Williams also differs from both Wollstonecraft and Paine in openly depicting the Revolution as a sublime, theatrical spectacle, stressing the theatricality that both Wollstonecraft and Paine denounce, albeit reproduce, in their respective works. In *The French Revolution,* Wollstonecraft had criticized the theatrical posturing of revolutionary "actors" and denigrated the Parisian theaters as a corrupting influence. Williams, in contrast, enjoys the Parisian theaters and their "comic actors," but considers the English theater superior for its production of tragedy (*Letters,* 1:1.90; cf. 1:2.77). Indeed, she initially sees the Revolution as a comedy—the happy spectacle that ends the Old Regime's tragedy—a formulation she later inverts when the Revolution becomes a terrorist tragedy. At the beginning, however, Paris is a delightful spectacle; there are at least twenty theaters, exhibiting "charming acting," and the Parisians' love of the theater illustrates their superior *joie de vivre* (1:2.77, 79–80).

Her descriptions of revolutionary events are replete with theatrical metaphors. The Festival of Federation (14 July 1790) was "the most sublime spectacle, which, perhaps was ever presented on the theatre of this earth" (*Letters,* 1:1.2). The majestic *Fête* was a "spectacle" electrifying French "spectators" (5; cf. 16), and she herself was "a spectator of the Federation" (108). She uses the word *spectacle* in the sense of a public display or entertainment (*OED,* def. no. 1), as well as the French usage of *spectacle* as theater. Williams continually returns to the Festival as a dramatic representation of the true Revolution: an exhilarating theatrical event presented to an applauding audience of four hundred thousand people, re-presented in her *Letters* for the English people.

The Revolution is a sublime spectacle, a divine comedy displaying the reconciliation of the French people and the incipient regeneration of humanity. Later, when the Revolution appears threatening to European spectators, it is still an ongoing "extraordinary drama" (1:4.121).

Although her description of the programmatic orchestration of the Festival unwittingly exposes her ingenuous emotional response, she astutely notes that the Revolution's "leaders" connect the French people to the Revolution by engaging them emotionally:

> The leaders of the French Revolution are men well acquainted with the human heart. They have not trusted merely to the force of reason, but have studied to interest in their cause the most powerful passions of human nature, by the appointment of solemnities perfectly calculated to awaken that general sympathy which is caught from heart to heart with irresistible energy, fills every eye with tears, and throbs in every bosom.
>
> *(Letters,* 1:1.61–62)

She suggests again the superiority of her emotional response and endorses as "natural" the studied calculation that could appear, to hostile observers, as manipulative and artificial. In describing the Festival of Federation, Williams (and practically everyone else who experienced it) emphasizes the emotional participation of the audience and "the effect it produced on the minds of the spectators" (*Letters,* 1:1.5)—an event in which the spectators were part of the spectacle. Wondering how she can possibly provide "an adequate idea of the behavior of the spectators" (5), she subsequently describes the people weeping and embracing each other, noting that her "heart caught with enthusiasm the general sympathy" and her eyes "filled with tears" (14). Thematically, this is both the "natural" language and response that the French leaders "calculated to awaken"—the "general sympathy . . . caught from heart to heart," throbbing "in every bosom," filling "every eye with tears" (1:1.62)—the same emotion and response she hopes the reader also catches. Moreover, Williams, like Wollstonecraft, in *The Rights of Men,* makes Burke's *Enquiry* an issue in her work and reinscribes, *mutatis mutandis,* one of Burke's insights in the *Enquiry:* descriptions of the effect of (revolutionary) beauty on the observer are more powerful than descriptions of beauty per se. In the *Reflections,* Burke had allusively dismissed the Festival of Federation: "Their confederations, their *spectacles,* their civic feasts, and their enthusiasm, I take no notice of; they are nothing but mere tricks"

(306). Williams, in contrast, emphasizes the spectacle and enthusiasm Burke rejects.

From the beginning, of course, a series of new festivals (from the planting of liberty trees to the grand, orchestrated *fêtes*) celebrated the Revolution as a communal spectacle. These festivals "were intended to be spectacles in which the people would be both spectators and actors"; Bernard Poyet, one of the planners in charge of the Festival of Federation, wrote that "Public festivals inspired by lofty considerations of common interests have this special characteristic, that the sentiment of each person becomes that of all by a sort of electrification which people can scarcely resist."[4] In crystallizing the revolutionary leaders' intent and in describing the people's reaction—each citizen catching "the general sympathy" from "heart to heart," seeing a reflection of each other in happy, tear-filled eyes—Williams underscores the emotional and visual *identity* of the spectators with each other and with the Revolution that is one and indivisible. She wonderfully captures both the spirit and intent of the revolutionary festivals; indeed, her description mirrors Rousseau's proposal for popular, communal *fêtes* in the *Lettre à d' Alembert sur les spectacles,* a proposal probably enacted by the Revolution's "leaders": after assembling the people at a focal site, "you will have a festival. . . . let the spectators become an entertainment to themselves [that is, display the spectators as spectacle]; make them actors themselves; do it so that each sees and loves himself in the others so that all will be better united."[5] Although Williams does not see the potential for coerced conformity in her unified celebration, she subsequently contrasts the natural Festival of Federation with the artificial Festival of the Supreme Being (8 June 1794).

Since the latter is Robespierre's festival, she emphasizes the programmatic conformity of the spectators' scripted roles, in which language represents beforehand what the people are supposed to enact: "mothers are to embrace their daughters . . . fathers are to clasp their sons . . . the old are to bless the young, and . . . the young are to kneel to the old" (*Letters,* 2:2.86). Williams' contrast is thus between spontaneous freedom and artificial coercion:

> Ah, what was then become of those civic festivals which hailed the first glories of the revolution! What was become of that sublime federation of an assembled nation which had nobly shaken off its ignominious fetters, and exulted in its new-born freedom! What was become of those moments when no emotions were pre-ordained, no feelings measured out, no acclamations decreed; but when every bosom beat high

with admiration, when every heart throbbed with enthusiastic transport, when every eye melted into tears, and the vault of heaven re-
sounded the bursts of unpremeditated applause!

(2:2.87)

Williams had faithfully read Rousseau who, in the *Lettre à d'*
Alembert sur les spectacles, laments rhetorically: "Ah! Where are
the games and festivals of my youth? Where is the concord of the
citizens? Where is the public fraternity? Where is the pure joy and
the real gaiety? Where are the peace, the liberty, the equity, the
innocence?"[6] As Jacobin tragedians coercively rewrite the Revolution's primal script, Williams contrasts the Revolution's fall with
the first festival and the original representation, which she remembers in nostalgic, romantic terms. Recollecting the spontaneous
overflow of natural feelings in her wistful, ubi sunt lament, the first
Fête is, for her, a prelapsarian spot of time.

The distinction between natural and artificial festivals complements the distinction between the Revolution as good theater—a
comedy played out naturally—and the Revolution as bad theater—
a terrorist tragedy in which natural roles are betrayed. The Terror
forced Williams to re-emplot the comedic revolution as a French
tragedy. In this Jacobin tragedy, however, the good "actors" still
react naturally to the unnatural parts they are forced to play. The
victims of the Terror display their natural feelings: all the sincere
tears shed over friends or family members imprisoned or guillotined, tears resulting from unnatural, forced separations. Similarly,
Williams' Girondins face the guillotine bravely. Conscious of their
invulnerable innocence, they die in the best Roman tradition of
Plutarch and other classic scripts. The change of genre reinscribes
the Revolution's betrayal through a series of multiplying tragedies:
a Jacobin tragedy that causes the national "French" tragedy, a
domestic tragedy for persecuted French families, and a personal
Girondist tragedy for Williams and her beloved friends. In the end,
her feminine Girondists—progressively emotional, profusely lach-
rymose, and valiantly vulnerable—are like the Trojans in Burke's
Enquiry: an endearing race, "whose fate [Homer] has designed to
excite our compassion" by giving them "infinitely more of the amiable social virtues than he has distributed among his Greeks" (*Enquiry,* 158).

The Jacobin terrorists script everyone, including Williams, into
the French tragedy. In a letter dated four days after the King's
execution (25 January 1793), Williams is a "spectator of the [revolu-
tionary] representation," a great drama she experiences directly,

in contrast to English spectators who view the Revolution "from a distance": "I am placed near enough the scene to discern every gesture of the actors, and every passion excited in the minds of the audience" (*Letters,* 1:3.2). During the Terror, however, she is forced to become a reluctant actor, "a sad spectacle to the crowd" that watches her ascend "the steps of the Luxembourg" and enter prison (2:1.13). There is an allusive contrast between her earlier role as a privileged spectator, happily watching the exciting revolutionary comedy unfold, and the unhappy prisoner who is forced to experience both France's national tragedy and her own.

Her principal dramatic villain is Robespierre, a frustrated metaphoric actor who, as a young man, fancied himself a genius destined "to act a splendid part on the theatre of the world" (*Letters,* 2:1.229). But this is a false part, and he fails miserably: a mediocre lawyer and orator, he must leave Paris and return to his provincial home in Arras (230). A frustrated failure, he finally succeeds when he ruins the Revolution's happy representation, becoming the Terror's primary author and actor. For Williams, Robespierre is the director of the Revolution's tragedy—manipulating people behind the scenes, sending others to death, pretending to befriend while he betrays—and he tragically fulfills his evil role: "While Robespierre behind the scenes was issuing daily mandates for murder, we see him on the stage the herald of mercy and of peace" (2:3.142). She contrasts the illusion of his public role with the reality of his private in(script)ion. Robespierre, the envious despiser of literary authors, also suppresses drama for political reasons and plans "to abolish the theatrical entertainments all together" (2:1.231). He is, for her, the ironic Puritan dramatist of France's national tragedy.

Since Williams sees the Revolution as a dramatic event, whoever controls the "representation" directs the Revolution to its conclusion. In a letter dated 10 February 1793, she recounts the failed censorship of a play reportedly written before 10 August, the *journée* on which the fictional monarchy finally ended and the royal family was forced to flee to the National Assembly. Since the play contained a caricature of "patriots" as lovers of anarchy resembling Robespierre and Marat, the Paris Commune prohibited its performance, but people protested by surrounding the theater and insisting that the play be performed. The Commune responded by sending the Parisian National Guard "to prevent the representation of the piece": suddenly the control of the drama becomes an allegorical struggle over control of the Revolution's direction and meaning—a conflict between the Girondist Convention (which previously declared that the Commune "had no right to control the representation") and the Jacobin Commune, which, failing to prevent the play, takes its revenge by "ordering all public places to be shut for a week" (*Letters,* 1:4.15–18). Linking artistic freedom to political freedom, Williams equates the Jacobins' attempted control of French *representation* with their flawed terrorist tragedy.

Another principal villain who contributes to the Jacobin (mis)-representation is Collot d' Herbois, a member of the Committee of Public Safety and former terrorist responsible for the repression (including the infamous *mitraillades*) in Lyon (November–December 1793). Lyon, of course, was one of the federalist cities that revolted against the Jacobin purge of the Girondins in June 1793. In his prerevolutionary years (1769–89), Collot had been both an actor and playwright, the producer of mediocre comedies and romantic dramas that lauded royalty, aristocracy, and the institutions of the Old Regime. In 1787 he became director of a theater in Lyon and assumed the stage name of d' Herbois. Like many others, he became a revolutionary in July 1789.

Williams focuses on his acting career in Lyon and his motive for subsequently "exterminating" Lyon's citizens: the people of Lyon had previously repudiated Collot's acting ability—Collot was a "comedian who had been driven from the stage for his professional incapacity." For Williams, the terrible irony is that the frustrated, failed comedian produces the horrible "tragedy" of Lyon (*Letters,* 2:2.157–58). Collot "was led to this vengeance on the people of Lyon for having hissed him when he acted on their stage. Thousands of victims have atoned for the insult offered to a wretched comedian" (166). Referring to Collot's role in Lyon's tragedy, she maintains that he modeled his role on Genghis Khan, avenging, like him, "private injuries" (160). Collot became a "tragic ruffian" acting "his part at Lyon"; later, she refers to him as "the tragedian of Lyon" (167; 2:3.54). The thematic link between Robespierre and Collot is that they are both failed artists who seek to punish others for their previous "artistic" failures.

After the fall of Robespierre, author of his own tragedy, Williams relates how one of Collot's agents, a comedian named Fusil, who had participated in the Lyon massacres and who subsequently became an actor in the Theater of the Republic, was forced by the audience to read the condemnatory verses of "Le Révil du peuple," the popular anti-Jacobin song sung after Robespierre's death. The audience, in effect, forces Fusil to play a self-condemnatory part and then refuses to let him proceed with an "after-piece" (*Letters,* 2:4.26–29).

In Williams' own dramatic presentation, the true revolutionaries act out their parts faithfully while the false (counter)revolutionaries betray both their roles and the Revolution. Williams writes Dantean comedy, while the Jacobins engage in "low" comedy, paradoxically resulting in the Jacobin tragedy that ruins her original representation. Her revolutionary comedy—the happy spectacle of the Festival of Federation—becomes a tragic travesty. As a poet and self-conscious writer, she sees the betrayed Revolution as bad and evil art—a monstrous mixture of genres, resulting in the botched revolutionary drama and the terrorist tragedy produced by tragic comedians and failed artists.[7] In the *Reflections,* Burke had viewed the Revolution similarly: "Every thing seems out of nature in this strange chaos of levity and ferocity, and of all sorts of crimes jumbled together with all sorts of follies. In viewing this monstrous tragicomic scene, the most opposite passions necessarily succeed, and sometimes mix with each other in the mind; alternate contempt and indignation; alternate laughter and tears; alternate scorn and horror" (92–93). Like Wollstonecraft, the closer Williams is to the Terror, the closer she is to Burke's representation.

In her revolutionary tragedy, the true artists, the genuine actors, are persecuted. The Paris Commune conducts an ideological purge, an "epuration" of actors "who had been in the habitude of personating princes, and nobles, and queens, and countesses"—corrupting roles that supposedly militate against "habits of equality." Significantly, the tragedians who act out royal roles are "sent to prison," while the comedians who represent lower-class characters are considered ideologically correct, "since they had acted their parts on the stage of the world without any disguise" (*Letters,* 2:2.179). The revolutionary comedians perform their roles without "disguise" (that is, they act out their true lower-class origins); they play and reveal their "real" and natural selves while the tragedians are supposedly tainted by masks and disguises. Williams alludes to the Jacobin obsession with virtuous "transparency" and the antithetical hatred of costumes, veils, and masks—the mystifying "wardrobe" of both the Old Regime and revolutionary impostors, which must be ripped off, revealed, and exposed.[8] In an inversion of this ideological formulation, Williams suggests that their obsession with transparency leads them ironically to mistake appearance for reality. The accoutrements of fictional representation are identified with real counterrevolution; the Jacobins mistake illusion for reality and imprison actors supposedly contaminated by their fictional roles. Theatrical costumes become reflexive signs, since theatrical disguises supposedly reveal both counterrevolutionary sympathies and hence counterrevolutionary actors as they really "are."

At times the real tragedies the Jacobins produce degenerate into farce.[9] Referring to the notorious revolutionary ceremony (10 November 1793) when the "church of Notre Dame was changed into a temple of Reason," Williams sarcastically notes that the "Goddess of Reason was a fine blooming damsel of the opera-house, and acted her part in this comedy . . . to the entire satisfaction of her new votaries" (*Letters*, 2:2.181). The irony resides in the inappropriate mixture of genres and roles: the common actress (conventionally considered low and "loose"—in England she was reported to be a prostitute) playing a virginal "damsel" in a farcical travesty of reason. The travesty continues when the Goddess of Reason introduces another actress representing the Goddess of Liberty (182). For Williams, true reason and liberty have been usurped (like the appropriated church) and misrepresented in grotesque parodies. There is an additional reflexive irony, since Williams had also played the part of Liberty in a play performed earlier at the chateau of the Du Fossés (*Letters*, 1:1.203–5)—the "charming little piece" that ended with the dancing of *Le Carillon National,* a "spectacle" that seemed "an enchanting vision (1:203, 205, 207) corresponding to her vision of the Festival of Federation, the happy comedy of 14 July. In the reader's mind, the three scenes intersect to signify both the degeneration of Liberty's representation and Williams' naive optimism.

In Williams' formulation, the Jacobins produce either bad farcical comedy or real terrorist tragedy. Williams herself envisions France's tragedy as a Girondist disaster. She sees the latter as a tragedy scripted by Jacobins who force Girondins to perform coerced roles, beginning when the National Convention is surrounded by Jacobin troops and the national "representation" is violated. This is a "prelude of that dark drama of which France has been the desolated scene, and Europe the affrighted spectator" (*Letters*, 2:1.28). The national "representation" refers to the deputies elected to represent the French people in the National Convention, and its "violation" (a standard Girondist phrase Williams frequently uses) refers not only to the insurrection of 31 May but to the violation of the true revolutionary representation the Girondins had produced. Williams' own representation accords with her Girondist tragedy, a *representation* entailing the "exhibition of character and action upon the stage; the . . . performance of a play" (*OED,* no. 3). As the Jacobins turn the true revolutionary comedy into a real tragedy, Williams additionally suggests that the crisis in representation constitutes a counterrevolutionary misrepresentation—a distortion of the true Revolution and its correspondent reality. Control of the national representation is not only a battle over control of the Revolution's direction, it is a war over whose representation will prevail.

Williams bases her account of the Jacobin tragedy on her personal authority as both spectator and coerced actor—the "witness of the scenes I describe," who knows "personally all the principal actors." In her mind, the sad scenes "rise in sad succession like the shades of Banquo's line, and pass along my shuddering recollection" (*Letters*, 2:1.2–3). She had earlier remembered Louis XVI, on trial for his life, being brought back to the Temple, and the "long page of human history rushed upon the mind—age after age arose to memory, in sad succession, like the line of Banquo; and each seemed disfigured by crimes or darkened by calamity" (1:4.11). Like Wollstonecraft, Williams often turns to *Macbeth*, with its themes of regicide and betrayal, to present France's tragedy. Likewise, she places herself in the position of Macbeth, who sees Banquo's line, suggesting again a tacit sense of guilt. Like Wollstonecraft, she wishes to blot out the "terrifying picture" and find "'some sweet oblivious antidote'" that would "drive from my brain the remembrance of these things" (*Letters*, 2:2.212; see *Macbeth* 5.3.44). Referring to France, she rearticulates its tragedy in Ross's words for Scotland (*Letters*, 2:2.65–66; see *Macbeth* 4.3.165–72). The terrorist Marat "feels like Macbeth, that he has stepped too far in crimes to recede" (1:4.70–1); Hébert and his terrorist "associates" are finally brought to justice, "while the knife of the guillotine, like Macbeth's aerial dagger, hung suspended before their affrighted imagination" (2:2.17, 18). During the king's trial, the Girondists fear a Jacobin massacre of both the royal family and themselves: "Imagination already beheld, like Macbeth, aerial daggers, and anticipated a sort of dark unknown danger, to which it could set no limits" (1:4.14–15). The last allusion unwittingly implicates the Girondins in the royal tragedy, since in the play, the guilty Macbeth is haunted by a vision of the regicidal dagger just before he kills the King (*Macbeth* 2.1.34–40; for other references to *Macbeth*, see 1:1.61; 2:4.15).

Dramatic tragedy is the Terror's primary trope. The guillotine concludes the "bloody tragedy"—a "daily spectacle" of victims watched by the assembled "crowd"—a spectacle replacing previous spectacles of innocent entertainment: "Such was the daily spectacle which had succeeded . . . the itinerant theatres . . . the dance, the song, the shifting scenes of harmless gaiety, which used to attract the cheerful crowd" (*Letters,* 2:2.7). The "spectacle" of the guillotine also replaces the "spectacle" of the Festival of Federation as the dominant perspective, in which Paris is "the theatre of crimes" (1:4.212). The surviving victims of the Nantes *noyades* are brought to Paris "to treat the Parisians with a *spectacle,* knowing their present taste for bloody sights" (2:3.40). For Williams, the degradation of aesthetic taste is an objective correlative for the betrayal of the Revolution.

But as the Terror finally ends, there is a sense of cyclical return to the comedy that commenced the Revolution. Williams presents the last stage of the Terror as the "last scenes" of the "foul tragedy" she compellingly records, anticipating the time when "the tyrant [Robespierre] grown bolder by success, intoxicated with power, . . . reached the climax of his crimes, and accelerated the moment of his fall" (*Letters,* 2:1.255). In her representation of the rise and fall of Robespierre, Robespierre is the dramatic overreacher, the tyrant who causes his own end. Thus she will soon "wind up the singular drama of revolutionary government conformably to the most rigid rules of poetic justice" (2:3.191). Her *Letters* end with the restoration of order: evil is punished, and the people are *again* liberated.

The *Letters* are essentially a three-act play, opening with a comedy and, as we will see, a mythical romance followed by the terrorist tragedy, concluding with the poetic re-establishment of justice.[10] Compelled to present the Revolution as a violated representation— the mixed genres of Jacobin tragedians and comedians—Williams finally regains control of the script, ending with a restoration of the magical possibilities of 1789. It is as if she wishes that the Revolution could begin over in the terms of her original comedy. Williams had concluded volume one by observing that the Revolution was still progressing even though the rest of Europe hoped that the "extraordinary drama" was "winding up" (*Letters,* 1:4.121).[11] Toward the end of volume two, she is ready to "wind up the singular drama of revolutionary government" (2:3.191) and end the Revolution. The Revolution, for her, is not what it became but what it was. By rewriting the Revolution's betrayal in the traditional tropes of tragedy, Williams makes its deviation from her comedic script understandable and even familiar: we have seen these terms before. Similarly, her repeated returns to the genres of comedy and romance suggest that the French tragedy will ultimately be happily resolved.

II

Williams' use of theatrical metaphors coincides with her use of romance (as in a romantic story of adventure) and other aesthetic categories (the sublime and beautiful) to explicate the Revolution. But by continually representing her revolutionary history aesthetically, she calls attention to her *Letters* as a work of fiction. This is, in fact, a paradox she inscribes in her epistolary history, although it has usually been seen as a contradiction. Indeed, her *Letters* have often been dismissed as partial (to the Girondins), exaggerated, and overwrought—and they often are. By emphasizing the fictional nature of her *Letters,* she inadvertently helped discredit them, supplying hostile or skeptical readers with the very terms by which they could be condemned—a romance, a tragedy, a comedy, a fiction. In retrospect, this seems clear enough. In addition, her topics and, for the eighteenth century, the gendered genres that she uses (romance, the epistle) perpetuate the very stereotypes that have made her unfashionable in this century. Although she had previously written on politically safe subjects endorsed by most enlightened liberals (the slave trade, the Spanish exploitation of South America), she probably sensed that the controversial nature of the Revolution might lead to accusations that she had transgressed sexual boundaries and had dirtied herself with masculine, political matters. This, in fact, did happen, but all the criticisms of her style and content miss the radicalness of her response: Williams suggests that her emotional, "feminine" reading of the Revolution is *ipso facto* superior to intellectual, "masculine" readings. In addition, her reader response to the Revolution is central to her revolutionary romance. Jay Fliegelman notes that, in the eighteenth century, a "new model of representation that defines truth as truthfulness to feelings rather than to facts subordinates history to the word pictures of romance. What happens within the text is judged by what happens within the reader."[12] Williams continually recurs to this model of representation.

Throughout the *Letters,* Williams' implicit contention is that her romantic "fiction" is truer than superficial fact—that the French Revolution is so extraordinary and wonderful that only the genres of fiction can convey such an astonishing event—an event defying the conventional modes of historical discourse.

In 1784 Williams had published *Peru, A Poem.* In the introduction, she stated that she had not attempted "a full, historical narrative of the Peruvian empire" but had instead produced a "romantic

History; where the unparalleled sufferings of an innocent and amiable people afford the finest subjects for true pathos."[13] Similarly,
in the *Letters,* her strategy is to engage the reader emotionally—
to make the reader share her own emotional commitment to the
Revolution by describing her feelings of how the Revolution affects
her. This is, as I have suggested, an insight she gleaned from
Burke's *Enquiry.* Her history of the Du Fossés illustrates this strategy. She narrates their tribulations, emphasizing how they affected
her, and assumes they will produce a similar effect in the English
reader, who will also endorse the revolution that saved her friends.
In the first series of letters, she periodically alludes to their forthcoming history, promising that she will soon make us "acquainted
with incidents as pathetic as romance itself can furnish" (*Letters,*
1:1.72). When she finally relates the Du Fossés' history (1:1.123–
94), it becomes the climax of her allegory of the repressive Old
Regime and the glorious French Revolution. She subsequently asks
rhetorically if her history has "the air of romance," if the reader
is glad that the "dénouement" is "happy" and that the evil baron
dies "exactly in the right place; at the very page one would
choose?" (1:1.193).

In *A Tour in Switzerland* (1798), she refers to her "romantic
history" of the Du Fossés.[14] By characterizing her history as a
"romance," Williams does seemingly subvert the accuracy or truth
of her narrative by enmeshing it with a word commonly associated
with feminine fiction.[15] In Samuel Johnson's 1755 *Dictionary,* a
romance is "[a] lie; a fiction" (Def. no. 2; cf. *OED* no. 3, no. 5). In
the seventeenth and the eighteenth centuries, it "was one of the
stock dismissals of incorrect histories to term them 'romances' or
fictions, rather than histories."[16] Williams thus provides the terms
for a counterrevolutionary reading of her history as a romantic
fiction—a lie that openly betrays itself. The skeptical reviewer in
the *Gentleman's Magazine* (January 1791) exploited this apparent
contradiction, referring to her "pathetic tale" of the Du Fossés:
"The writer herself fears it has the air of romance, and we should
perfectly agree with her as she is used to such writing," adding
with sarcastic emphasis, "that every incident is made to tally, did
we not know, from *undoubted* authority that the tale was true."[17]
In the *Letters,* Williams realizes that her history, which she insists
is true, can be dismissed as fiction, so she exploits the contradiction and turns it into a paradox: in the 1790s, France is a marvelous
land where miraculous realities occur; consequently, romance is
the only genre that can convey accurately the Revolution's electrical excitement and do justice to events that would appear incred-

ible and fanciful in conventional historical discourse. To many readers, this undoubtedly comes across as clever evasion, but it is a paradox that Williams insists is true.

In letter 21 she tells her anonymous and fictional correspondent that she will transcribe a narrative sent by a friend, adding that a novel writer might be tempted to exaggerate and heighten some of the details and circumstances and "almost spin a volume from these materials." Williams, however, will send the "story exactly" as she received it, since "nothing is so affecting as simplicity, and nothing so forcible as truth." Insisting that her letters are stranger and truer than fiction, she contrasts the reality of her narrative with the illusion of fiction and hence has it both ways: she uses the genres of fiction to convey her affecting truths. She prefaces the story by admonishing the correspondent and reader to "recollect that you are not reading a tale of fiction; and that in real life incidents are not always placed as they are in novels, so as to produce stage effect" (*Letters*, 1:2.156–57). But by continually blurring the line between fiction and history, she suggests that history necessarily involves the emplotments of fiction. She herself raises questions about the status of her *Letters* by continually blurring and transgressing traditional generic boundaries. She seems to be teasingly defensive about how her story will be received, for when she observes "that in real life incidents are not always *placed as they are in novels,* so as to produce stage effect," she allusively (or perhaps unwittingly) reminds the reader of her history of the Du Fossés and her rhetorical affirmation that the evil baron dies "exactly *in the right place;* at the very page" the reader would choose (*Letters*, 1:1.193; my emphasis). In this reading, Williams subverts the authenticity of her "history" by betraying its fictional nature, or does she suggest that human history necessarily entails a teleologic story line? Even the defensive reminder that she, unlike novel writers, does not manipulate incidents "to produce stage effect" seemingly raises just that possibility in the reader's mind. The reminder, in fact, seems to be a defensive response to Burke's contention that revolutionary writers employ dramatic scenes to produce their false revolutionary dramas: "There must be a great change of scene; there must be a magnificent stage effect; there must be a grand spectacle to rouze the imagination" (*Reflections,* 156). Williams' depiction of the Festival of Federation as just such a "grand spectacle" seems either to confirm or challenge Burke's formulation. In both *The Rights of Men* and the *Rights of Man,* Wollstonecraft and Paine reverse Burke's representation and as-

cribe it to him, whereas Williams works within the fictive frame-
work they reject, albeit reproduce.

In the narrative that Williams intends to relate "exactly as [she]
received it," she realizes that she implicates herself with a genre
associated with imaginative fiction:

> In some parts of the narrative you will meet with a little romance; but
> perhaps you will wonder that you meet with no more; since the scene
> is not in the cold philosophic climate of England, but in the warm
> regions of the south of France, where the imagination is elevated, where
> the passions acquire extraordinary energy, and where the fire of poetry
> flashed from the harps of the Troubadours amidst the sullen gloom of
> the Gothic ages.
>
> *(Letters,* 1:2.157)

She con(text)ualizes her narrative within the genre of romance
and the imaginative realm of poetry; her revolutionary romance
transcends the cold, intellectual boundaries and "climate" of traditional English historiography. Feeling contextualizes fact.

She continues to insist that only in revolutionary France is romance really true: ". . . living in France at present appears to
me somewhat like living in a region of romance. Events the most
astonishing and marvellous are here the occurrences of the day,
and every newspaper is filled with articles of intelligence that will
form a new era in the history of mankind" (*Letters,* 1:2.4–5). Even
when the Revolution is apparently unraveling, she still believes in
a happy, romantic ending, even though the most "ardent" person
would have "considered himself as reading the last page of this
romance of the republic," given all that had gone wrong (1:4.79–
80). The "romance of the republic" reflexively refers to her romantic *Letters,* and it is significant that all her concluding epistles that
close respective volumes of the *Letters* end propitiously, predicting
regeneration and joy in a mythical future. In this sense, Williams'
dramatic comedy and republican romance end happily. At the beginning of volume two, she describes herself returning to France
after Robespierre's death and witnessing poetic justice, as guilty
Jacobins are punished and innocent victims are liberated: "We
seem to live in regions of romance," thus "returning" to the romantic region and spirit of volume one (*Letters,* 2:1.178; 1:2.4). In
Julia (1790), Williams' heroine had announced that she had "no
pleasure in being led into regions of romance," but the marvelous
possibilities of the French Revolution transformed this sentiment.[18]

By ultimately envisioning the Revolution as a republican romance, Williams ensured an inevitable, storybook ending. Ro-

mance, of course, entails conflict before the happy ending occurs. In Northrop Frye's terms, there is a mythic quest (the Du Fossés' and—by extension—France's search for true love and justice and later the meaning of the "true" Revolution) as well as epic confrontations between heroic characters (Du Fossé and the Girondins) and despotic villains (the baron, the Old Regime, and Jacobin "monsters"). Frye's analysis of comedy also applies to the Du Fossé episode and the first series of Williams' *Letters:* In comedy "[w]hat normally happens is that a young man wants a young woman; that his desire is resisted by some opposition, usually paternal; and near the end of the play some twist in the plot enables the hero to have his will." The uniting of the two lovers corresponds to the crystallization of a new society, "frequently signalized by some kind of party or festive ritual."[19] Just before she leaves France to return to England, Williams performs the part of Liberty, in a play celebrating the French Revolution, which ends with everyone dancing and singing patriotic revolutionary songs. Appropriately, the play is performed at the Dú Fossé *château,* "where the gentlemen danced with the peasant girls, and the ladies with the peasants" (*Letters,* 1:1.203–7). Williams' first series of *Letters* (1:1.1–223) is a romantic comedy, "an enchanting vision" (207), displaced by the terrorist tragedy of subsequent *Letters.*

In the final section of the *Letters,* Williams observes "that no story which has been invented is so pathetic as what has really happened" and applies this "observation . . . to the period of the [terrorist] revolutionary government": "the pencil of fiction has no colouring more gloomy than that which truth then presented, and the stories of romance offer no stronger conflicts of the passions, no incidents more affecting, or sorrows more acute, than what has passed, and what has been suffered, during the tyranny of Robespierre" (*Letters,* 2:4.53). The discrepancy between fact and fiction is both inscribed and written "out" in a Revolution that paradoxically embodies both. As a romantic historian, Williams represents the Revolution in the genres through which she sees it: starting as a romantic comedy, degenerating into a tragedy (with romantic interludes), and ending with a happy, comedic resolution. The Revolution's contradictions are paradoxically played out through the fictive genres that represent them. The Jacobin attempt to rewrite the Revolution results in a mixture of styles and genres that Williams implicitly criticizes as bad art and bad revolution.[20] But as the revolutionary comedy is forcibly changed to a Jacobin tragedy, she represents this change in oppositional genres that explain how and why the pristine Revolution degenerated.

It has always been facile to dismiss Williams' *Letters* in the fictive terms she presents them. But there is a larger sense in which Williams recognized the fictive dimension of history—that history entails a selection of facts telling a story, explaining the events that make up a phenomenon as complicated as the French Revolution. Given the extraordinary nature of a revolution that seemed, at turns, magnificent, terrible, and thus contradictory, there was a tacit (often unwitting) acknowledgment by both revolutionary and counterrevolutionary writers that only the genres of fiction could express and explain a revolution that seemed suprareal and hence unreal. Paine's *Rights of Man* is, among other things, a disguised drama; Wollstonecraft's *French Revolution* is, inter alia, her version of *Macbeth*. While both Paine and Wollstonecraft deny that the Revolution is a theatrical event, the Revolution's theatricality is a documented commonplace in the Revolution's historiography: from the beginning, the Revolution was represented as a dramatic spectacle, with its actors and *mise en scène*—a representation embraced and endorsed by the revolutionaries themselves.[21] While the implications are still being discussed and explored, Williams' *Letters,* in this context, are truer to the Revolution's spirit than many of her canonical contemporaries.

11

The Sublime and Beautiful in Williams' *Letters from France*

WILLIAMS' use of tragedy and romance also complements her use of the sublime and beautiful. Not surprisingly, Burke's *Enquiry* figures in her *Letters:* after a brief skirmish with its values, she incorporates them into her revolutionary allegory. Just as she considers revolutionary France a region of romance, she also notes that revolutionary events have led her "into regions of hitherto undiscovered beauty and sublimity" (*Letters*, 2:3.51). In contrast to Wollstonecraft's hostile reading of the *Enquiry*, in *The Rights of Men*, Williams embraces its masculine and feminine polarities. She also realizes there are distinct versions of the sublime in the *Enquiry*—a remote sublime viewed from a distance and experienced as an aesthetic event and an impending sublime whose power and terror threaten the spectator with death. In the *Enquiry*, Burke noted that "ideas of pain, and above all death, are so very affecting, that whilst we remain in the presence of whatever is supposed to have the power of inflicting either, it is impossible to be perfectly free from terror" (65). Both Burke and Williams retrospectively applied this dictum to the Terror. Similarly, there are two distinct kinds of the beautiful in the *Enquiry*—a feminine beauty associated with sexual attraction that leads to social union and the preservation of a country's beautiful values and institutions—and a dangerous, seductive beauty that leads to enervation and death. Williams uses the positive sublime to depict the Revolution as an awe-inspiring aesthetic event and the pejorative sublime to depict the Terror. She uses the feminine beautiful to characterize both the true Revolution and the Terror's victims, while pejorative beauty characterizes the seductive artificiality of the Old Regime.

I

In a perceptive essay, Matthew Bray has shown that Williams is "dealing with Burke's definition of the sublime and beautiful implicitly from the very first letter of her work" in order to criticize the binary opposition of the sublime and beautiful, but that she nevertheless produces a text that resembles Burke's own rethinking of this opposition in the *Reflections*.[1] I will argue that the real presence of the Terror compels Williams to change her initial criticism of Burke's political-aesthetic *Reflections* into a profound reading of and identification with Burke's antirevolutionary text. Williams begins rewriting the Revolution by reinscribing a series of Burkean texts that she had previously criticized.

In the beginning, the Revolution is a series of thrilling emotional events that she experiences as a "spectator." For Williams, the Festival of Federation is the supreme sublime event, embodying the Revolution's true spirit. It was "the most sublime spectacle" probably ever "represented on the theater of this earth," and the Revolution is an ongoing sublime event (*Letters*, 1:1.2, 65). There are echoes from the *Enquiry*, even when she responds to events that are not revolutionary. When she describes the emotional effects produced by Roman Catholic ceremony, she notes, approvingly, that although "the Roman Catholic worship" is a "stumbling block to reason," it is "striking to the imagination" (1:1.113). In the *Enquiry*, Burke notes that sensibility involves a higher pleasure of the imagination than judgment, which is "employed in throwing stumbling blocks in the way of the imagination, in dissipating the scenes of its enchantment, and in tying us down to the disagreeable yoke of our reason" (25). Using Burke's language, Williams changes his formulation: the emotional Catholic service is a "stumbling block to reason" but striking to the imagination. Her superior sensibility allows her to feel emotionally the "service for the dead," allowing the heart to "delude itself with the belief" that prayers may help loved ones in purgatory (*Letters*, 1:1.113). Her emphasis on emotion, heart, and imagination is again proto-Romantic, but her reference to the heart's delusion retrospectively prefigures her own disillusionment: the Revolution as an emotionally enchanting "vision" dissipates when confronted with "the stumbling block" of the Terror.

Early in the *Letters*, Williams refers to Burke's *Enquiry* to distinguish Paris from London: London is beautiful (its streets are "broad, airy, light, and elegant"), while Paris is sublime (the streets are "narrow, dark, and dirty"). London thus has "most of the beautiful, and Paris of the sublime, according to Mr. Burke's definition of these qualities"; indeed, a "sensation of terror" complements the "sublimity of Paris," since Parisian coachmen whip through the streets, and "one expects" the corresponding death of pedestrians (*Letters*, 1:1.73–74). The possibility of a collision is a spectacle

Williams watches safely, while those who experience the "terror" blame the counterrevolutionary streets, not the French drivers: the "streets of Paris are Aristocrates." Her tone is light, the pejorative sublime is hyperbolically counterrevolutionary; the Counterrevolution is not yet an imminent threatening presence. Since the Old Order has been destroyed, the counterrevolutionary sublime can only depress her, as when she visits the impotent Bastille, whose "gloom and horror" nevertheless affect her (25).

In her history of the Du Fossés, however, the Old Order's terror is contrasted with the Revolution's beauty. The malicious baron (Augustin Du Fossé's father) microcosmically represents the Old Order's severity; his domestic tyranny reflects the political tyranny of the era: he utilizes the infamous *lettre de cachet* to imprison his son, who loves literature and possesses "the most amiable dispositions, and the most feeling heart" (*Letters,* 1:1.124–25). The father represents the oppressive sublime, while the son represents the beautiful. The link between domestic and political terror reappears when Augustin is imprisoned by his father in a "subterraneous cell" (148), evoking the subterranean cells Williams saw in the Bastille (23). Similarly, in a cell adjacent to Augustin's, an old man, who has been confined for forty years, is "chained by his neck to the wall," evoking again Williams' visit to the Bastille, where she saw "those chains by which the prisoners were fastened round the neck, to the walls of their cells" (155, 22–23). After the baron dies, Augustin returns to France on 15 July, "the very day after . . . the Bastille was taken" (189). Revolutionary beauty suddenly replaces old oppression as Augustin is finally free to return to liberated France: "a country where iron cages were broken down, where dungeons were thrown open, and where justice was henceforth to shed a clear and steady light, without one dark shade of relief from *lettres-de-cachet*" (193–94).

In contrast, Williams' history of Auguste and Madelaine, a narrative containing "a little romance" (*Letters,* 1:2.157), is an allegory of the revolutionary sublime and the Old Order's artificial beauty. In 1788 Auguste, a young, aristocratic Frenchman, travels to Bareges, the French Bath. Since he has "some taste for the sublime scenery of nature," he gladly leaves the artificial beauty of the Old Regime: "the regular walks which art has planted in the Tuilleries, and the trim gardens and jets-d'eaux [that art] has formed at Versailles" (158). He thus enjoys the sublimity of the Pyrenean mountains that inspire his mind with "strong emotions of awe, astonishment, and admiration" (159)—the strong effects of the "sublime in *nature,*" in Burke's *Enquiry* (57).

In Bareges, Williams contrasts the artificiality of the wealthy, who amuse themselves with cards and scandal, with the simplicity of Madelaine, a young but poor French woman who has accompanied her aged and ailing father, seeking the relief of Bareges' medicinal waters. The pampered aristocratic ladies are "dressed in style of expensive variety and profusion," while Madelaine wears "only a plain linen gown, which, though . . . clean, was coarse; and her dark hair was left unpowdered and without any ornament whatever" (*Letters,* 1:2.160–61). Madelaine's natural beauty is opposed to the aristocrats' artificial beauty, and her style of dress prefigures the revolutionary simplicity that Williams previously had contrasted with ci-devant aristocratic style (see 1:2.81). Indeed, Madelaine represents a new revolutionary beauty—neither dazzling nor "very beautiful," she has a "sweet" expression "which answered the end of beauty by exciting love and admiration" (161)—the two passions Burke opposed in the *Enquiry:* "we submit to what we admire, but we love what submits to us" (*Enquiry,* 113). Williams, in effect, fuses the sublime and beautiful that Burke separates, depicting Madelaine as the happy combination of natural simplicity and republican virtue. Not surprisingly, the decadent male aristocrats neither recognize nor appreciate Madelaine's natural beauty, and while they "admire" Madelaine's "amiable qualities" and "graces," they refuse (because she is a commoner) to love her. The aristocratic women, consequently, are not jealous or envious, since they know that the men will marry a woman only of their own class: "Although the French [R]evolution had not yet happened, these ladies were aware that, with respect to marriage, the age of *calculators* was already come, and therefore no rival was to be feared in Madelaine" (*Letters,* 1:2.163). In the *Reflections,* Burke had lamented that "the age of chivalry is gone" and that "of . . . calculators, has succeeded" (170). Ironically reversing Burke's formulation, Williams makes the Old Regime the age of calculators and the death of romantic, chivalrous love—opposing aristocratic "heads" to romantic, revolutionary "hearts."

Auguste, prefiguring the good aristocrats who will renounce their titles and distinctions and embrace the Revolution, admires and loves Madelaine. He is not "dazzled by the polished graces of a fine lady rouged, powdered, perfumed, and equipped for conquest." He prefers Madelaine's "simple manners, . . . natural smiles and unstudied blushes"—all of which "were far more in union with the Pyrenean mountains" (*Letters,* 1:2.164)—the natural "sublime scenery" Auguste had sought when he left the artificial beauties of Paris and Versailles (158). Madelaine's "natural" beauty is "in union" with the natural sublime, while the artificial beauty of the Old Regime ("regular walks . . . trim gardens and jets-d'eaux," 158) is associated with the artificial beauty of its women: "the polished graces of a fine lady rouged, powdered, perfumed . . . artificial attractions [that] might have accorded well enough with clipped trees and angular walks" (164). The Revolution, for Williams, constitutes the natural and historical union of the sublime and the beautiful. Her romantic narrative is yet another parable of the Revolution and the natural union of ci-devant aristocrats with beautiful commoners. Thus, as Auguste ceases his class "reasoning" and abandons "his heart" to "unconquerable passion" (168), he resists the reactionary endeavors of his aristocratic father to banish Madelaine and, instead, marries her (saving her from a life in a repressive nunnery, 174–82). Williams, in effect, presents another version of the Du Fossé romance: the Revolution is again a triumph of the heart.

II

The Revolution is both sublime and beautiful—a stupendous emotional event generating beautiful benefits for the French people. Even after the execution of Louis XVI, Williams quotes approvingly a French acquaintance who maintains that the Revolution's theory is "beautiful" and its principles "sublime." Many of the "actors" are, however, "detestable," and hence the "present race" is not worthy of a Revolution that will only be consummated in the future (*Letters,* 1:3.25–26). This was, as we have seen, a standard explanation of the Revolution's *dérapage:* the superiority of the revolutionary "tenor" to the French "vehicle." It illustrates that Williams uses the sublime and beautiful as ideological categories to explain a Revolution deviating from enlightened theory and principle.

Revolutionary beauty is, for Williams, always naturally feminine. In *A Tour in Switzerland* (1798), she employs the conventional pictorial distinction between the sublime and beautiful by contrasting the landscape's "awful wildness of terrific grandeur" with the "luxuriant charms of [nature's] beauty."[2] In the *Letters,* "charms" signify the Revolution's prelapsarian beauty. In Williams' works, hostility to feminine beauty and charms is always pejorative. In *Julia* (1790), the beautiful heroine's rivals, the disagreeable Miss C____s, have "an unconquerable antipathy to female beauty."[3] Early in the *Letters,* Williams extols "a young English lady . . .

whose appearance is calculated to give [the French] the most favourable idea of English beauty" (*Letters*, 1:1.41). Her subsequent account of a revolutionary procession in Paris is an allegory of the liberation of captives by revolutionary beauty: five hundred young ladies dressed in white and adorned with cockades led "by silken cords a number of prisoners newly released from captivity," who were then "conducted to a church where they returned thanks for their deliverance." Williams provides the revolutionary moral: "Thus have the leaders of the revolution engaged beauty as one of their auxiliaries" (62).

Her references to Henry IV (1553–1610), the French king initially celebrated as a model and precursor to that good patriot king, Louis XVI, is in the Burkean vocabulary of the beautiful. In 1790 celebrations of Henry IV constituted a veritable revolutionary cult. Henry is Williams' "favourite hero" and although other kings may have been great conquerors and hence "terribly sublime," she gives Henry her "love" and the others her "admiration" (*Letters*, 1:1.93). The sentence alludes again to Burke's comment in the *Enquiry* that "we submit to what we admire, but we love what submits to us" (113). In the *Reflections*, Burke referred sarcastically to the revolutionary cult, observing that if Henry had been alive in 1790, enthusiasm for him would have quickly evaporated, given his exercise of sublime, punitive power when he was living: "He never sought to be loved without putting himself first, in a condition to be feared" (241–42). In contrast, Williams' Henry was an "amiable prince" (*Letters*, 1:1.93); on the Pont Neuf his statue is "decorated" with "a scarf of national ribbon" (20); "[l]ittle statues of Henry IV" are ubiquitous (93); Williams loves to be reminded of him; he is the only hero, ancient or modern, of whom she is "enamoured"—"a hero who united a taste for letters with all the great, and all the amiable qualities" (103; 1:2.15). Although she describes him in the recognizable language of the beautiful ("amiable," "little," and beloved), the last reference suggests he united the sublime ("the great") and the beautiful ("the amiable"). Likewise, Williams frequently describes the French people as "pleasing" and "amiable," but hopes that in acquiring, through the Revolution, "great," (that is, sublime) qualities, they never lose "amiable" ones (*Letters*, 1:2.145). By uniting the sublime and the beautiful, Williams was, like Wollstonecraft, in *The Rights of Men,* rewriting the terms of Burke's *Enquiry*. Similarly, the Du Fossés' microcosmic "misfortunes" cause her "to love, as well as admire, the [macrocosmic] revolution": "while we contemplate the deliverance of millions with a sublime emotion of wonder and exaltation,

the tears of tenderness, the throbbings of sympathy, are reserved
for the moment when we select one happy family from the great
national groupe [and hear] amidst the loud acclamations . . . the
soothing sounds of domestic felicity." Combining the language of
the sublime and beautiful, she beholds "with awful astonishment
the sun of liberty," while tracing that "benignant beam" that dispels
darkness from the Du Fossé "dwelling" (1:2.1–2).

As the Revolution, however, becomes more problematic, so do
her sublime and beautiful equations. For instance, she states that
the "French [R]evolution is not only sublime in a general view,
but is often beautiful when considered in detail"—even though
contemporaries are too close to see the real Revolution: "The
French [R]evolution is viewed too near to excite the same veneration in the present age which it will probably awaken in the minds
of posterity" (*Letters,* 1:2.22). In Burke's *Enquiry,* veneration is
associated with the sublime, but Williams does not suggest that the
Revolution's sublime terror is too close to the spectators but that
familiarity breeds contempt: "the old remark that no man is a hero
to his valet . . . may be applied to great events, as well as great
characters." Since she is indirectly alluding to the revolutionary
violence (referred to as early as 1:1.81–82 in the *Letters*) that is
"too near" European contemporaries and that keeps them from
seeing the Revolution as either sublime or beautiful, it is significant
that she refers to it as if it were a banal, ordinary occurrence. She
talks around this troublesome violence by establishing a future
perspective, a temporal distance, that will mysteriously justify the
violence by making it disappear "in the minds of posterity"—displaced in time and space. The Revolution is supposedly beautiful
"in detail," but it is precisely the *closeness* of those details that
cannot be examined, since they are currently not considered beautiful. Noting that the Revolution needs "that mellowed tint which
is produced by time," Williams then employs a Burkean solution
to current revolutionary violence.

In the *Enquiry,* Burke had discussed how time mellows the sublime authority of grandfathers (imposing and intimidating) into the
beautiful: "we generally have a great love of our grandfathers, in
whom this authority is removed a degree from us, and where the
weakness of age mellows it into something of feminine partiality"
(111). Likewise, in the *Reflections,* Burke argued that prescriptive
time occasionally "mellows into legality governments that were
violent in their commencement" (276). For Burke, time mellows the
threatening sublime into the aesthetically beautiful, and Williams
echoes both his formulation and language, adding the following

twist: since the closeness of the Revolution makes it appear banal and ordinary, time will transform it into the extraordinary event it really is, since, in her reading, the Revolution is both sublime and beautiful. But since the beautiful is associated with the minute "detail" of the Revolution, a perspective that posterity (too far away) will not "see," Williams suggests that time will ultimately turn the Revolution into a venerated, sublime event: "[s]ucceeding generations will perhaps associate the Tennis-court of Versailles, and the Champ de Mars [the site of the Festival of Federation] with the Forum and the Capitol" (*Letters,* 1:2.23). As she imagines a grateful posterity visiting these revolutionary shrines, she envisions the Revolution as a venerated legacy and tradition. Like Wollstonecraft, she contends that "prejudices" presently "obscure" the Revolution, keeping contemporaries from seeing the big picture, so she returns to the future sublimity of the event: "Posterity . . . will contemplate the revolution in the same manner as we gaze at a sublime landscape, of which the general effect is great and noble, and where some little points of asperity, some minute deformities, are lost in the overwhelming majesty of the whole" (23).[4]

The "little points of asperity" and "minute deformities" are euphemisms for the present violence happily removed from posterity's perspective. Williams softens and disguises this violence, which is "lost" in the overwhelming whole—in which the language of the beautiful ("little" and "minute," modifies the "asperity" and "deformities") of the mellowed violence invisible to future eyes overwhelmed by the Revolution's sublime totality. In the *Enquiry,* Burke referred to the power and terror of the sublime that is impendingly present: ". . . the ideas of pain, and above all death, are so very affecting, that whilst we remain in the presence of whatever is supposed to have the power of inflicting either, it is impossible to be perfectly free from terror" (65). Similarly, Williams later refers to the violence contributing to France's "dreadful condition," noting that "[w]e are too near the events to consider them with coolness or impartiality" (*Letters,* 1:4.82). Too close to the violence that keeps her from seeing the Revolution as a sublime spectacle and from aesthetically appreciating its beautiful details, Williams disguises present sublime, revolutionary terror in the language of minute beauty—the former lost and overwhelmed in a future time and space. The French people are "too close" to see the Revolution's "beauty" because they are too close to the terror that she disguises as "too ordinary and familiar." Likewise, posterity is "too far away" to see the perspectively small violence that is mellowed and lost in space and time.

This aesthetic displacement dramatically changes in the second volume. In the *Enquiry*, Burke had contended that "[w]hatever is fitted in any sort to excite the ideas of pain, and danger . . . whatever is in any sort terrible, or is conversant about terrible objects, or operates in a manner analogous to terror, is a source of the *sublime;* that is, it is productive of the strongest emotion which the mind is capable of feeling" (39). In volume two, Williams again uses the *Enquiry*'s language and categories to construct a political enquiry into the desecration of the Revolution's beauty by Jacobin Terror. Burke himself had incorporated the aesthetic values of the *Enquiry* into his critique of the Revolution, and Williams, like other contemporaries, realized that the category of the sublime could be applied to the Terror. Indeed, Burke's emphasis on the impending power of the sublime to produce *terror* and death corresponds to Williams' depiction of the Terror that produces horror and death. *Terror* is a core word in the *Letters,* and it seems fortuitous that Burke had previously used a word and concept that was used frequently to refer to revolutionary violence, even before the National Convention declared that "Terror is the order of the day" (September 1793), and that was subsequently the thematic word used to characterize Robespierre's reign.

In volume one, Williams had criticized the terrified Parisians for permitting the September massacres by remaining "in a state of stupified astonishment and terror" (*Letters,* 1:3.17), a phrase that she also uses, in various forms, in volume two to criticize their passive reaction to Robespierre's reign (2:2.64; 2:3.2, 164, 174, 185; 2:4.7). She believed that Thermidorean France had "just seen one of these epochas, which are the astonishment, the terror, and the shame of human nature" (2:3.149). In the *Enquiry,* Burke noted that "astonishment . . . is the effect of the sublime in its highest degree," a "state of the soul, in which all its motions are suspended, with some degree of horror." Likewise, fear is a passion that "robs the mind of all its powers of acting and reasoning" (57). Using the criterion of the pejorative, impending sublime, Williams sees the Jacobin sublime violating "natural" beauty.

Trying to forget Paris, a city "petrified with Terror," Williams escapes to the countryside and walks "amidst the noble parks of St. Cloud, the wild woods of Meudon, or the elegant gardens of Bellevue . . . "seats" that were "once the residence of fallen royalty" (*Letters,* 2:2.4, 2). But she finds these places desecrated by Jacobin terrorists who hold "their festive orgies in those scenes of beauty, where they dared to cast their polluting glance on nature, and tread with profane steps her hallowed recesses" (2–3). Consequently, those "regions of decorated beauty" become "forbidden ground" (3). The desecration of nature's beauty is explicitly sexual, a violation of her feminine essence. While the bestial Jacobins seem to add insult to injury by holding their orgies in the ci-devant retreats of fallen royalty, the references may also conjure up aristocratic "orgies" supposedly engaged in by Marie Antoinette and her lovers at Trianon and other royal sites, in the political pornography of the time. If this is so, Williams may be establishing a repetitive link between the Jacobins and the Old Regime.[5]

Paris, as in Wollstonecraft's history, is the locale of terror and horror—"that den of carnage, that slaughter-house of man" (*Letters,* 2:2.4). Even Danton, a former terrorist ironically imprisoned by the Terror, "expatiated continually on the charms of nature, on the beauties of rural scenery" (28). For Williams, nature is beauty's refuge from the Jacobin sublime. After the fall of Robespierre, luxuriant nature seems to revive and return again to Paris—a return that simultaneously marks the return of feminine beauty, as women "indulge in their dress the full extent of female caprice, as well as extravagance" (2:3.9; cf. 2:1.193–94). As Parisians return to their pre-Terrorist entertainments, there is a return to the style of the Old Regime and a contextual erasure of Williams' previous praise of the "revolution in dress and manners"—previously posited as revolutionary naturalness versus old-order artificiality (1:2.81). This counterrevolution in style had been prefigured by the terrorist Hébert's death. The Jacobin "winter," associated with political and sexual repression, ends and beauty is released: "Immediately after his execution . . . black wigs, red caps, sailors' jackets, and pantaloons were cast aside; and the eye was refreshed with the sight of combed locks, clean linen, and decent apparel." The prerevolutionary masculine style complements the liberation of "beauty" as "women, who for some months had reluctantly bound up their hair beneath the round cap of the peasant, now unfolded their tresses, perfumed and powdered, to the vernal gales" (2:2.22). (In her allegory of Auguste and Madelaine, Auguste prefers Madelaine's natural revolutionary beauty to the artificial beauty of aristocrats "rouged, *powdered,* [and] *perfumed*" [1:2.164], my emphasis.) The Terror evidently compelled Williams to rethink and reinscribe the "style" she had formerly rejected. For Williams, the Terror's murder of women coincides with the Jacobin repression of feminine beauty. Similarly, the violation of natural beauty is equated with the assault on feminine beauty.

Consider her account of the destruction of the village of Bedouin by revolutionary troops (*Letters,* 2:3.86–87). The village is "situated in a country of the most romantic beauty," so when the troops raze both "the village and territory," spreading "desolation and death" (86–87), Williams equates the assault on nature's beauty with the murder of its innocent inhabitants. While her emphasis is often on her beautiful female victims, innocent males also partake of the vulnerable beauty assaulted by Jacobin terrorists.

Her central focus, however, is on female suffering—women either guillotined or forced to watch their loved ones expire. The guillotined women are usually mothers or "blooming beauties, who in all the first freshness of youth, in the first spring of life, submitted to the stroke of the executioner with placid smiles on their countenances, and looked like angels in their flight to heaven" (*Letters,* 2:1.213). Her description of the murder of young, beautiful females evokes a murderous sexual violation consummated by the guillotine, as when the executioner "cuts," with his coercive scissors, "the lavish tresses of the youthful beauty," whose "tender hands" were tied "behind her waist with cords" (2:2.100). This rape of the lock, in which the phallic scissors metaphorically violate both her sex and beauty, corresponds to the guillotine that literally violates her body, cutting off her head. Similarly, the young beauties who watch their mothers or fathers guillotined are themselves guillotined or destroyed by the emotional aftermath, like the faithful daughter who suffers imprisonment with her innocent father and then dies of "a broken heart" and a body "wasted by fatigue, anguish, and want" following his murder: "multitudes in the bloom of youthful beauty have felt her sorrows, and have shared her fate" (2:4.126). Since Williams was herself imprisoned and witnessed the death of "beauty," she becomes the historian of female tragedy, in which terrorist assaults on womanhood signify the Revolution's tragedy as well.

The tragedy of France causes her to revise previous metaphoric equations. The prelapsarian Revolution—a sublime, aesthetic spectacle—is displaced by the Jacobin, terrorist sublime, and liberated prelapsarian "beauty" is either reimprisoned or killed. Early in the *Letters,* Williams defended the Revolution by formulating absurd, antirevolutionary arguments that ironically made the revolutionary case. The French "have led beauty from the solitary cell, where its charms might have bloomed in security, and have exposed those dangerous attractions to the love and admiration of society" (*Letters,* 1:2.72). Beauty, here, corresponds to liberation, light, and the enlightened "charms" released by the Revolution as

well as the mental emancipation of France and of course the national liberation of the Old Regime's victims. Williams exploits the
irony of reactionaries who prefer Liberty's "charms" confined, and
she mocks the suggestion that revolutionary beauty is a temptress
exposing society to seductive attractions and charms (Burke's pejorative beauty). She presents the true benefits of the Revolution
as natural feminine attractions and charms, but her equation subsequently redounds on her sarcastic dismissal when "beauty" is again
confined during the Terror. In one sense, however, this ironic repetition connects the Terror with the Old Regime: in the *Letters*, the
Terror is often a magnified reflection of the Old Regime's
repression.

In volume two, she remembers "the first days" of the Revolution,
a "moral revolution" electrifying Europe with "sublime and immortal principles," lamenting that Liberty "has fallen into the hands
of monsters ignorant of her charms, by whom she has been transformed into a Fury . . . and driven us back to regions of guilt
hitherto unknown" (*Letters*, 2:2.211–12). Williams deplores the
transformation of the revolutionary sublime and beautiful into its
Jacobin perversions. The beautiful "charms" imprisoned by the
Old Regime (1:2.72) are also ignored by Jacobin "monsters" who
forcibly replace the positive revolutionary sublime (the Revolution's "sublime and immortal principles") with the terrorist, Jacobin sublime—transforming revolutionary beauty (Liberty and
her "charms") into a Burkean "Fury." This change corresponds,
as will be seen, to the change of beautiful revolutionary women into
ferocious Jacobin monsters. In her tragedy of the Fall of Beauty,
"regions of guilt" replace "regions of romance," and the regression
that drives "us back" constitutes a counterrevolutionary turn to
the repetitive past.

Williams' initial imagery of beauty being "led from the solitary
cell" (*Letters*, 1:2.72) is also contrapuntally reminiscent of another
beauty—Helen Maria Williams—later arrested and then led into
the Luxembourg, a "sad spectacle" to the crowd (2:1.13). In the
Luxembourg, Williams and her family (her mother and two sisters)
are terrorized by Henriot (the *septembriseur* and commander of
the Paris National Guard) who looks as if he longed "to plunge his
sabre" in their "bosoms" and "drink a libation of [their] blood"
(2:1.29). Against women, phallic Jacobin terror is a suggestive
combination of violence and violation. Just before she and her
family were imprisoned, they had consoled themselves that "being
a family of women," they would be "spared," but the Jacobins
respect "neither sex nor age" (7). Her account of their arrest rever-

berates with Burkean echoes of another family awakened by terrorist forces—the royal family who, in the *Reflections,* after a day of "confusion, alarm, dismay, and slaughter, lay down . . . to indulge nature in a few hours of respite, and troubled melancholy repose"—before the palace was invaded and they were conducted to their prison, "a Basti[l]le for Kings" (164–65). Similarly, after a day of "terror," Williams and her family go to bed, overcome "with fatigue and emotion" but are awakened by a loud knocking and then confronted by a "revolutionary committee" and "a guard, two of whom were placed at the outer door with their swords drawn" (*Letters,* 2:1.7–8). They are finally conducted to the Luxembourg where, after suffering "too much fatigue of body, as well as disturbance of mind," they find "refuge from sorrow in some hours of profound sleep" (15). Likewise, Henriot, who "looks" as if he longed "to plunge his sabre" in their "bosoms" (2:1.29), conjures up Burke's lament that "the age of chivalry is gone," since "ten thousand swords" did not leap "from their scabbards to avenge even a *look* that threatened" Marie Antoinette "with insult" (*Reflections* 170, my emphasis). These Burkean echoes intensify when Williams discusses the Terror.

She, in effect, returns to reaffirm Burkean sentences she previously mocked. Burke's lament for chivalry in the *Reflections* was the principal passage that his respondents loved to ridicule, and Williams sarcastically alludes to it at various points. After commenting that France seems like a "region of romance," she notes that she sometimes thinks that "the age of chivalry, instead of being passed forever, is just returned"—given the marvelous events and the generous emotions inspiring the French people. She allusively opposes her republican romance to Burke's Gothic romance—erroneous notions of chivalry she associates with "dwarfs, giants, and imprisoned damsels" (*Letters,* 1:2.5). Indeed, since "beauty" had already been liberated from her "solitary cell" (72), Burke's tears for queens and damsels in distress were absurdly irrelevant. If anything was extinguished forever, it was the old French government that, like Burke's "age of chivalry," was "past for ever" (107). In another sneer at Burke, she notes that since Frenchmen are now preoccupied with sublime, revolutionary politics, they no longer engage in idle gallantry. Thus "[n]ot only the age of chivalry, but the age of petits maîtres [dandies] is past" (81).

In volume two, however, as the Jacobin sublime kills or suppresses female beauty, she nostalgically returns to Burkean chivalry and the defense of female innocence. Quoting a flattering French poem addressed to her by a French admirer, she notes

wistfully that "the French language is still that of gallantry, although the days of French chivalry are gone for ever" (*Letters,*
2:2.119). The masculine gallantry dismissed previously (1:2.81) is
now flatteringly recalled. Likewise, her previous mockery of
Burkean chivalry and "imprisoned damsels" (1:2.5) contrapuntally
returns when Williams and her family become imprisoned females
in the Luxembourg. The young Frenchman engaged to her sister,
Cecile, "haunts" the appropriate revolutionary authorities, risking
"his own personal safety a thousand times, and at length, like a
true knight, vanquished all obstacles, and snatched his mistress
from captivity" (2:1.205). The mocked imagery of damsels in distress and anachronistic chivalry is now reaffirmed; indeed, Williams' history of persecuted "beauty" evokes Burke's remark in
the *Enquiry* that "Beauty in distress is much the most affecting
beauty" (110).

Burke's chivalric text also reverberates incrementally in other
passages in the *Letters.* In volume one, Williams pauses to lament
the disappearance of her revolutionary "visions":

Ah! what is become of the delightful visions which elevated the enthusiastic heart?—What is become of the transport which beat high in every
bosom, when an assembled million of the human race vowed on the
altar of their country, in the name of the represented nation, inviolable
fraternity and union—an eternal federation! This was indeed the golden
age of the revolution.—But it is past!—the enchanting spell is broken,
and the fair scenes of beauty and of order, through which imagination
wandered, are transformed into the desolation of wilderness, and
clouded by the darkness of the tempest.

(*Letters,* 1:3.6)

These "delightful visions" elevating the "enthusiastic heart"—a
"golden age of the revolution" now "past"—are Williams' version
of those "pleasing illusions, which made power gentle," incorporating "into politics the sentiments which beautify and soften private
society," a golden age of chivalry now "gone" and "extinguished
for ever" (*Reflections,* 170–71).[6] "[S]cenes of beauty" are "transformed" by the Jacobin sublime. Williams proceeds to accuse the
Jacobin "faction" of declaring "war against every improvement,
and every grace of civilised society—all that embellishes human
life—all that softens and refines our nature" (*Letters,* 1:3.23–24)—
echoing again Burke's contention that the Revolution destroyed the
"glory of Europe," the chivalry that "mitigated ferocity," ennobling
"whatever it touched," making "power gentle," beautifying public
politics while softening private society (*Reflections,* 170–71).

A third version of Burke's chivalric lament culminates in her description of the Terror's intrusion into the departments of Vaucluse, where formerly "the Troubadours flung their early harps" and Petrarch "poured forth his impassioned strains": "those dear illusions have for ever vanished—that delicious country, the pride of France, the garden of Europe, the classical haunt of Petrarch no longer presents the delightful images of beauty, of poetry, of passion; the magical spell is broken" (*Letters*, 2:3.84–85). Now compare Burke again: "But the age of chivalry is gone . . . and the glory of Europe is extinguished for ever . . . all the pleasing illusions, which made power gentle, and . . . incorporated into politics the sentiments which beautify and soften . . . are to be dissolved by this new conquering empire of light and reason" (*Reflections*, 170–71). Similarly, in Williams' romance of Charles and Adelaide, the two romantic lovers view scenic "romantic beauties," the "contemplation of which softens while it elevates the affections." But the reality of the "revolutionary government" (which had persecuted their Girondin fathers and now separates them—Charles is called up for active duty in the army) dispels these enchanting visions, and the two lovers are "awakened" from "those dreams, those delightful illusions" (*Letters*, 2:3.101). In another letter, Williams remembers her prison apartment and a tapestry "which described a landscape of romantic beauty," through which she imaginatively escaped the sorrow and horror of the Luxembourg into "pleasing illusion" (2:1.36–37)—Burke's phrase ("pleasing illusions") for chivalry in the *Reflections* (171).

Like Burke, Williams unwittingly subverts her "vision" by suggesting that it was only a pleasing, imaginative "illusion," although, like him, she understands that an imaginative, cultural construct is a reality in the eyes and hearts of believers. The fact that Burke also opposes "natural" human feelings to cold revolutionary reason suggests another reason for Williams' sublimated attraction to his chivalric text. Her evocations of Burke's lament are allusively anti-revolutionary, since her condemnation of the Terror is in context of Burke's condemnation of the Revolution, in toto. Like Wollstonecraft, the closer she is to the Terror, the closer she is to Burke. In Williams' case it seems a belated acknowledgment, a disguised identification with a text she previously mocked. Referring to Burke's dismay that all "homage paid to the sex in general . . . is to be regarded as romance and folly" (*Reflections* 171), Madelyn Gutwirth perceptively notes that while Burke "idealizes the status quo . . . he . . . exposes the . . . gender hatred implicit in the new order's incommensurable vituperation against Marie Antoinette, and reveals its implications not only for her class, but for the whole of her sex."[7] In the *Letters,* Williams' vision of the prelapsarian Revolution was also regarded as "romance and folly," but the Terror compelled her to change her romance into the tragedy of feminine beauty. She reinscribes Burke's characterization of a bestial, misogynous revolution as a murderous, misogynous Terror. In doing this, she understood that chivalry, for Burke, constituted the historical modification of terror and power—chivalry "mitigated ferocity" . . . it subdued the fierceness of pride and power," compelling "stern authority to submit to elegance, and gave a domination vanquisher of laws, to be subdued by manners" (*Reflections,* 170, 171). Williams realized that, for Burke, chivalry "made power gentle" and incorporated into the political order the "beauty" that had softened domestic, private life (*Reflections,* 171). In other words, chivalry constituted the historical transformation of sublime terror into the aesthetic sublime that complimented ("homage paid to the sex") and complemented the feminine beautiful. For Burke, the Revolution violently ruptured this crucial historical fusion. Williams, in effect, reformulates Burke's reading of the reemergence of terror and power. In her formulation, Jacobin Terror violates the Revolution's "charms" and "beauty," a violation corresponding to its misogynous assault on women.

Williams was, in many ways, a luminous reader of both the *Enquiry* and the *Reflections.* Burke's defense of chivalry is still read by some as a sentimental, rococo fantasy that disguises reactionary power and terror in beautiful "drapery." Williams seems to have understood that, for Burke, chivalry was, in men, the self-imposed discipline and suppression of threatening power and terror, mitigating masculine "ferocity" by confronting it in themselves and others. The faithful knight incarnated the chivalric sublime, humbling and disciplining himself, confronting masculine terror, which he either defeated or kept at a safe distance.[8] Burke contended that, historically, the Christian, chivalric sublime made the politics of beauty possible, incorporating the "feminine" into the Western political order. For Burke, the Revolution reintroduced pejorative sublime power magnified in new, ferocious forms. For Williams, the Revolution initially liberated the political, social beauty suppressed by the Old Order; thus the terrorist reimprisonment and *murder* of beauty constituted a tragic regression.[9]

The Terror changed her vision of the Revolution irreparably. As the Terror continued to become increasingly close and as she tried to escape it by fleeing to Switzerland, the pristine Revolution became increasingly identified with the "charms" and "beauties" of literature, especially poetry. It was ultimately through literature that Williams escaped terrorist time; in her romantic *Letters,* the golden age of the Revolution is forever pure. Before the Revolution, she had referred to poetry as an enchanting "illusion," a metaphor that constitutes her final revolutionary vision.[10]

Previously she had lamented that the "golden age of the revolution" was "past": "the enchanting spell is broken, and the fair scenes of beauty and of order, through which imagination wandered, are transformed into the desolation of the wilderness, and clouded by the darkness of the tempest" (*Letters,* 1:3.6). Her vision of the prelapsarian Revolution is one of imaginative "beauty," an "enchanting spell" broken by the sublime terror that ominously gathers in the sterile and stormy imagery that now "clouds" her "vision." The imagery of her various enchantments—magic, beauty, and illusion, illustrates that the pristine Revolution is retrospectively an aesthetic literary event—a beautiful illusion broken by real terror. The "spell" that is broken inscribes her *disenchantment* (her disillusionment) and the possibility that the Revolution was only a pleasing "illusion"—a beautiful, imaginative romance.

In her third version of Burke's chivalric text, she had lamented that "the classical haunt of Petrarch no longer presents the delightful images of beauty, of poetry, of passion; the magical spell is broken, the soothing charm is dissolved" (*Letters* 2:3.85).[11] Even when Williams records her disenchantment and disillusion, she still longs to be reenchanted with the pleasing illusions of 1789. By associating her beautiful revolutionary romance with pleasing illusions broken by the Terror, she seemingly betrays a preference for past illusion rather than present reality. Wollstonecraft, in her Versailles apostrophe, had also referred to the "charm" broken by Jacobin terror (*Works,* 6:85), but she could return to the quotidian English world and forget the Revolution. Williams did not have that luxury. Self-exiled, she had totally committed herself to the Revolution, and the Revolution completely changed her life.

When the Terror ended with "the fall of Robespierre," she returned romantically to the revival of nature and beauty that had inspired her first prelapsarian visions: "Upon the fall of Robespierre, the terrible spell which bound the land of France was broken; the shrieking whirl winds, the black precipices, the bottomless gulphs, suddenly vanished; and reviving nature covered the wastes with flowers, and the rocks with verdure" (*Letters,* 2:3.190). In her romantic account, revolutionary beauty returns with the death of the Jacobin sublime—a restoration recorded in the previous language of disenchantment. Reversing her previous imagery in which the Terrorist sublime breaks the enchanting spell and transforms the "scenes of beauty" into the "desolate wilderness and dark tempest" (1:3.6), she now suggests that the Terror was only a bad nightmare, an evil spell broken by the wicked magician's fall. In other words, her previous revolutionary vision is ultimately more real than the Jacobin "illusion." She suggests that her revolutionary vision—what she previously thought and felt—was and is truer than the "spell" or re-vision that momentarily interrupted her innocent enchantment. Her beautiful vision, her idea of the Revolution, is thus kept pure and protected—safely removed from "sublime" reality.

In a fundamental sense, this was an escapist literary fiction, a verbal magical trick, allowing her the consolation of her romantic illusion. It again highlights her proto-Romantic reading of the superiority of imagination and feeling to reason and reality. Towards the end of her *Letters,* she recalls that, in prison, those condemned to the guillotine "indulged their imaginations in all the fond illusions of life, and all the gay chimeras of glory," until Williams and her companions "awakened them from those vain illusions" (*Letters,* 2:4.78)—a phrase that reflexively evokes all of her correspondent illusions. The language of their illusion is reinscribed in the language of her beautiful revolutionary romance, seemingly destroyed, as her friends are, by the reality of the Terror. In *Julia* (1790), she had written that "[p]erhaps the most precious property of poetry is, that of leading the mind from the gloomy mists of care, or the black clouds of misfortune, which sometimes gather around the path of life, to scenes bright with sunshine, and blooming with beauty."[12] In a letter dated 1794, she included a poem, in French, dedicated and written to her by a friend. In the footnote, Williams observes that even though "the days of French chivalry" are forever gone, "fiction is the privilege of poets." The observation alludes to the poem in which her friend speaks of her leaving England to find the revolutionary "promised land" and caressing this "delectable illusion," just "as children amuse themselves with bright dreams of fable" (*Letters,* 2:2.118, 119; my trans.). Her friend proceeds to equate her idealistic illusion with her enthusiasm for poetry. The fact that Williams showcases the poem acknowledges her retrospective admission that the Revolution had been a "delectable illusion" that reality had destroyed: "For me, the world has lost its illusive colouring; its fairy spells, its light enchantments have vanished" (*Letters,* 2:2.100). In the end, however, literature, the poetry of imagination and illusion, constituted a momentary stay against the reality that compelled her ubi sunt lament, "Ah what is become of the delightful visions which elevated the enthusiastic heart?" (1:3.6; cf. 1:4.143).

Years later, physically and emotionally exhausted, Williams enjoyed an evening with William Wordsworth, as she informed a friend in a letter dated 25 October 1820: "You will therefore easily believe with how much pleasure I left politics, the laws of election, and the charter—to take care of themselves, while I was led by Mr. Wordsworth's society to that world of poetical illusion, so full of charms, and from which I have been so long an exile."[13] Her "exile," one feels, also refers to the enchanting English world she had left thirty years before, but Wordsworth's visit and the talk of poetry returned her momentarily to the charm and beauty—to those romantic regions where she had formerly been "led." If they also talked about the Revolution, as F. M. Todd suggests,[14] the reference to "that world of poetical illusion, so full of charms" could also refer to her previous revolutionary vision restored by a nostalgic conversation about the Revolution with Wordsworth, a poet who had tried unsuccessfully to locate Williams in 1792 and who had based "Vaudracour and Julia" on Williams' account of the Du Fossés.[15] In *The Prelude,* Wordsworth had also recorded his enchantment and disillusionment with the Revolution, so his attraction to Williams was not only for her poetry, which he admired, but for the fact that she had also experienced the Revolution as he had—as a crisis of emotional and imaginative faith. The "poetical illusion" and "charms" to which Williams refers in her 1820 letter is the same language that she had previously used to describe her revolutionary enchantment. The reference to her exile from "that world of poetic illusion" also evokes her disenchantment—momentarily dispelled—on that autumnal evening when she and Wordsworth shared their youthful illusions.

12

Feminine Representation: Helen Maria Williams' *Letters from France*

WILLIAMS' refiguration of the sublime and beautiful impinges, as we have seen, on her representation of women. In the *Letters*, women in the Old Regime are initially split between those who are pampered aristocrats and those young women of the Third Estate who are confined in convents. These convents are suggestively sterile prisons, prisons in which the young nuns' sexual natures are repressed through coerced chastity. In Rouen Williams visits "a convent of Benedictine Nuns" and sees a room divided by iron bars, with "a young man sitting on one side of the grate, and a young nun on the other." This is a "gloomy barrier," and the nun is dressed in that "dismal habit that seems so much at variance with youth and beauty"—a "melancholy symbol" renouncing the "world" and its "pleasures" (*Letters,* 1:1.114; cf. 115–20).

In her romance of Auguste and Madelaine, the former's haughty, aristocratic father tricks Madelaine (a commoner) into confining herself in a convent, where she is to become a nun. Madelaine is of course still in love and associates the incipient Revolution with the freedom to marry. Having lost contact with Auguste, however, she resigns herself to the inevitable: "The day was fixed, when, prostrate with her face towards the earth, and with flowers scattered over her, and a part of her long tresses cut off, she was to enter upon that solemn trial preparatory to her external renunciation of the world—of Auguste!" (*Letters,* 1:2.179). Symbolically buried and dead to the world, the ritual cutting of her hair also symbolizes her renounced femininity—retrospectively evoking the similar enforced rite for female victims of the guillotine. All ends happily, however, as Auguste arrives just in time, bringing with him the revolutionary authorities who declare that the National Assembly had prohibited "any nuns to be professed" (180). As she prepares to leave the convent, Madelaine thinks of her love for the liberating Revolution and, laying aside her white wedding gown, contemplates what would have happened if the National Assembly's decree had "come too late": "At this idea Madelaine took up the veil for her novitiate . . . and bathed it with a flood of tears" (181). Relieved that the Revolution has freed her from coerced chastity and liberated her to love, she bathes the nun's "veil" (contrastingly evoking the wedding veil) in tears of happy release.

In 1793, when Williams herself is confined in an English convent after her release from the Luxembourg, she delights in conversing with the beautiful Sister Theresa, "that amiable nun who so much wished to hide a face which nature had formed to excite love and admiration" (*Letters*, 2:1.192). Since Theresa is apparently an English nun, Williams equates the Revolution with the liberation of French, feminine beauty: "It was impossible to converse with [Theresa] without feeling that the revolution was a blessing, if it was only for having prohibited vows which robbed society of those who were formed to be its delight and ornament" (192). For Williams, the Revolution's prohibition of unnatural religious "vows" frees women to take natural wedding vows. Her reference to women as "those who were formed to be [society's] "delight and ornament" underscores her attachment to traditional, gendered values.

Because Williams showcases her feminine response to the Revolution, in which her feminine reading signifies the Revolution's true meaning, her vision of women's role within the Revolution complements her readings of the sublime and beautiful. We have seen that her favorite hero is Henry IV, whose masculine qualities are modified by feminine beauty. Her other favorite is Joan of Arc, the Maid of Orléans and savior of France. While Williams is always pleased to fix her eyes on the statues of Henry, she feels ashamed of her country when she passes the spot "where the Maid of Orléans was executed, and on which her statue stands, a monument of our disgrace" (*Letters*, 1:1.103). Williams seems "haunted" by Joan of Arc (1:2.41). Her account of how the French celebrate Joan's cult in Orléans centers on a ceremony in which a "young girl" is chosen, a girl considered "the most amiable, the most modest, the most virtuous," in a word "the most distinguished for those qualities which are the best ornament of her sex." The young woman—the embodiment of the traditional femininity Williams endorses—"is married on this day to the lover of her choice" (43). In this celebration of female virtue, there is a tacit contrast between the heroic and masculine "virgin" and the beautiful maid who will marry. If the girl is the chosen representative of her beautiful sex, Joan transcends her sex.

Joan's gender is, in fact, blurred by Williams with a masculine roughness. Her statue is placed on one side of the Virgin Mary holding the dead Christ; on the other side is a statue of Charles VII, but both statues "are so rude, misshapen, and grotesque, that it requires some deliberation to determine which is Charles the Seventh, and which is the Maid of Orléans." In the procession honoring Joan, "a young boy, dressed in a fantastic manner," represents her (*Letters,* 1:2.42). While Williams continues to suggest that Joan possesses both feminine and masculine qualities, she initially emphasizes the latter. Joan's "hat" is "religiously kept" in a "convent" of monks, a masculine confine where "no women could be admitted," although "the reverend fathers" relax "from the usual severity of their order in favour of so extraordinary a woman as Jeanne d' Arc." The "rest of [Joan's] sex must not expect the same indulgence," including Williams, who leaves Orléans without seeing her hat (44). Although Williams describes what she actually sees (the rude statue and the boy who represents Joan) or refers to what she does not see (Joan's masculine "hat" enshrined in a male "convent"—one expects the word *monastery*—an ecclesiastical site that the Revolution, as we have seen, liberates), her selection of details illustrates her fascination with the Revolution's androgynous nuances. But these nuances are also disturbing.

Thus she prefaces another tribute to Joan with a contrast between Mary Queen of Scot's "weakness" and Elizabeth's greatness (*Letters,* 1:2.66). This standard contrast between Mary's femininity and Elizabeth's "masculinity" is in context of Williams' preference for Mary, whom she had sympathetically described in a 1786 poem titled "Queen Mary's Complaint."[1] "Unfortunate Mary['s] . . . calamities" make her "forget every weakness of Mary, and every great quality of Elizabeth" (*Letters,* 1:2.66). She then describes an old painting of Joan of Arc: "The countenance is uncommonly beautiful. It seems that nature, while she bestowed on the Maid of Orléans the heroic qualities of the other sex, did not deny her the soft attractions of her own." The sexual extremities of Mary and Elizabeth (excessive femininity versus excessive masculinity) seem united in Joan, who is a complementary fusion of both the sublime and beautiful. Williams, however, seems anxious to emphasize that Joan's feminine "attractions" are not overpowered by "the heroic qualities of the other sex." She softens Joan's masculinity which she had stressed in her visit to Orléans.

Joan's military exploits were of course overtly masculine, so Williams emphasizes her beauty to soften her heroic qualities. This is also how she represents the women who resist the powers of the Old Regime, for, like Joan, they are saviors of their country, albeit in a more traditional supporting role. During the siege of the Bastille, French women bravely defy the enemy canon and, instead of "indulging the fears incident to our feeble sex," bring food to their "sons and husbands; and, with a spirit worthy of Roman matrons, encouraged them to go on." Guarding the streets, they "boldly" demand that people identify themselves (*Letters*, 1:1.27–28). In the *Reflections,* Burke had referred to Marie Antoinette's "lofty sentiments . . . she feels with the dignity of a Roman matron" (169), so perhaps Williams is counter-responding with a plurality of revolutionary matrons, although the reference to Roman matrons was fairly commonplace, especially among the revolutionaries. As in her reference to Joan of Arc, the allusion to Roman matrons establishes another precedent that prefigures the heroism of women in the Revolution. Revolutionary women are the historical culmination of sublime-and-beautiful female heroism; the Revolution does not create sublime, heroic women—it inspires and elicits latent qualities that are intrinsically part of female nature.

Beautiful, bountiful femininity, "those generous affections which belong to the female heart," culminates in sublime acts of selflessness. Thus patriotic, aristocratic women, like the women of ancient Rome, sacrifice their jewels for *la patrie,* "even the personal ornaments, so dear to female vanity, for the common cause" (*Letters,* 1:1.37). In *The French Revolution,* Wollstonecraft referred to this episode as an exercise in ostentatious frivolity (*Works,* 6:169); Williams' point is that the Revolution elicits what is really true and sublime in female nature, empowering women to conquer female weakness, the vanities and fears "incident to our feeble sex" (*Letters,* 1:1.27). For her, the Revolution opens the political and social space that allows women to participate in the sublime, albeit behind the scenes. She insists that women play a vital role in the Revolution: "The women have certainly had a considerable share in the French [R]evolution: for, whatever the imperious lords of the creation may fancy, the most important events which take place in this world depend a little on our influence; and we often act in human affairs like those secret springs in mechanism, by which, though invisible, great movements are regulated" (37–38). The aggressive challenge to men, "the imperious lords of creation" (cf. Robert Burns, "The Twa Dogs," 1.45), and her articulation of the crucial role of women in the Revolution is not so much a feminist assertion as it is a claim for women's secret influence, a cultural commonplace she reinscribes in a revolutionary context, suggesting that women are also behind history's progressive "events."

In volume two, women's sensibility and "constancy" again illustrate what is true and sublime in female nature:

> While men assume over our sex so many claims to superiority, let them at least bestow on us the palm of constancy, and allow that in the fidelity of our attachments we have the right of pre-eminence. Those prisons from which men shrunk back with terror, and where they often left their friends abandoned lest they should be involved in their fate— women, in whom the force of sensibility overcame the fears of female weakness, demanded and sometimes obtained permission to visit, in defiance of all the dangers that surrounded their gloomy walls.
>
> (*Letters*, 2.1:40–41)

The sentence starts with a deceptive concession to masculine "claims to superiority," implicitly questioned by the verb "assume," suggesting both the false assumption and the presumption of asserting "so many claims to superiority." The modest female claim to "constancy" actually rejects an entire misogynous tradition in which women were characteristically fickle and inconstant and makes the masculine sex the suggestively inconstant betrayers of women, since the latter are preeminent in the "fidelity of our attachments."[2] Moreover, in crises, men betray the "female weakness" of fear, what she formerly referred to as "the fears incident to our feeble sex" (1:1.27): men shrink "back with terror" and abandon friends, "lest they should be involved in their fate." In this sexual role reversal, female "weakness" is projected onto men while women display the superior, sublime qualities of constancy and bravery. In Burke's *Speech on American Taxation* (1774), "the great masculine virtues" are "constancy, gravity, magnanimity, fortitude, fidelity, and firmness." The bravery and magnanimity Williams ascribes to women in the Revolution (*Letters*, 1:1.27–28, 37) are the same virtues exhibited by women oppressed by the Terror. Williams suggests again that different sublime events (the prelapsarian Revolution and the postlapsarian Terror) elicit what is naturally there. While the Terror suppresses women, it cannot ultimately suppress their true natures.

Williams herself is the explicit example of female constancy and fidelity, visiting imprisoned friends, like Madame Roland, or, when she herself is imprisoned, allowing secret visits from La Source and Sillery, two members of the National Convention, confined in a room next to hers. She notes that the "discovery of these visits" would have endangered her family, "but our sympathy prevailed over our fears" and, regardless of the consequences, they could not "refuse our devoted friend this last melancholy satisfaction"

(*Letters,* 2:1.44). When Williams and her family are told that they will be moved to a convent, La Source and Sillery thank them "a thousand times" for "the dangers we had risqued in receiving them, and for the sympathy which had soothed the last hours of their existence" (2:1.55).

Madame Roland is the preeminent revolutionary heroine of the *Letters,* a splendid fusion of the sublime and beautiful. Brave and true, she is faithful to her Girondist values. Visiting her in the prison of St. Pelagie, Williams finds her resigned to her fate, stoically reading Plutarch, but bursting into tears when she recalls her husband and daughter: "the courage of the victim of liberty was lost in the feelings of the wife and the mother" (*Letters,* 2:1.197). Roland, for Williams, represents woman as victim, the embodiment of "oppressed innocence"—Roland's representation of herself in her memoirs. Her description of Roland crying and losing herself in maternal, wifely "feelings" has a historical context, for Roland had been accused of transgressing her feminine role and trying to be a man. In her memoirs, Roland is conscious of this charge and goes out of her way to deny it.[3] In an appendix in the *Letters,* Williams quotes Roland's denial that she had ever "overpassed the limits prescribed me by my sex" (2:1.283), illustrating the anxiety over proper sexual roles that characterizes both revolutionary and counterrevolutionary discourse.

Williams' description of Roland's degrading trial and treatment is similar to that of Marie Antoinette's (cf. *Letters,* 2:1.153–55, 197), suggesting the Terror's hostility to the opposite (and oppositional) sex. After her eloquent defense (of herself) and her stoic acceptance of the death sentence, Roland goes to the guillotine dressed in virginal white, "her long dark hair" flowing "loosely to her waist," dying heroically, "one of those illustrious women whose superior attainments seemed fitted to exalt her sex in the scale of being" (*Letters,* 2:1.199, 201). Since Williams does not mention the cutting of Roland's hair, she suggests that Roland dies "pure," preserving her innocent virtue. Roland is the historical culmination of Joan of Arc and all those valiant Roman matrons; her role in Williams' sexual drama illustrates the constancy of woman's beautiful and sublime nature.

Like Madame Roland, Charlotte Corday (another valiant Girondin) studies history and assimilates "the examples of antiquity," which inspire her to kill the terrorist Jean Paul Marat (*Letters,* 2:1.129). As Patrice Higonnet notes, the Jacobins considered Corday's archetypically "masculine" act (the stabbing of Marat) to be "doubly defiant, politically and sexually."[4] Although almost all of

Williams' heroines are innocent victims, Corday is the one example of sublime, female vengeance against the violators of revolutionary purity. After her capture, however, she is also victimized and guillo- tined. Like Roland, she defends herself bravely at her trial, em- bodying both the sublime and the beautiful: "Her face sometimes beamed with sublimity, and was sometimes covered with smiles" (*Letters,* 2:1.132). Since Corday committed a violent "masculine" murder (her "femininity" was an issue at her trial), Williams empha- sizes the effect of her beauty on those who see her, suggesting again Burke's point, in the *Enquiry,* that the described effect of beauty on spectators surpasses beauty's description (*Enquiry,* 171– 72). In a long footnote (*Letters,* 2:1.134–35), she recounts how Adam Lux, a young man who accidentally saw Corday being led to her execution, was struck "instantly" by Corday's beauty and bravery; Lux, consequently, fell obsessively in love and published a pamphlet praising her as "Greater than Brutus." He was quickly imprisoned and then condemned to the guillotine—an "altar" on which he considered it a privilege to die by "the identical instru- ment by which [Corday] had suffered." (Lux develops a guillotine fetish, becoming "enamoured not of her only, but . . . of the guillotine.")

Significantly, the government tried to discredit Corday's femi- nine beauty in a publicly distributed article: "This woman, said to be pretty, was not at all pretty; she was a virago, brawny rather than fresh, without grace, untidy as are almost all female philosoph- ers and eggheads. . . . Charlotte Corday was 25 years old; in our customs that is practically an old maid, especially with a masculin- ized bearing and boyish look. . . . Thus, it follows that this woman had thrown herself absolutely outside of her sex."[5] Corday's own death is presented, by Williams, as a Jacobin violation of feminine purity. After tying her to a plank, the executioner removes the handkerchief covering her face (a grotesque parody of the removal of the wedding veil), causing her to blush "deeply; and her head, which he held up to the multitude the moment after, exhibited this last impression of offended modesty" (*Letters,* 2:134–35). Williams apparently added the details of the handkerchief and the maidenly blush to suggest the insult to Corday's femininity, so mocked and exploited. Indeed, her reference to Corday's "blush" is a delicate allusion to the fact that the executioner held up Corday's decapi- tated head and slapped it two or three times. As Madelyn Gutwirth notes, "even the radical *Révolutions de Paris* of July 19 was im- pelled to remark 'there was but one cry of horror against the man who allowed himself such an atrocity!'"[6] Williams' imagery suggests violated virginity, a murderous rape witnessed by a multitude of voyeuristic spectators in a Revolution that has degenerated from the spectacle of the Federation to the spectacle of the guillotine. She sees the Terror as a murderous violation of woman's body as well as the body politic. (There is a connection between the "violation of the national representation"—the Girondist phrase she frequently uses—and the "violation" of women, especially Girondist women.) Although Williams could not have known that Jacobin authorities (in an attempt to discredit Corday's "beauty") had Corday's body anatomically examined to determine whether or not she had been a virgin (she was)—necrophilically enacting the literal terms of Corday's violation, she repeatedly connects Jacobin terror and repression with the repression and violation of women.

In a repetition, or rather degeneration of the Corday episode, Cecile Renault, "young and handsome" seeks, à la Corday, the house of Robespierre (24 May 1794), but instead of successfully killing him, is captured and interrogated. Self-dressed with "care" and perhaps with "coquetry," she is humiliatingly "stripped" and "covered with squalid and disgusting rags" before being sent to the guillotine with her innocent family (*Letters*, 2:2.68–69). Later, in a more faithful enactment, a young lady whose father had been guillotined, "filled with the terrible sentiment of vengeance," plunges "a dagger into . . . the judge who had condemned her father to die" (2:4.153–54). Interestingly, this incident is in context of the "White Terror" (1794–95) against former Jacobin terrorists. It is a parable of innocence vindicated, the one incident where sublime female violence is not punished.

Even Williams' disdain of aristocrats and royalty, so pronounced in her earlier sections, changes into a subjunctive vindication of the king by the women of Paris. She contends that if Louis XVI had been allowed to return to the National Convention on the day of his execution, the Parisian women, who had spent that day "in tears of unavailing regret, would have rushed between the monarch and his guards, and have attempted his rescue, even with the risk of life" (*Letters*, 1:4.37). While her contention that the Parisian women would, under the right circumstances, have tried to save the king is perhaps exaggerated, Williams' emphasis on their emotional response is historically grounded. Citing Restif de la Bretonne (1734–1806), Madelyn Gutwirth observes "that women in particular appeared stricken at the king's death."[7] Daniel Arasse quotes a revealing misogynous report by a municipal official who blamed the somberness of 21 January on the emotional weakness of women:

The women—and it would be unreasonable of us to expect them immediately to grasp the significance of political events—were, for the most
part, somewhat sad; and this played a considerable part in the sullen
air that Paris wore all that day. There were perhaps a few tears shed;
but we know that women abound in tears. There were some reproaches
also, and even some insults. All this is quite excusable in a frail and
light-headed sex, which has seen the radiant last great days of a bril-
liant court.[8]

Writing during the Terror and referring to an execution that was
undoubtedly a traumatic event for millions of the French people,
the Jacobin official reduces women to cryptoroyalists, aggrieved
over the loss of the gay, frivolous pleasures of the rococo court.
Williams' contention that women would have, under the right conditions, tried to rescue the king suggests both their bravery as well
as the conspicuous absence of men willing to do the same. Later,
"many young women who had lost their parents or their lovers on
the scaffold" cried out, "Vive le roi!" This counterrevolutionary
cry predictably earns them, as they had hoped, "a passport to the
tomb" (Letters, 2:2.65). In a sense, their cry is also Williams.'

Not all women, of course, are victims, since Jacobin women also
perpetuate the Terror, betraying both the Revolution and their sex.
If French women represent beauty and the Girondin heroines a
happy fusion of the sublime and beautiful, Jacobin women represent the degeneration of the beautiful sex into masculine monsters.
As Charlotte Corday is being led to the guillotine, a group of tricot-
euses gathers to insult her, "furies of the guillotine" who are, nevertheless, "awed into silence" by her "demeanour" (Letters,
2:1.133–34). After Robespierre's fall, the Parisians become
alarmed when they see "the female furies of the guillotine" and
realize that the Jacobins are again trying to gain control (2:4.35).
As in Wollstonecraft's account of the October Days, these Burkean
furies have lost their sex. Referring to the Jacobin assault on the
National Convention (31 May 1793), Williams focuses on Robespierre's "body guard of revolutionary women, who were in the van
of the attack" and who, "armed with poniards," pointed them "at
the bosoms of such of the deputies as attempted to leave the hall"
(2:1.73). The heroines of the Bastille, we will remember, supported
their men in a battle of liberation; in contrast, the militant participation of these Jacobin women suggests the masculinization of their
sex. The female terrorists pointing their poniards (the weapon of
the "assassins" who tried to kill the queen in Burke's Reflections,
164) at the "bosoms" of male deputies (the feminine Girondins!)

also evoke the male terrorist, Henriot, who terrorized Williams' female family in the Luxembourg: "he looked . . . as if he longed to plunge his sabre in our bosoms" (*Letters*, 2:1.29). Williams later notes that she is not "skilled in the art of war," as some French women are (2:4.180).

Referring to "a certain class" of Parisian women "who gave themselves the title of revolutionary women" (that is, Claire Lacombe and the *Republicaines-Revolutionaires*) and who had replaced the *poissardes*, she presents them as women who had aggressively transgressed their natural roles and intruded into male political space. These women were presumptuous "female politicians" who held "deliberative assemblies," presented their views in the National Convention, and "influenced" its debates by unfeminine "vociferations in the tribunes, which they . . . exclusively occupied." In the days preceding the Jacobin coup of 31 May, they "mounted guard" at the Convention and "prevented the execution of certain orders they disliked." Afterwards they demanded that the Convention pass repressive laws, arrest "every suspected person," and require women to wear sans-cullotic red caps (*Letters*, 2:1.139–40). There is an allusive, historical context to Williams' references to the *poissardes* (the fishwomen who figured so prominently in earlier *journées*) and the failure of the revolutionary women to get what they wanted (the requirement of women to wear red caps) from the Convention, which quickly bans their activities and their club (*Letters*, 2:1.140). Just before the Convention effectively disempowered the revolutionary women, the *poissardes* had violently beaten a group of them (28 October 1793), providing the Convention the pretext to close their club and all other women's clubs and political "societies" as well (30 October 1793). Williams' reference to the red cap is significant, since the wearing of the cap was considered a masculine privilege and was deeply resented by the *poissardes*. The revolutionary women were consequently discredited for trying to transgress their sexual roles and become "men."[9]

After Robespierre's fall, the Jacobins try to repeat their terrorist tactics. Referring to the events of the Prairial Uprising (20–23 May 1795), Williams notes that the Jacobins tried to intimidate the Convention with insurgents, "headed as usual by women, who filled the tribunes, and passages leading into the assembly, with vociferations for bread and a constitution; but whose furious looks and menacing gestures indicated more strongly a thirst for blood" (*Letters*, 2:4.132; cf. Henriot's ferocious look, indicating a thirst for blood, 2:1.29). The return of terror is a return of these monstrous, masculine women.

Williams' principal focus, however, is on masculine Jacobin violence against women who prefer to die with their loved ones: "Among the victims of the tyrants, the women have been peculiarly distinguished for their admirable firmness in death. Perhaps this arose from the superior sensibility that belongs to the female mind, and which made it feel that it was less terrible to die, than to survive the objects of its tenderness" (*Letters,* 2:1.213). With the exception of the ci-devant Madame Du Barry, who fearfully shrinks from the guillotine (2:2.42, 44, 48), women are either Girondin martyrs or apolitical daughters, wives, and lovers who make the ultimate sacrifice, proving women's sublime fidelity to truth and beauty. Williams stresses again superior female sensibility, a faithful fusion of thought and feeling. She sees the Terror as, among other things, systematic Jacobin misogyny directed against feminine "beauty": "those blooming beauties, who in all the first freshness of youth, in the very spring of life, submitted to the stroke of the executioner with placid smiles on their countenances, and looked like angels in their flight to heaven" (2:1.213). She contrasts feminine beauty (youth, spring, life, and angels) with Jacobin death, a contrast also suggesting the superior Christian forgiveness of beauties who smile on the executioner, conscious that they will be meeting their maker as they angelically ascend to heaven. But her allegory of defenseless beauty is also sexual: these young virgins submit to the executioner's phallic stroke, suggesting the repetitive "violation" of feminine "innocence." If decapitation represents public castration within the polysemantic system of the Terror's signs and symbols, it also represents, for Williams, the public violation of the feminine Revolution's virginity, its forced loss of innocence.

The symbolism includes wives such as Lucile Desmoulins, who is imprisoned on trumped-up charges and guillotined. Dressed, à la Madame Roland, in virginal white, she makes the "sacrifice of life in all its bloom and freshness" (*Letters,* 2:2.35–36). Williams does not pursue the imagery for obvious reasons, but in the reader's mind, the deflowering of these innocent victims who lose their "bloom and freshness" evokes the imaginative blood that stains white virginal dresses once the (maiden) head is pierced. Williams, in this context, was the first to suggest that the Terror constituted the misogynous, sexual fury of Jacobin men against women:

The fury of these implacable monsters seemed directed with peculiar
virulence against that sex, whose weakness man was destined by nature to support. The scaffold was every day bathed with the blood of
women. Some who had been condemned to die, but had been respited
on the account of their pregnancy, were dragged to death immediately
after their delivery, in that state of weakness which savages would
have respected.

(*Letters*, 2:1.214–15)

The "implacable monsters" are the Jacobin judges who send innocent women to their deaths. Thus the Terror inverts the "natural"
roles of men as well: masculine protectors chivalrously "destined
by nature" to support female vulnerability become "implacable
monsters" who assault the softer sex. It is almost as if these misogynous monsters resent the reproductive capacity of women, reluctantly allowing them to give birth before they are murdered.
Williams proceeds to stress the unnatural separation of mothers
from their babies, in the history of "the wife of a peasant."

The woman is breast-feeding her baby when the Jacobin authorities arrive to take her to the guillotine: as "they take away the
infant who was hanging at her breast, and receiving that nourishment of which death was so soon to dry up the source," the woman
rents "the air with her cries, with the strong shriek of instinctive
affection, the piercing throes of maternal tenderness." The fact
that she is a peasant woman, along with nineteen "other [con-
demned] women of the same class," suggests the murderous betrayal of the very class the Jacobins promised to liberate, and her
"cries" conjure up the baby's cries, separated from the "source"
that gives them life. The baby's precarious presence disappears
with the mother's death: "the infant was torn from the bosom that
cherished it, and the agonies of the unfortunate mother found respite in death" (*Letters*, 2:1.215). The "agonies" of the mother
complement Williams' allegory of "the agonies of beauty"
(2:4.47)—the suffering of women whose roles and nature are repeatedly violated.

In the *Letters*, victimized women are usually virgins or young
mothers, fecundly filled with life. The young and beautiful Polish
princess, Lubomirska, is, despite her attachment to the Revolution, arrested and imprisoned by Robespierre on account of her
"friendship for some members of the Gironde." Pregnant in prison,
the "unhappy princess" miscarries and is then executed. Two days
before Robespierre's fall, eight women, including the princess of
Monaco, who had previously pleaded their bellies, are "dragged

to the scaffold" (*Letters*, 2:2.106–7). Williams again suggests the Jacobin hatred of woman's nature and "life," since the women are still ambiguously pregnant.

Jacobin Terror against women is especially ferocious in the counterrevolutionary Vendée. Williams translates a report from J. M. Lequinio, a member of the National Convention *en mission:* "We have seen republican soldiers shoot or stab rebel women in the public roads. We have seen others carrying infants torn from the breast, on the ends of their bayonets, or the pikes that had pierced with the same blow the child and the mother" (*Letters*, 2:3.18).[10] As bayonets impale rebel babies and phallic pikes pierce "with the same blow the child and the mother," Jacobin gynocide is simultaneously matricide and infanticide, almost as if the Terror abhors women's bodies and wombs. These terrorist assaults on women cut across ideological lines—aristocrats, Girondins, peasants, and rebel women oppressed equally—but the Vendean women are especially humiliated and mutilated. Thematically, one notes, just as Jacobin furies are really not women, Jacobin "monsters" are not really men: both are unnatural, unsexed murderers. Although there are many male victims in the *Letters*, Williams links the violation of women with the violation of the Revolution.

In counterrevolutionary Nantes, Jacobin troops kill "women in a state of pregnancy" as they do "[p]regnant women, who were under the protection of a special decree" (*Letters*, 2:3.44, 47). In the Vendée, unlike the rest of France, women and the *life within* them are literally murdered. Williams was one of the first to contend that the Jacobins were engaged in a systematic policy of genocide in the Vendée, and the imagery of gynocide suggests a Jacobin endeavor to extinguish all resistant, oppositional "life." Until recently, the Revolution's dominant historiography has ignored or dismissed "counterrevolutionary" charges of genocide. Similarly, in many accounts of women in the French Revolution, counterrevolutionary women have been marginalized, ignored, or dismissed. Williams' account, despite her typical Girondist bias, is atypically inclusive of these women. For Williams, after the suppression of the Federalist revolt, the Vendée is the only place where the Terror is forcibly resisted. She seems to sense and to suggest that the Jacobin endeavor to represent (and annihilate) all opposition as "counterrevolutionary" coincides with the gynocidal extermination of resistant, oppositional "life" in the Vendée. She senses a murderous ideological connection between the representation of opposition and difference as a counterrevolutionary "Other" and the misogynous representation of the gendered "Other."[11] It is true that while she denounced the genocide and was sympathetic to Vendean victims, she considered the Vendée a region of reaction and royalism, but it is equally true that the Vendée, in the *Letters,* is the region where terrorist misogynism kills with particular horror.

In her account of the *noyades* at Nantes—the "drownings" of prisoners packed in barges set adrift in the Loire river and sunk by cannon fire—"innocent young women were unclothed in the presence of [male, Jacobin] monsters; and, to add a deeper horror . . . were tied to young men, and both were cut down with sabres, or thrown into the river; and this kind of murder was called a republican marriage" (*Letters,* 2:3.42–43). Although young men also die, her emphasis is on the suggestively sexual murder of the young women. The fact that they were "innocent" not only suggests that they were not guilty of aiding the rebels but that they were young "virgins." Their humiliating horror is especially suggestive, since they were tied naked to the (naked) young men, a detail Williams delicately suggests without saying. The Jacobins, in turn, are sadistic, public voyeurs who delight in tying "counter-revolutionary" men and women into forced positions of sterile intercourse, in a grotesque "marriage" of the soon-to-be dead. If the Old Regime, for Williams, represents the forced confinement of female beauty, the Terror represents beauty's degrading death.

Williams, we have seen, envisions the guillotine as woman's violation—the female victim's hair is shorn by the male executioner, and her head is cut off by the guillotine's stroke. Since woman's cascading hair represents her sexual beauty, the enforced cutting of her hair represents the violation of her femininity—a rape of the lock, doubly consummated in the cutting off of her head. The guillotine, as I have suggested, is a murderous phallic machine, and the "spectacle" of the guillotine is a degrading, murderous rape witnessed by frenzied crowds. The suggestive splattering of white dresses contributes to the sense of sexual violation, the coercive loss of the woman's virginity when she loses her (maiden) head. More comprehensively, Williams sees the Terror as an assault on women per se, orchestrating her imagery to produce an allegory of violated feminine innocence. This allegory encompasses the betrayed Revolution, for the Revolution's fate reflects the fate of its faithful, feminine followers.

Perhaps the most vivid image of the gynocidal guillotine occurs in the history of the peasant woman who is arrested and tried for previously expressing sympathy for some "victims" being led to the guillotine. Her gender and class again underscore the irony of the oppression of those who were supposed to be liberated. During the trial, she suckles her infant, but when she hears "her sentence of death," exclaims "What! for that one word I said, will you part the child and its mother?" Upon receiving "the fatal stroke, the streams of maternal nourishment issued rapidly from her bosom, and, mingled with her blood, bathed her executioner" (*Letters*, 2:3.121–22).

In Williams' sexual allegory, what does woman's blood mean? Her blood of course is simultaneously her own life and the life she gives to her infant. The maternal milk and blood are both nourishing, and the decapitation ends the motherly connection—the "maternal nourishment" sustaining the infant, separated and cut off from the mother by the causal blade that also ends its existence. Unmentioned, the infant simply disappears. The guillotine represents Jacobin hatred of woman's reproductive life: cut off by the sterile blade, this Jacobin "rape" reproduces impotent death. For the eighteenth-century reader, the violation of the woman's motherhood is an assault on her most fundamental nature and role. As is well known, by the end of the eighteenth century, a veritable cult of motherhood had been established and celebrated in England and France—a cult that stressed domestic bliss and the pleasures of breast-feeding—the latter pushed enthusiastically by Enlightenment writers, most notably Rousseau. The Revolution continued this fetishistic celebration of the female breast, simultaneously sexual and maternal, in the voluminous prints of Liberty, Nature, and Equality—allegoric female figures displaying prominent inviting breasts, most amply in Boizot-Clement's drawing of *Republican France Offering Her Breast to All Frenchmen*. In the Festival of Regeneration (10 August 1793), milk (actually water) flowed from the breasts of a gigantic statue of Nature. During the Revolution, woman's fetishized breast simultaneously suggested available sexual pleasures for true republicans and maternal nourishment for the nation.

Both are suggestively combined (and betrayed) in Williams' account, for the mingling of the woman's blood with her milk focuses "the fatal stroke," suggesting that the maternal breast has also been pierced. But the sterile stroke only reproduces another repetitive death. Interestingly, the sterile rapist, the executioner, is "bathed" with this feminine mixture of blood and milk—something difficult to imagine, since the executioner stood behind the victim. If he were bathed it would probably be around the feet—the released milk from the covered breasts of the woman tied face down would mix with the blood but would not, one supposes, fly upwards. The phrase is written, however, to suggest that the executioner has been drenched by both, suggesting the woman's vulnerable exposure and nakedness. The blood and milk staining the executioner seem both a stigmatic reproach and a redemptive purification, as if the woman finally washes the executioner clean in the blood of her sacrifice. Indeed, in Williams' depictions of women ascending the scaffold—valiant victims whose sacrifice shines in the blood shed for parents, loved ones, and the Revolution—another meaning of their blood is their Christly Sacrifice during the Terror, the Calvary of French womanhood.

As the Revolution turns into the Terror, Williams' representation of women changes from the union of the sublime and beautiful to the Jacobin suppression of feminine beauty. The *Letters* correspondingly reflect her anger and anxiety over the Revolution's course. In the final chapter, I explore a different kind of anxiety—the fear that she may have been wrong about the Revolution—and its expression in her ambiguous, ambivalent *Letters*. Specifically, I will show how her imagery contextually contradicts and hence revises her earlier pro-revolutionary pronouncements.

13

Rewriting the Revolution: Contextual Contradiction in Williams' *Letters from France*

I

THERE are two events in the first volume of Williams' *Letters* that are subverted and contextually "unsaid" in the second: her celebration of the Festival of Federation and her visit to the Parisian Jacobin club. The first was the primal scene of the Revolution—an event enchanting her imagination—the second was a defense of maligned Jacobin patriots, stigmatized by reactionaries.

On 13 July, the day before the *Fête,* Williams attended a ceremony at the Cathedral of Notre Dame commemorating the fall of the Bastille and recalling "images" of "horror" prevailing the year before. In the ceremony, she remembers that these words were spoken: "People, your enemies advance .". . They come to bathe their hands in your blood" (*Letters,* 1:1.3). The last phrase reappears repeatedly in the *Letters.* Later, she disappointedly decides that the present French race will not taste the "golden fruit" of revolutionary regeneration, although they "may plant the seeds of general prosperity, sown with toil and trouble, and bathed in blood" (1:4.12). The initial image of counterrevolutionary enemies threatening to bathe their hands in the people's blood now turns into the blood bathing the "seeds" that will eventually flower into "general prosperity." The allusion to *Macbeth* ("toil and trouble"), however, conjures up witches and "bloody hands," suggesting the guilty blood staining revolutionary hands as well. During the Terror, the imagery of bloody hands returns as Barère, a member of the Committee of Public Safety, "bathe[s] his hands in the blood of the innocent" (2:1.171). Likewise, Jacobins "bathed themselves in the blood of the innocent," and the scaffold was daily "bathed with the blood of women" (2:4.23; 2:1.214–15; cf. 289). Jacobin "terror-

215

ists . . . had dyed their hands in the blood of their fellow-citizens" (2:4.152). The Jacobins are allusively associated with the initial counterrevolutionary enemy, whom they easily surpass in "horror" (1:1.3).

In her early celebration of the *Fête,* Williams had noted that the people had enjoyed the day despite the bad weather, especially the torrents of rain: the people, though "drenched by the rain," enthusiastically exclaim that they "are wet for the nation," that the "French [R]evolution is cemented with water, instead of blood" (*Letters,* 1:1.14–15). But this contrast (pure water versus impure blood) soon becomes a bloody imagistic nexus. Initially, the rain falling on the people complements the tears of joy falling from their eyes (9, 13), but later these happy tears and pristine waters retrospectively conjure up tears shed by the Terror's victims as well as terrorist torrents like the *noyades*—"'Quel torrent revolutionnaire que la Loire'" (2:3.38). In this context, the *Fête's* bad weather retrospectively prefigures the ominous weather symbolizing the Terror or victims "drenched" in blood and made "wet for the nation." It is as if the Terror retrospectively stains the joyful waters of the *Fête.* Robespierre's dominion spread from "the ensanguined banks of the Loire to the mourning waters of Vaucluse"; the French republic was "stained with the blood of the patriot, and bathed with the tears of the mourner" (2:1.169; 2:3.1). The initial celebratory images of the *Fête* (the rainy weather, the happy tears, the people shouting they are wet for the nation and that the Revolution is cemented with water, not blood) are conjured up in an ironic, retrospective reversal of the prelapsarian imagery that fallingly prefigures the water and blood of the Terror. Williams fleshes out her lament of the Festival's fall ("Ah, what has then become of the civic festivals that hailed the first glories of the revolution! . . . when every eye melted into tears" [2:2.87]) with the Terror's water and blood.

Jean-Sylvain Bailly, one of the Revolution's founders, is made wet for the nation, forced to stand "drenched in rain" for hours before he is guillotined at the Champ de Mars (*Letters,* 2:1.241), the original site of the Festival of Federation and subsequently, the massacre of 17 July 1791.[1] Lamenting that the Revolution's "magic spell" has been broken, Williams writes that "the waters are tinged with blood" (2:3.85). She spells out her disenchantment by continually subverting her initial imagery. There are explicit, ironic echoes of the people exclaiming that the Revolution is cemented with water instead of blood. Williams quotes Collot d' Herbois (terrorist and member of the Committee of Public Safety) exulting over the massacres of the Lyonnais Girondins: "More heads every day, more heads are falling. . . . What cement for the republic!" (*Letters,* 2:2.163). She notes that the temporary "coalition" of two terrorist committees "had been cemented . . . by crimes and by blood" (2:3.155). Even her optimistic prediction that with the establishment of the 1795 Constitution, the "vessel of the state, built with toil and trouble, and cemented with blood, will soon be launched" (2:3.191–92)—subverts the optimism, since the reader remembers that innocent blood has cemented the Terror and that the allusion to *Macbeth* and the witches again evokes guilty hands bathed in blood. Other intertextual specters possibly haunt these passages, since Jean-Paul Marat had often exclaimed that "[w]e must cement liberty in the blood of the despot" and Madame Roland, Williams' principal revolutionary heroine, had insisted, before she herself was guillotined, that "there must be blood to cement revolution."[2] More significantly, perhaps, just before he was guillotined, Louis XVI expressed his hope that his "blood" would "cement the happiness of the French."[3]

We will recall that, despite the bad weather, the Festival of Federation was a jubilant event and that Williams subsequently uses bad weather to symbolize the Revolution's tragic change. Although Williams sometimes contrasts the beauty of the season or weather with Jacobin terror or "polluted" Paris (*Letters,* 2:1.165, 172), she also contrasts natural vernal beauty with the moral "tempest" that increases with terrorist turbulence (1:4.52; 2:2.1). Her initial comment that the "weather proved very unfavourable during the morning of the Federation" (1:1.14) subsequently turns into an ironic, prophetic prefiguration. For instance, she had also noted, with amusement, the comment of a ci-devant duchess who had told her that the Revolution had changed the seasons and "that the climate of France had become stormy and disagreeable." Likewise, Williams observed that the fall of the Bastille "appeared to the court of Versailles as miraculous as if the course of nature had been changed, and the order of the universe broken" (1:2.28, 37). But she subsequently incorporates this mocked counterrevolutionary criticism into her own imagery. The terrorist government, for instance, metaphorically produces tremendous revolutionary storms:

> The effects resulting from the terrible impulse of revolutionary government upon the moral world, may perhaps be compared to those produced upon the natural scene by the tremendous tempests which sometimes sweep along the western islands; when the mingled ele-

ments rush forth in irresistible fury, when the deluging waters bear
away vegetation, trees, and rocks, and the shrieking whirlwinds shake
the dwellings of man to their foundations.

(*Letters*, 2:2.116–17)

The fact that, in the second volume, she often uses *revolution* and
revolutionary pejoratively[4] reinscribes her disenchantment with
the Revolution, even though she predictably sees a return of philo-
sophic light: "The storm is passed . . . a soft light hovers on the
horizon" (*Letters*, 2:2.117).

During the Festival of Federation, the stormy weather was, at
one magical point, broken. As soon as the king and National Assembly pronounced a solemn oath, "the sun, which had been ob-
scured by frequent showers in the course of the morning, burst
forth" (*Letters*, 1:1.13). Similarly, following the execution of Robespierre, light metaphorically reappears: generous affections "burst
forth" and "summer awakens . . . her fresh foliage and her luxuriant flowers," evoking "the flowers of summer" she had earlier predicted (2:3.2; see 1:2.155). The Jacobins had previously broken
the Revolution's "magical spell" (2:3.85), but the death of Robespierre breaks "the terrible spell" binding France, as "reviving nature" replaces the revolutionary storm (2:3.190). She compares
this return of summer and light to "the reviving influence of a
benign sky" after a "mighty convulsion of nature" (2:4.52). The
conventional imagery of cyclical nature, however, qualifies her suggestion that the Revolution is back on track and "progressing,"
since the return of "light" also suggests that terrorist storms can
return to a Revolution that is imagistically and thematically repetitive. Her optimistic return to joyful imagery is further modified by
the reader's predominant experience: optimistic pronouncements
are subsequently questioned and subverted.

Remembering friends that had been guillotined, Williams feels
that "a funeral veil" seems to "be spread over nature" and that
"neither the consciousness of present, nor the assurance of future
safety, neither the charms of society, nor all the graces, nor all the
wonders of the scenes I am now contemplating, can dissipate the
gloom" (*Letters,* 2:1.4). The words *charms* and *graces* had been
previously associated with her revolutionary romance and subsequently with the poetic "illusion" that allows her to escape the
disenchanting revolutionary world, a world where bad magic dis(-
s)pels good magic.

Williams frequently used images of magic wands reviving nature
or malignant magicians producing evil spells.[5] In the *Letters*, the
imagery of magic wands initially expresses her revolutionary en-

chantment. Wandering among the ruins of the Bastille, she sees the scene "suddenly transformed, as if with the wand of necromancy, into a scene of beauty and of pleasure" (*Letters*, 1:1.21). But after her return to England in September 1790, she reprobated journalistic misrepresentations of the magical land of revolutionary enchantment. Alluding to Burke's *Reflections* ("Amidst assassination, massacre, and confiscation, . . . at the end of every visto, you see nothing but gallows" [*Reflections*, 161, 171–72]), she is weary of hearing about "crimes, assassinations, torture, and death . . . that every street is blackened with a gallows": "To me, the land which these mighty magicians have suddenly covered with darkness, where waving their evil wand, they have reared the dismal scaffold, have clotted the knife of the assassin with gore, have called forth the shriek of despair, and the agony of torture—to me, this land of desolation appeared dressed in additional beauty beneath the genial smile of Liberty" (*Letters*, 1:1.217). The "mighty magicians" are Burkean counterrevolutionaries misrepresenting the Revolution with the malignant pen ("evil wand"), transforming revolutionary "beauty" into a terrorist sublime that is actually a counterrevolutionary "illusion." But the fact that she also tropes her own magical enchantment suggests, ironically, the possibility that she is also conjuring up and seeing a revolutionary illusion. Indeed, the malicious imagery she condemns (French "darkness," magicians waving evil wands, the scaffold, the "shriek of despair") subsequently returns in her representations of Jacobin France.

Maignet, the terrorist representative-on-mission, invades the Vaucluse, destroying its "romantic beauty" with "desolation and death." His mandate is "fatal as the fabled wand of an evil magician," striking "the luxuriant soil with sudden sterility" (*Letters*, 2:3.87, 88). The Jacobin rape of nature is again "sterile," and the terms of the previous counterrevolutionary misrepresentation (a terrorist sublime where she sees revolutionary beauty) are now prophetically realized. She had prefaced her vision of paradise lost with this Burkean lament:

> . . . those enchanting dreams, those dear illusions have for ever vanished . . . the classical haunt of Petrarch no longer presents the delightful images of beauty, of poetry, of passion; the magical spell is broken, the soothing charm is dissolved; the fairy scenes have been polluted, the wizard bowers profaned . . . the waters are tinged with blood . . . shrieks of despair reecho from the cliffs; the guillotine has arisen amidst those consecrated shades where love alone has reared its altars!
>
> (2:3.85)

I have suggested that Burke's lament for chivalry reverberates through this passage and that the latter contextually criticizes her earlier "enchanting dreams" by making her revolutionary "vision" a self-deceptive "illusion." More pertinently, the imagery reinscribes as "reality" the previous counterrevolutionary misrepresentation, for here is the darkened "land of desolation"—"the shriek of despair" and the raised "scaffold" (guillotine) that she earlier dismissed as a counterrevolutionary illusion (1:1.217). Indeed, her subsequent identification with Burke reechoes in the tribulations of the young lovers, Charles and Adelaide, harried by the Jacobin government. The despondent Adelaide sees "the guillotine behind [the] trees," and it looms in Williams' imagination, compelling her to acknowledge that Burke's "gloomy prediction" had been fulfilled: "I thought of that passage in Mr. Burke's book, 'In the groves of *their* academy, at the end of every vista, I see the gallows!'" (*Letters,* 2:3.106; 2:2.89–90; see *Reflections,* 171–72).

This reflexive, contextual unsaying of previous positions is similarly repeated in her visit to the Jacobin club, another embarrassing event that reechoes through the *Letters.* In her account of the visit (*Letters,* 1:2.106–16), she had defended the Jacobins as patriots who had been misrepresented by their antirevolutionary enemies. Since the Jacobins subsequently become the heinous betrayers of the Revolution, she responds to her mistaken account in a variety of ways. In the first volume, Williams had objected that revolutionaries were being compared "with the most rude, ferocious, and barbarous levellers that ever existed" (1:1.219). Likewise, in her visit to the Jacobin club, she implicitly mocks anti-Jacobin misrepresentations: "To the Jacobins is owing every outrage committed by popular fury, and every treasonable design conceived by the aristocratic factions. The Jacobins are contrivers of all disorder, the levellers of all distinctions, and the enemies of all subordination. It is their intention to overturn the present system of government, and divide the French empire into eighty-three republics, governed by Jacobins" (1:2.107). "Such is the cry," she remarks, of aristocrats and reactionaries, but it becomes her cry as well, since she incorporates this "misrepresentation" into her subsequent anti-Jacobin critique.

She ascribes to the Jacobins "every outrage" and "every treasonable design." In the midst of the Terror, the Jacobins are "horrible levellers" who destroy commerce and establish "an equality of misery, throughout the republic" (*Letters,* 2:2.166). She subsequently affirms the previous (mis)representation of those insisting that the Jacobins intended "to overthrow the present system of

government, and divide the French empire into eighty-three republics": the Jacobin leaders intended "the immediate overthrow of
what remained of the then-existing system, and meant to establish
a government of municipalities, Mr. Burke's forty-four thousand
republics" (1:3.9–10). Her affirmation of Burke's criticism underscores her allusive adoption of the "misrepresentations" she previously mocked. The misrepresentations are retrospectively true.
Thus when she noted that the Jacobins had been accused of "every
outrage committed by popular fury, and every design conceived
by the aristocratic factions" (1:2.107), she subsequently accuses
them of the same things: they are "guilty of the late outrages that
have been committed in Paris, of exciting the people to revolt and
assassination; of being concerned with that [aristocratic] faction
which, by means of those disorders, had hoped to effect an overthrow of the government, and raise a dictator on its ruins, of whose
power they were to partake" (1:4.83–84). The Jacobins are behind
both the "popular" *canaille* and the aristocratic Counterrevolution;
hence they are "traitors and conspirators against their country"
(83). The "faction of the Mountain" had been "purchased by foreign
courts"—a "coalition" that produced anarchy so that the people
would reaccept tyranny (1:3.24). The "leaders of the Mountain
acted as auxiliaries of the aristocracy" (1:4.49; cf. 50, 54 and
2:1.78). Since, for Williams, Jacobins comprise the Mountain,
they are cryptocounterrevolutionaries, but she herself valorizes
representations she previously implied were false and counterrevolutionary.

There are other allusive echoes of her initial Jacobin visit. After
articulating the exaggerated misrepresentations of the Jacobins,
she had provided the sympathetic account of the Jacobins' "numerous" friends:

> Those persons declare that they never enter the hall of the Jacobins
> without respect, because they consider it as the cradle and the sanctu-
> ary of French liberty. They are convinced that those watchful, vigilant,
> jealous, noisy Jacobins are its best guardians; and that but for the
> extensive influence which they have acquired, in consequence of their
> correspondence with other patriotic societies, established in every part
> of the kingdom, with whom they constantly maintain a chain of connec-
> tion, the infant liberty of France would have been crushed in its birth
> by its numerous and formidable enemies.
>
> *(Letters, 1:2.110–11)*

Two series later, however, this Jacobin defense is contextually
criticized.

The "vigilant, jealous" (i.e., suspicious) Jacobins, who were liberty's "best guardians" and without whose endeavors "the infant liberty would have been crushed," are "now endeavoring to crush in its birth that liberty which they contributed to create, and of which they were so long the jealous guardians" (*Letters,* 1:4.55). The condemnatory sentence contrapuntally unsays the previous affirmative ones by allusively conjuring up not only the contradictory context but by repeating the very diction and imagery that it now reverses: the Jacobins betray their friends' representations; they murder the liberty they were supposed to defend. Williams does not explicitly refer to her "visit," a visit that occurred hundreds of pages back in a prelapsarian past, but her diction and imagery provide a contextual intersection contradicting her previous representation as a "mistake." Her contextual unsaying of her previous representations is also a revisionist rewriting of these representations.[6] Thus, the Jacobin club, characterized "as the cradle and the sanctuary of French liberty" (1:2.110) is changed by "the demon of Jacobinism" from "the cradle of infant liberty into a den of desolation and carnage" (2:4.128). Likewise, the Jacobins, liberty's "best guardians" (1:2.110), push for a show trial of the Girondins and are now sarcastically characterized as "guardians of the public weal," as are Jacobin terrorists in Lyon (2:1.156; 2:2.156). The Jacobins praised for preserving liberty by establishing a correspondence "with the other patriotic societies . . . with whom they constantly maintain a chain of connection" (1:2.110–11) are later the conspirators who make "proselytes to their system of anarchy by their affiliations and correspondence in the departments" (2:1.63). Embarrassed by her earlier visit to the Jacobins, Williams overturns her previous representations by reinscribing counterrevolutionary misrepresentations she now validates.

II

The Du Fossé episode also illustrates how she rewrites her previous prelapsarian history, especially since it signifies the revolutionary triumph of truth and justice. One day after the Bastille falls, Du Fossé feels secure for the first time in years: "no longer embittered with the dread of being *torn* from his family . . . It was then that he no more feared that his repose at night would be broken by the entrance of ruffians prepared to *drag* him to dungeons, the darkness of which was never visited by the blessed beams of day!" (*Letters,* 1:1.189–90, my emphasis). Although this never again happens to Du Fossé, it subsequently seems to happen to everyone else, including Williams, who was awakened at night and imprisoned. Since the Du Fossé episode is a domestic microcosm of the liberation of France's national family, it is significant that the subsequent imagery of friends and family members being dragged away suggests not only a return to the past but a tragedy of macrocosmic proportions.

During the September Massacres, the "executioners of that night . . . drag[ged] forth those victims to modes of death at which nature shudders" (*Letters*, 1:3.5). Williams sees her Girondin friends "torn" from her "forever" and "dragged to execution" (2:1.4); Girondin deputies are "dragged . . . to the scaffold" (81); Parisians see their "fellow-citizens dragged daily through their streets to the scaffold" (86); an "unfortunate young lady" sees "her father, her mother, and several of her relations dragged to the scaffold" (2:2.104); "unhappy [Vendean] fugitives" are ironically "dragged to the tree of liberty" and "coolly murdered" (2:3.34). A young aristocratic daughter sees her father "stripped" and "dragged" to Paris "to be tried" and then "dragged out of the court" to be executed (2:4.123–24). A young mademoiselle sees "her beloved father dragged to the scaffold" (153). During "the reign of Robespierre," the "gendarmes" were "constantly employed in dragging [Robespierre's] victims to prison" (149–50). Williams herself has witnessed similar scenes, and if she has been "led into regions of hitherto undiscovered beauty and sublimity," she has also been "dragged . . . into dens of undescribed and unknown monsters, whose existence we had never till now believed" (2:3.51). As the Terror repeats and yet exceeds the nightmare of the past, Williams' republican romance becomes a Gothic novel of unrelieved horror.

Chaumette, a key member of the Paris Commune, calls for an end to the Terror: "for the father no longer to demand in vain the liberty of his son unjustly torn from him; the husband that of his wife, and the brother that of his brother" (*Letters*, 2:3.68–69). After Thermidor, Williams enters the Revolutionary Tribunal and feels an "emotion of the deepest horror on entering the hall, where so many persons who were dear to me had . . . been dragged to death" (2:4.44). She imagines the famous English lawyer Thomas Erskine condemning Fouquier-Tinville (the public prosecutor, 1793–94), describing how "unhappy victims of each sex and every age" were "dragged slowly through crowds" to the guillotine (47). In retrospect, Augustin Du Fossé's (and Williams') confidence that he (and, implicitly, everyone else in France) would never again be dragged from the repose of his family (1:1.190) contextually implodes. Indeed, the Du Fossé episode constitutes a principal contradiction in the *Letters,* since Du Fossé's domestic tragedy represents the injustice of the Old Regime, and his "repose" justifies the Revolution's triumph: "I am glad you think that a friend's having been persecuted, imprisoned, maimed, and almost murdered, under the ancient government of France, is a good excuse for loving the revolution" (1:1.195). But as Williams' many friends are subsequently imprisoned, mutilated, and murdered under the revolutionary government of France, it is, by the same criteria (repeatedly amplified), a good excuse for hating the Revolution as well. Even though Williams tries to distinguish the prelapsarian Revolution from postlapsarian Terror, she either contradicts and "unsays" her optimistic predictions of the revolutionary future or reinscribes and valorizes the counterrevolutionary misrepresentations she had previously dismissed. In the *Enquiry,* Burke had referred to a terrorist sublime "too close" for aesthetic comfort. Similarly, in Williams' *Letters,* the Terror is too close to the Revolution, resulting in an ambiguous mix belying her Girondist distinction.

Similarly, the imagery of prisons and gloomy dungeons reinforces her contextual criticism of her previous ideological naiveté. In the beginning, she associates the Old Regime with these gloomy dungeons: the old French constitution is "connected in [her] mind with the image of a friend [Du Fossé] confined in the gloomy recesses of a dungeon" (*Letters,* 1:1.72). This constitution, like the Bastille, is an "old gloomy Gothic fabric" the French "have laid in ruins" (1:1.68). The Bastille itself is "a gloomy fortress" consisting of "gloomy dungeons" (1:2.94; 1:3.5) that "still haunt" her imagination after her visit. She contrasts its gloomy darkness with the superficial splendor of Versailles—dazzling light that does not keep her from seeing the gloomy despotism that she suggests supported the splendor (1:1.83). She had, similarly, referred to the "despotic throne" that shines "like the radiance of lightning, while all around is involved in gloom and horror" and prayed that "no such strong contrast of light and shade again exist in the political system of France!" (1:1.25; cf. 2:1.257).

The strong contrast, however, returns in a series of ironic historical repetitions through which she describes revolutionary repression with the same gloomy imagery that "still haunt[s]" her. Louis XVI is forcibly removed "from the radiant palace of Versailles" to the "gloomy tower of the Temple" (*Letters,* 1:3.1), where he exists in the "gloomy solitude of his prison" (1:4.32). Her imagery suggests a repetition of both the feudal past and the "contrast" she had prayed never to see again (1:1.25). Likewise, the murderous, revolutionary *lanterne* conjures up "gloomy images"—"so dark a shade . . . thrown across the glories of the revolution" (1:1.81). The king's sister, Elizabeth, is also imprisoned in the Temple, "the gloomy tower where she was immured" (2:2.51). After the execution of the king and queen, the only surviving member of the royal family is the younger daughter, "a blooming beauty confined in gloomy towers" (2:3.5). The confinement of royal "beauty" coincides with the Terror's attack on "multitudes in the gloom of prisons," awaiting the guillotine (2:3.93). A friend of Williams is confined for fifteen months "in one of the most gloomy prisons of Paris" (2:4.55). Through her imagery, Williams repeatedly suggests Jacobin repetitions of the old despotism she previously said could not return.

The September Massacres make her wonder if European nations will consider democratic anarchy worse than the old despotism, with "its gloomy towers and its solitary dungeons" (*Letters,* 1:3.19). She apostrophizes the slain "heroes" of 14 July, asking if it was "for this that ye overthrew the towers of the Bastille, and burst open its gloomy dungeons?" (1:3.5). This was also the crucial question asked by Wollstonecraft in *The French Revolution* (*Works,* 6:123), and Williams' cumulative answer resounds negatively.

The linkage between old despotism and new terror reappears in the imagery of subterranean cells. Augustin Du Fossé, the archetypal victim of the Old Order, is initially imprisoned by his tyrannous father in a convent converted into a dungeon (a telling connection), where he languishes in "a subterraneous cell" (*Letters,* 1:1.148; cf. 213). In Williams' earlier visit to the Bastille, she noted that many "subterraneous cells" had been discovered "underneath a piece of ground which was [e]nclosed within the walls of the Bastille." In this prison within a prison, despotism's "horrid secrets" were "disclosed": the remains of prisoners who had died silently, "skeletons . . . with irons still fastened on their decaying bones" (1:1.23–24).

Later, however, Williams herself is imprisoned in a convent, and her Girondin friends are "entombed in subterraneous dungeons" (*Letters,* 2:1.178). The brother of her good friend, Rabut de St. Etienne, is imprisoned in a "subterraneous dungeon" (2:1.210), just as the generous and brave Madame de L——, a pregnant, aristocratic Girondin, is "placed in a subterraneous grated chamber" (2:4.62). Williams' initial condemnatory imagery (the Old Regime's gloomy prisons and subterraneous cells) returns to indict the new Jacobin order, suggesting another repetition of the oppressive past.

The history of the Revolution, however, is also the history of its own repetitive prisons: "I have seen the Conciergerie, that abode of horror, that anti-chamber of the tomb. I have seen those infectious cells, where the prisoners breathed contagion, where the walls are in some places stained with the blood of the massacres of September, . . . I have seen the chamber, where the persons condemned by the revolutionary tribunal submitted to the preparatory offices of the executioner" (*Letters,* 2:2.99–100). The Conciergerie was the oldest prison in Paris, especially notorious during the Revolution for its crampt, cavelike vaults and underground *cachots* surrounded with walls ten to twelve feet thick. Prison authorities sealed air vents to prevent escape and permitted doors opened only to bring in food or remove waste. During the September Massacres, 378 of its 508 inmates were murdered. After the formation of the Revolutionary Tribunal (10 March 1793), it was infamously known as "the antechamber of the guillotine" and, in a phrase coined by Jacques-Claude Beugnot, "a vast antechamber of death"—a phrase Williams alludes to. Political prisoners such as Charlotte Corday, Pierre Vergniaud, J.-S. Bailly, Marie Antoinette, G.-J. Danton, Madame Roland, J.-R. Hébert, and Madame du Barry awaited trial and execution behind its walls.[7] For Williams, Jacobin terror continually repeats itself. Just as the Conciergerie's walls are "stained with the blood of the massacres of September," Williams contends that after the National Convention had passed the Law of 22 Prairial (10 June 1794), the September Massacres were, in effect, repeated, albeit institutionally: the revolutionary authorities invented a conspiracy-in-the-prisons myth—a "pretext" for the murders of political prisoners "dragged . . . to the guillotine" (*Letters* 2:2.98, 100–1).

Williams also connects old repression and the terror that exceeds it by repetitions of causal "madness." The link between imprisonment and madness first occurs in her narration of Du Fossé's history. When Du Fossé is imprisoned, another young man languishes in an adjoining cell by virtue of a *lettre de cachet* obtained by his evil, aristocratic mother. His younger brother is later imprisoned for ten years, via the *lettre,* by the same "unrelenting mother," angry that he had committed some unnamed "indiscretions." When the Revolution occurs and the National Assembly orders "all the prisons . . . thrown open," it is too late: "His reason was gone forever! and he was led out of his prison, at the age of five and twenty, a maniac" (*Letters,* 1:1.210–12). Similarly, during the Terror, Williams narrates the history of a young, imprisoned girl who sees her imprisoned parents "dragged to the scaffold" and consequently becomes "bereft of reason." When Robespierre falls, "the dungeon of this unfortunate young lady is thrown open—but . . . for her, redress and freedom have come too late—her reason is gone for ever!" (2:2.104–5). In Williams' narration of belated liberation, the two episodes contextually recall each other.

If, however, under the Old Regime, individual parents unnaturally imprisoned their aristocratic sons, Williams indicts the Jacobin regime for imprisoning and killing entire families. This familial genocide both exceeds and recontextualizes her prior indictment of the Old Regime: Du Fossé had been "persecuted, imprisoned, and *almost* murdered, under the ancient government of France" and hence Williams loves the liberating Revolution (*Letters,* 1:1.195; my emphasis). But as liberation becomes imprisonment and doors are "thrown open" belatedly, her history of terrorist prisons repeatedly mocks her previous celebration of liberated France: "a country which could no longer boast a Bastille; a country where iron cages were broken down, where dungeons were thrown open, and where justice was henceforth to shed a clear and steady light, without one dark shade of relief from *lettres-de-cachet*" (*Letters,* 1:1.193–94).[8] When the prisoners of the Luxembourg are finally released in July 1794 and ecstatic crowds gather to greet them, the reader has an ironic sense of *déjà vu,* as if we are witnessing again the liberation of the Bastille and another repetitive cycle of revolutionary history (see 2:3.185).

III

There are additional examples of how Williams subsequently rewrites her previous pronouncements. In preterrorist France, she wishes that antirevolutionary "critics" would not "repeat" the "trite remark, that the French have gone too far" (*Letters,* 1:1.68); she wonders rhetorically who could be so presumptuous "to assert" (i.e., Burke, *Reflections,* 182) that there is nothing left to discover in "the science of government" or "to say to the human understanding, thus far shalt thou go, and no farther?" (*Letters,* 1:2.71).[9] In the next series, however, she begins to modify her criticism, conceding contextually that "though the French may not be going too far, they seem to be going too fast" (1:3.223). But as the Revolution implodes, she herself repeats the "trite remark," praising the federalist *Marseillais* who appear at the National Convention and demand law and order: "They have said to [the Jacobins'] enthusiastic zeal, 'Thus far thou shalt go, and no farther'" (1:4.19). Suddenly the progressive Revolution has excessively gone too far. Referring to the Jacobin attack on the National Convention (31 May 1793), she notes that the Jacobins had passed the Rubicon and "had gone too far to recede" (2:1.73). In the last series, she speaks positively about "finishing the revolution": "To finish the revolution was an idea of all others the most soothing to the public mind, which, agitated for six years past by the most convulsive political tempests, felt perhaps, less the love of order, than the irresistible desire of repose" (2:4.171–72). By wishing the Revolution to be completed, she wishes it to go no farther, and hence she resays what she formerly condemned. In addition, the "convulsive political tempests" that have been agitating France "for six years" suggests that the Revolution was marred from the very beginning.

Williams' references to "tombs" also illustrate how her contrapuntal imagery contradicts her previous statements. Defending the revolutionaries against their critics, she had earlier proclaimed that the former had "invaded the grand monuments of the dead, and thrown open the melancholy tombs of the living" (Letters, 1:2.72; cf. A Tour in Switzerland, 1:21). The first clause is a sarcastic caricature of counterrevolutionary complaints that revolutionaries have no respect for the past. Indeed, it is, as we might suspect, a reference to the Reflections and Burke's veneration for the "grand monuments of the dead, which continue the regards and connexions of life beyond the grave" (Reflections, 272). Williams' second clause celebrates concrete revolutionary accomplishments: not concerned with the "dead," the French have liberated people from cells, prisons, and convents—"the melancholy tombs of the living." Later, when she discusses the Terror, however, these tombs reappear as Jacobin prisons; the Conciergerie, we will remember, is an "anti-chamber of the tomb" (Letters, 2:2.99). When the first prisoners are released from the Luxembourg, crowds gather to see them "snatched from their living tombs" (2:3.185). What she formerly mocked returns to haunt her.

Her initial sarcastic reference to revolutionaries who invade the monuments of the dead probably alludes to Burke's criticism of English Revolutionaries who, he suggests, may replicate the desecrations of the 1640s: "Do these theorists mean to imitate some of their predecessors, who dragged the bodies of our antient sovereigns out of the quiet of their tombs" (Reflections, 107). Burke later warns that the spirit of revolutionary vice (actually *old* vice) "assumes a new body" and is "renovated in its new organs with . . . fresh vigour": "It walks abroad; it continues its ravages; whilst [the French] are gibbeting the carcass, or demolishing the tomb" (*Reflections*, 248). Obsessed with an evil past, the French are terrifying themselves "with ghosts and apparitions" while the real monster (in another form) "walks abroad."[10] Both passages are *loci classici* of antirevolutionary criticism: revolutionaries as monstrous iconoclasts who invade graves and monuments and Frankenstein-like monsters who are created and rejuvenated out of dead limbs and organs. Lee Sterrenburg notes that in *Frankenstein*, Mary Shelley was drawing "upon political images and values that were already current," having been established by Burke and other anti-Jacobin writers: "She echoes such standard anti-Jacobin motifs as grave-robbing, reviving the dead, and monsters who destroy their own creators. Conservatives had often used these images to warn of the dangers of reform. They pictured the radical regeneration of man in demonic terms, as the unleashing of parricidal monsters and spectres from the grave."[11] All this impinges on Williams' subsequent depictions of monstrous revolutionaries.

Her sarcastic reference to the invaded monuments of the dead retrospectively prefigures the Jacobin monsters who desire "to throw down all the monuments of taste and genius, and to destroy all literature in one impious conflagration" (*Letters*, 1:3.24). Burke's allusion to English revolutionaries dragging dead "sovereigns" from their graves and Williams' reference to the invaded monuments of the dead intertextually conflate in her account of the desecration of the basilica of St. Denis, which had been the mausoleum of French kings since the sixth century. The background is as follows. On 1 August 1793, the National Convention had decided to commemorate the overthrow of the French monarchy (10 August 1792), decreeing that "The tombs and mausoleums of the former kings . . . all over the republic will be destroyed on 10 August." Several days later (6–8 August 1793), the desecration of the tombs began, and in October (12–25) the "embalmed bodies" were exhumed and thrown into a common pit. Among the desecrated kings was Williams' favorite—Henry IV, whose corpse was also "thrown unceremoniously into the Bourbin pit."[12]

Even though she does not specifically mention her beloved Henry, Williams records her outrage for "this violation of the dead" (*Letters*, 2:2.191):

> The bodies of these monarchs and heroes were not treated with equal respect; for, as the edict had gone forth against every vestige of royalty,

and every mark or remnant of aristocracy, the tombs in which they
had been for ages quietly inured were forced to open their ponderous
jaws; and those furious Jacobins, worse than "the hellish rout that tore
the Thracian bard in Rhodope," had the satisfaction to see the bones
and ashes of the long line of their Charles's, Henries, and Louis . . .
become the prey of famished dogs, and the sport of the winds.

(190)

In *A Tour in Switzerland* (1798), she was still outraged, referring
to "that sacrilegious period when the tombs of the illustrious dead
were savaged by [Jacobin] cannibals."[13] In the *Letters,* the "long
line" of French kings allusively echoes "the long line of Banquo,"
conjuring up the regicidal guilt that we have seen disturbing both
Williams and Wollstonecraft—here, however, projected on to frenzied Jacobins. Her citation from *Paradise Lost* (7.34–35; Williams
misquotes "wild Rout" as "hellish rout") equates the desecration of
the royal corpses with the murder of the poet Orpheus by frenzied
Bacchantes: she associates Jacobin necropolitan terror with
"mad," orgiastic ferocity.

She later refers again to Jacobin monsters and their necropha-
gous legacy by quoting Vergniaud's "famous speech on the trial of
Lewis XVI" (31 December 1792), in which he formulates the Jacobin response to French citizens asking for bread: "Go to the
charnel-houses, and tear from the earth the palpitating limbs of
the corpses we have heaped together. Blood and corpses—these
are all they have to offer you" (*Letters,* 2:3.81–82).[14] In Williams'
formulation, Jacobin hatred of the "dead" past ironically feeds their
present necrophilic frenzies. Corpses, monsters, and specters—all
the anti-Jacobin imagery of the Counterrevolution—informs her
Girondist discourse. In the first of the *Letters on a Regicide Peace*
(1796), Burke had written that "out of the murdered monarchy in
France has arisen a vast, tremendous, unformed spectre, in a far
more terrifick guise than any which ever yet have overpowered the
imagination, and subdued the fortitude of man." The Revolution is
a "hideous phantom" overpowering "those who could not believe
it was possible she could at all exist." In Williams' *Letters,* the
Jacobins are "hideous spectres" who have "haunted" the altar of
Liberty (*Letters,* 2:2.214). Even after Robespierre's death, the
possibility of his ghoulish return—like Burke's revolutionary spirit
that "assumes a new body" and "transmigrates" (*Reflections,*
248)—haunts her: "Although the great conspirator against the liberty of France had fallen, the colossal spectre of tyranny rising
from his tomb still hovered round the national convention" (*Let-*

ters, 2:4.2). The specter haunting Williams' imagination is similar to the one haunting the counterrevolutionary imagination.[15] As tombs are invaded and Jacobin monsters assume even more horrible forms, Williams ironically eats her earlier sarcastic words, reabsorbing the counterrevolutionary critique into her anti-Jacobin discourse.

In addition to unsaying previous positions or reaffirming what she previously denied, Williams' literary allusions also betray an ambivalence toward the Revolution, belying her favorable predictions. Her allusions subvert her celebrations of the Revolution by contextually contradicting the very thing she says. Confronting the contradiction that French revolutionary armies were invading "the Belgic provinces," despite the National Assembly's "former abjuration of conquest" (that is, the declaration of 22 May 1790), Williams observes that since French armies had been "checked" by enemy forces, the French had been taught a punitive lesson and would "probably relinquish their Quixote expeditions in favor of liberty": that is, the contradictory compulsion to force people to be free (*Letters,* 1:4.71). She then quotes a passage from *Paradise Lost* to illustrate that the French have heretofore "only proved that the passage from despotism to liberty is long and terrible— like the passage of Milton's Satan from hell to earth, when

> His ear was peal'd
> With noises loud and ruinous; — —
> — — — — — as if this frame
> Of heav'n were falling, and these elements
> In mutiny had from her axle torn
> The steadfast earth.
>
> (1:4.72)

The reference (*Paradise Lost* 2.920–21, 924–27) is to Satan's uncomfortable journey through chaos to reach earth, where he will commence mankind's fall, but not before creating another "passage" from hell to earth—the track by which Sin and Death follow him (see 11.1024–25).

Williams' allusion actually subverts her point that the French are following the difficult passage from "despotism to liberty," since Satan's passage and intent is to subvert and subsequently to introduce satanic despotism into the invaded earth. Since the satanic army has already considered different invasion schemes (*PL* 2.45– 105, 310–89) and will soon follow Satan, Sin, and Death's passage, the allusion ironically evokes the invading French armies it is supposed to "check." Williams reinforces this reading by noting that

once "the French have passed 'the wild abyss,'" then Europeans
will be able to judge the true nature of the Revolution (*Letters*,
1:4.72). She apparently means to suggest that once the French
pass beyond the momentary confusion (like Satan passing through
Chaos), they will proceed "to liberty." The "wild abyss," however,
is the empire of Chaos through which the "wary fiend" (*PL* 2.917),
"once past," commences the track Sin and Death follow in the
postlapsarian future, "soon after when man fell" (1023). It is at this
point that the devils, "spirits perverse," also enter the earth, "this
frail World," to "tempt or punish mortals" (*PL* 1030–32). Since
Williams compares France's passage to Satan's, her allusive prediction of the passage from "despotism to liberty" contextually places
the revolutionary future in a postlapsarian time of sin and death.
Her allusion turns into a counterrevolutionary reading of satanic
French armies invading the vulnerable, prelapsarian European
world, creating the conditions for its corresponding "fall." One can,
of course, argue that Williams uses the allusion carelessly by not
thinking it through, but she prefaces the quotation by specifically
comparing France's passage to Satan's. The discrepancy between
what she says she is allusively saying and what she actually says
is too glaring—it is another example of intertextual blindness in
eighteenth-century discourse.

Towards the end of the *Letters,* after documenting Jacobin Terror, Williams typically insists that "anarchy and vandalism can return no more" and celebrates the "foundation" of (yet another)
French Constitution (the third in five years)—the 1795 Constitution, which, she predicts, will inaugurate a new enlightened era:
"The new constitution, like the spear of Romulus thrown with a
strong hand, will fix itself in the earth, so that no human force can
root it up, and will become, like the budding wood, the object of
a people's veneration" (*Letters,* 2:4.179). The allusion is to Plutarch's life of "Romulus," which she probably read in Dryden's
translation (cf. Williams, *Poems,* 2:17). The reference is not, as
one might expect, to a Roman "foundation" act but to a "holy
cornel tree," where "Romulus once, to try his strength, threw a
dart from the Aventine Mount, the staff of which was made of
cornel, which stuck so deep into the ground, that no one of many
that tried could pluck it up, and the soil being fertile, gave nourishment to the wood, which sent forth the branches, and produced a
cornel stock of considerable bigness."[16] Williams predicts that the
1795 Constitution, "like the budding wood," will become "the object of a people's veneration" (179); Plutarch says that the cornel
wood was preserved by posterity and "worship[ed] as one of the

most sacred things."[17] Although Romulus was the mythic founder of the Roman monarchy and not the Roman republic, the allusion works up to this point: like the firm spear transformed into a cornel tree and rooted firmly in the fertile earth, the French Constitution will be firmly established and venerated by posterity. But this is not the end of the cornel tree or Plutarch's account. In the same paragraph, the Romans proceed to build a wall around the sacred tree, and when it seemed "to pine and wither," they douse it with water: "But when Caius Caesar . . . was repairing the steps about it, some of the labourers digging too close, the roots were destroyed, and the tree withered."[18] In the end, the spear of Romulus, transformed into the sacred wood, dies. The entire allusion subversively deracinates Williams' budding prophecy by situating the 1795 Constitution within the con(text) of Plutarch's narrative. Ending with an allusive act of mythic revolutionary faith (cf. *Letters,* 2:3.192), Williams, like the revolutionaries themselves, allusively sanctifies the new era and the "beginning" with the authoritative tradition of the past. Rather than establish a new, mythical beginning, however, the allusion suggests another repetitive failure: the 1795 Constitution fated to wither like Romulus's budding spear (there was yet another doomed French Constitution in 1799 after the coup of 18 Brumaire). The allusion reinforces the readers' experience of the *Letters:* Williams insists that "anarchy and vandalism can return no more" (179), but we have heard this before, insistently and repetitively. Like Wollstonecraft's ambiguous history, Williams' Revolution is exposed and written "out."

IV

In retrospect, Williams' *Letters* are notable for paradoxical reasons. Historically, they encapsulate Girondist readings of the Revolution, some of which were apparently lost. For instance, while Williams argues, correctly, that the Jacobins tried to discredit the Girondists by linking the federalist revolt with the Vendean revolt, she also insists that the Jacobins initially allowed "royalist" armies to escape or be victorious (allowing them to link up with enemy emigrants and the English) so that they could later justify their ferocious repression (*Letters,* 2:3.29, 31–32). She connects the repression in the counterrevolutionary Vendée with the repression of the federalist cities, arguing that both were an interconnected plot to exterminate rebels and patriots (2:2.150–68; 2:3.5, 26, 36). With regard to the Vendée, she was, as far as I know, the first

British contemporary to insist that the Jacobins were engaged in systematic genocide ("the general extermination of the inhabitants of the Vendée" 2:3.13)—an argument that has recently been addressed by twentieth-century scholarship.[19]

Williams understands that history is often written by the conqueror: "Of [the Vendean] war we yet know but little, and what we do know is only the history written by the party which persecuted" (*Letters,* 2:2.193). She hence sees a connection between military and historical suppression, and her sources are often revealingly Jacobin: she quotes members of the Convention and the Committee of Public Safety who mandate the Vendée's "extermination" (2:3.12–15, 20–21, 26, 36, 49, 72). More than any other British contemporary, Williams also evokes the atmosphere of both the prelapsarian Revolution and the subsequent Terror. Her depiction of the Revolution as a theatrical event impinges on a dimension fundamental to the Revolution: from the beginning, both revolutionaries and counterrevolutionaries depicted the Revolution as a stupendous dramatic event played out on the world's stage. The revolutionaries represented themselves as actors, observed by the world, whether through dramatic speeches in the Assembly and Convention or dramatic events on French and foreign soil. They presented themselves in a theatrical language of true "parts" and roles and discredited their enemies as false actors, counterrevolutionary betrayers whose "masks" and "disguises" were to be ripped off, so that their insincerity could be exposed to the world. Williams' *Letters* embody the themes that are currently being explored by contemporary criticism: the Revolution as theater, the link between revolution and Romanticism (the superiority of passion and the heart, the Absolute and the Ideal), *sensibilité* and sentimentalism, the obsession with transparency, with sincerity and pure emotion—all the resounding *leitmotifs* characterizing revolutionary and counterrevolutionary discourse.

"I am a spectator of the representation," she had exclaimed at the beginning of 1793 (*Letters,* 1:3.2), and her *Letters* thematically crystallize the variety of ways the Revolution was represented in the 1790s—as a dramatic *representation,* "[t]he exhibition of character and action upon the stage; the . . . performance of a play" (*OED* no. 3), or a *representation,* a statement, account or presentation of facts, especially "one intended to convey a particular view or impression of a matter" (*OED* no. 4), "a formal and serious statement of facts, reasons, or arguments, made with a view to effecting some change . . . etc." (*OED* no. 5), "the operation of the mind in forming a clear image or concept" (*OED* no. 6b), "[t]he fact of standing for, or for some other thing or person" (*OED* no. 7). She herself becomes the primary representative of the true Girondin Revolution as well as a victim of the Terror "violating" the "National representation" (*Letters,* 2:1.69, 71, 87, 259, 265)— breaking the correspondence between the Revolution and reality— all that the Revolution meant and "stood for" in the halcyon days of 1790.

More fundamentally, Williams seems more conscious than her canonical contemporaries that history is, in many ways, a story that highlights certain facts, while ignoring or downplaying others—that it depends on a mode of emplotment determining how the story will be told as well as how it will be resolved. She seems to realize that, as Hayden White and others have noted, the writing of history necessarily involves the selection and arrangement of facts to make sense of conflicting or ambiguous information. In acknowledging the fictive dimension of history, Williams sees that it is part of the imaginative apprehension of human reality—the interpretive reading "in" and "out" that constitutes her version of the French Revolution. Williams' history is openly her own personal history and experience of the Revolution—the vehicle and tenor of her *Letters* are wedded to the Revolution she contradicts but never ultimately betrays. In perhaps a self-conscious reaction to her sexual demonization in England, she is forever faithful to the first Revolution she lovingly represents. She contextually criticizes her early errors and the deviant Terror, but never her heartfelt experience of the true Revolution. In contrast to her contemporaries, like Paine, who distinguish between "sober history" and reactionary theater, repeating the conventional fiction of Enlightenment historiography,[20] Williams openly acknowledges that her personal fiction is her French Revolution and not, as her contemporaries present it, *the* French Revolution. Like everyone else writing about the French Revolution, Williams of course believed that her version was truer to the Revolution's reality, and she illustrated (in Leo Damrosch's words) that "every piece of writing, whether it presents itself as fiction or not, is committed to a version of reality."[21] In acknowledging the fictive dimensions of human history that her contemporaries denyingly disguised, Williams, in her vulnerable *Letters,* paradoxically illustrated a more complex understanding of both herself and the history that her contemporaries continued to write.

Epilogue

THE French Revolution was radically different from any historical event that preceded it, yet writers in the 1790s continually connected it to past paradigms. In one respect, this was due to the human need to make sense and explain the strange and unrecognizable by comparisons with previous models. Even contrasts with these models helped define the Revolution's identity. Prorevolutionary writers had initially recurred to the paradigms of radical British and American tradition which the Revolution revivified in ways that seemed contemporaneously new. Subsequently, they returned to the paradigms of "reactionary" history to explain the Revolution's fall. In both cases, the past that the Revolution had supposedly transcended ironically provided the Revolution its causal significance. After 1792 and with the crisis in representation, the Revolution resembled "repeatable" fallen history: Roman dictators and the fall of the republic, Goths and Vandals (Helen Maria Williams, *Letters*, 2:1, 234, 239), Norman robbers, traitorous Tories, and other indelible traces of the old feudal order. When the Revolution seemed additionally to repeat its own fallen history, it was as if its original significance were being parodied and mocked. There were, of course, initial comparisons with the American and Glorious Revolutions, but these parallels could not be sustained after 1792. Instead of the creation of a new time and history, the Revolution, in the end, seemed complicit with the past it had defined itself against. The past became a "cause" of both the Revolution and its betrayal. Confronted with their original representations of a revolution they no longer recognized, radical writers changed their mode of emplotment from Romantic and Comic to Tragedy and Satire. From the beginning revolutionary rhetoric had been overdetermined: it had claimed too much. For writers such as Wollstonecraft, Mackintosh, and Williams, revisions of the Revolution flickered with self-reflecting irony. For Paine, there could be no irony, since the Revolution was the intimate history of himself; for the Revolution's opponents, the Revolution's irony was retrospectively tragic. But for all those who had exuberantly promoted the Revolution and who had intimately linked their lives to its

236

history, the rewriting of the Revolution ultimately entailed the rewriting of themselves as well.

Conservative historiography conventionally plots a fall into chaos, beginning with an Ur-Fall and repetitively continuing to the end, when fallen history will be transcended outside of time. For the past two centuries, within the perpetual fall of history, this historiography has reconceived the French Revolution as a second primary Fall, reversing humanity's transient recuperations. In varying repetitions of Burke, this historiography locates the fatal origin of totalitarianism in the prefiguring ideologies of the French Revolution.[1] Similarly, radical historiography repeats the same plot with its own ideological variations: there is a fall from unity into chaos and a subsequent recovery of unity, prophesied and projected in a future—a new transcendent historical order. This suggests that the rebellions of writers in the 1790s were really revisions, not rejections, of the same plot: the "fall" into contradiction and the recovery of unity. For the past two centuries, the Left's historical identification with the Revolution as "the mother of us all"[2] has similarly resulted in representations of the Revolution as a transfiguring event—betrayed—but, nevertheless, a nostalgic adumbration of the future. Even Marx's revision of the Revolution as a *révolution manquée* plots the Revolution as a necessary stage in the progressive unfolding of history—the dissolution of contradiction. In the twentieth century, the Bolsheviks were obsessed with resemblances between the Russian and French Revolutions, especially fatal repetitive parallels and a "Thermidor" reaction that would again delay humanity's best hope. In *Interpreting the French Revolution,* François Furet observes how left-wing historiography incorporated the French Revolution into the macrocosmic Russian Revolution, making the former "the mother of a real, dated, and duly registered event—October 1917."[3] For two centuries, the Revolution has haunted the Western imagination. Like the writers of the 1790s, to write about the Revolution is to write simultaneously about resemblances between the past and present—about betrayals and falls. In many ways, the plots of late eighteenth-century historiography have been absorbed into the ongoing text of the Revolution.

For radical writers in the 1790s, there was a timeless pristine moment between the fall of the Bastille and the Festival of Federation, but events subsequently, perhaps necessarily, were written with repetitive irony. Jules Michelet, in the nineteenth century, is the culmination of late eighteenth-century historiography and writers like Helen Maria Williams, who nostalgically look back at

1789 and 90, but whose perspective is ironic the further they write from the original pristine moment. But whether they recurred to the paradigms of the past or to a utopian revolution deferred in the future, or to a displaced revolution that would finally be successfully reconsummated in the future, writers in the 1790s used a variety of repetitious models to explain, "look away," or to rationalize a "present" that was bewilderingly problematic.

The thematic and strategic repetitions that I have explored are continuations of a concurrent book dealing with resemblances between Burke and the writers who opposed him in the great intertextual wars of the 1790s. Like the print of Robespierre and the guillotine, repetition and resemblance complement each other—both are reflective replications of a prior model, and both are based on a concept of correspondence and identity. Supporters and opponents of the French Revolution were similarly preoccupied with an original, pristine model and true or deviant "copies," and both plotted a series of respective "falls." There is, in the writings of the 1790s, a revealing Platonic dimension.

This resuggests that as both sides rebelled against each other's (author)itarian readings, they simultaneously wrote in and "out" of the same system of representation. Reinscribing the same preconceptions, each told the same (disguised) story in a repetitive search for the true ground of history. Each side represented itself and the Revolution in opposition to either radical or counterrevolutionary "difference," and each respective difference was written out in terms of the writers who opposed it. Difference was invariably the recurring problem of the "Other." While the Terror constituted the climactic crisis in representation for the Revolution's supporters, there were, from the beginning, a variety of representational crises. Writers returning to the recognizable paradigms of the past reinscribed difference as an explainable, hence as a reassuring, similarity. But this was to erase or misrepresent what was truly different about the Revolution, for each historical event exists sui generis, and even writers cannot step into the same historical flux twice.

In *Difference and Repetition*, Gilles Deluze argues that the concept of identity and its negative (or absence) constitutes the limits of Western representation, and consequently difference can never be represented in terms of itself, because it is always contrastively expressed and defined in terms of its privileged opposition. Difference hence reinforces the illusion of repeatable identity or resemblance, since it is expressed within concepts that provide it its bogus identity.[4] This suggests that the underlying crisis of the

French (or any) Revolution was that its writers could not represent its existential difference, and that the problem of writing the history of the "other" is always the problem of inadequate representation.

There are, at the same time, covert similarities and resemblances in different oppositional texts, no matter how they are written out. I have emphasized this side of the revolutionary story; the other, more complex side, remains to be explored. The fact, however, that the Revolution was and continues to be constituted on its difference to the ci-devant past reposes a primary historical problem confronting rebellious readers and writers of revolutions: how is revolution represented when rebellion is written "out" (repeatedly erased and exposed) within the textual space of the tradition it resists? Since "tradition" even provides the "terms" of rebellion, revolutionaries necessarily write within the very system of representation they rebel against. They are profoundly implicated in the representations they react against.

In *The Marriage of Heaven and Hell* (1790–93), William Blake had contended that Milton was "of the Devil's party without knowing it." But Blake and other revolutionary writers blindly replicated the tradition they subversively read. While the radical readers of the 1790s antithetically rewrite the traditional canon, their inversions are reinscribed within a representational system of divergence and correspondence, a value system of good and evil, of fallen and unfallen worlds. Hence they reproduce, mutatis mutandis, the same Manichean readings of the traditional texts they demonize. In this reflective intertextual juncture, Blake and Burke dialectically conflate, so that rereading rebels and Romantics rewriting Burke and the French Revolution is, two centuries later, to recognize again that they are, like Blake's devil, complicit with the tradition they refuse to acknowledge.

Appendix: Paine's Letters to Burke

In early 1790, when Paine, in Paris, learned that Burke intended to publish a pamphlet critical of the Revolution, he felt personally betrayed: he considered Burke an ideological ally and had sent him a glowing account of the Revolution's course in a letter dated 17 January 1790. On 9 February, in the House of Commons, Burke had declared that he would break with his closest friends over the issue of the French Revolution. Then, within a week, came the announcement of his intention to publish a public letter on the Revolution. Paine, however, was unaware that Burke had previously received a letter (4 November 1789) from a French correspondent requesting his views or that he had read Richard Price's *A Discourse on the Love of Our Country* (1789) in mid-January, just about the time Paine was writing to him from Paris. Paine, consequently, assumed a causal relationship between Burke's attack on the Revolution and what he took to be Burke's rejection of his letter and hence himself.

In the *Rights of Man*, he angrily refers to his correspondence with Burke, mentioning his January letter on three occasions. First, he notes that when Burke made his "violent speech" against the Revolution (9 February), Paine was in Paris "and had written to him but a short time before, to inform him how prosperously matters were going on. Soon after this, I saw his advertisement of the pamphlet he intended to publish" (*CW*, 1:244). The temporal proximity of the two events indicate that, for Paine, there is a causal connection between his January letter and Burke's betrayal of both the Revolution and himself.

Second, Paine refers to his January letter when he quotes Thomas Jefferson, "in a letter which I communicated to Mr. Burke," as his anonymous source for the characterization of "Count de Broglio" (Victor-François, Duc de Broglie, commander of the king's troops in July 1789) as a "high-flying aristocrat, cool and capable of every mischief" (*CW*, 1:261). Although Paine, in the *Rights of Man*, does not identify Jefferson, he insists that the characterization comes "from an authority which Mr. Burke well knows was good" (261). Indeed, in his letter to Burke in January,

Paine had quoted approvingly from a letter Jefferson had sent him on 11 July 1789, three days before the Bastille's fall.

Finally, he notes that he "used sometimes to correspond with Mr. Burke, believing him then to be a man of sounder principles than his book shows him to be," referring, for a third time, to his affirmative account of the Revolution in his January letter (*CW*, 1:297).

But Paine's January letter, as Thomas W. Copeland and others have noted, probably reconfirmed Burke's increasing mistrust of the Revolution.[1] For instance, Paine refers to the political use of the term *Aristocrat* to stigmatize anyone hostile to the Revolution, and he quotes approvingly Jefferson's comment that the National Assembly intended "to set fire to the four Corners of the Kingdom and perish with it themselves, rather than relinquish an Iota of their Plan of a total Change of Government."

Paine proceeds to relate that when Louis XVI entered Paris (17 July 1789), he was surrounded by a crowd armed with "Scythes, Sickles, Carpenters Chissels and Iron Spikes fixed with Sticks Blacksmith's with sledge Hammers and in short every thing and any thing that could be got." When the king arrived at the Hôtel de Ville, "he had to pass through an Alley of Men," who crossed their weapons "over his head under which he had to pass, impressed perhaps that some one was to fall upon his head." Amazingly, Paine mentions this "to show how natural it is, that [the king] should now feel himself tranquil.—The Revolution in France is certainly a forerunner to other Revolutions in Europe."[2] Paine's letter undoubtedly did not make Burke feel tranquil, reconfirming ironically his worst suspicions.

But there is, in addition, another letter that Paine cites in the *Rights of Man* as yet another example of Burke's reactionary betrayal: the letter that the Abbé Morellet returned to him in August 1787, agreeing with Paine's assessment of Anglo-Franco relations and supporting, along with Loménie de Brienne (the Archbishop of Toulouse and Minister of Finance), Paine's proposal to show it to selected British statesmen. In the *Rights of Man,* Paine notes indignantly that he had "put this letter into the hands of Mr. Burke almost three years ago, and left it with him," hoping that Burke would make good use of it by promoting a new, amicable understanding between Britain and France. Since Burke had the "opportunity of doing some good" by showing the letter to British authorities, especially when the Revolution broke out, but apparently did nothing (*CW,* 1:246)—this confirmed, for Paine, Burke's betrayal of his former principles as well as Paine's authoritative sources. Burke, according to him, had the opportunity to do something but instead did "nothing"—a charge he would hurl at George Washington five years later. Burke had, in fact, received Morellet's letter; in a letter (7 August 1788) to Burke, Paine mentions enclosing it, adding that "I have not a copy of my own letter here . . . but you will easily see the points I went upon by the abbe's answer."[3] Paine would not, in any case, have shown Burke his (August 1787) letter to Morellet, since it underscores his anti-English sentiments, including his proposal to wage a propaganda war in England, because "the best Conquest that can be gained over an Enemy is that which is gained upon their Mind."[4]

Burke was probably underwhelmed with Paine's source, for he had met Morellet in Paris in 1773. In a letter to Burke's future enemy, the earl of Shelburne, Morellet referred critically to the meeting: "*Je veux vous parler un peu de M. Burke: il est très aimable et plein d'espoir et de chaleur; mais, mylord, j'ai cru lui voir une philosophie incertaine encore des principes, qui ne sont ni bien fixes, ni bien liés les uns aux autres.*"[5] In 1782 Shelburne was instrumental in sabotaging what remained of the Second Rockingham Administration (culminating in Burke's and Charles James Fox's resignations), and "his close association with French liberal thinkers such as the abbé Morellet,"[6] undoubtedly heightened Burke's mistrust of Paine's source.

Later, in the *Rights of Man,* Paine unwittingly subverts both his source (Brienne) and his criticism of Burke for ignoring the letter, when he observes that Brienne, the Archbishop of Toulouse, "turned out [to be] a despot, and sunk into disgrace, and a Cardinal" (*CW,* 1:304). For Paine, however, the battle lines had been drawn: by rejecting his unimpeachable sources (Jefferson, Morellet, and Brienne), Burke had, he believed, decided to attack both the Revolution and himself in the *Reflections.*

Notes

Introduction

1. Hayden White, *Tropics of Discourse: Essays in Cultural Criticism* (Baltimore: Johns Hopkins University Press, 1978), p. 63.
2. Thomas Paine, *Rights of Man*, in *The Complete Writings of Thomas Paine*, ed. Philip S. Foner, 2 vols. (New York: The Citadel Press, 1945), 1:266. All subsequent quotations from Paine are from this edition and will be cited as *CW* (see Abbreviations).
3. Thomas Christie, *Letters on the Revolution of France* (London: J. Johnson, 1791), pp. 126–27.
4. Mary Wollstonecraft, *A Vindication of the Rights of Men*, in *The Works of Mary Wollstonecraft*, 7 vols., ed. Janet Todd and Marilyn Butler (New York: New York University Press, 1989). Hereafter cited as *The Rights of Men* in the *Works;* Edmund Burke, *A Philosophical Enquiry into the Origin of our Ideas of the Sublime and Beautiful*, ed. J. T. Boulton (New York: Columbia University Press, 1958). Hereafter cited as *Enquiry; Reflections on the Revolution in France*, ed. Conor Cruise O'Brien (Harmondsworth: Penguin Classics, 1986). Hereafter cited as *Reflections* (see Abbreviations).
5. Mary Wollstonecraft, *An Historical and Moral View of the French Revolution* (1794); hereafter *The French Revolution* in *Works* (see Abbreviations).

Chapter 1. In the Beginning: Thomas Paine's Two Revolutionary Careers

1. Frances Sherwood, *Vindication* (New York: Farrar, Strauss, and Giroux, 1993), pp. 147, 204.
2. Alfred Owen Aldridge, *Thomas Paine's American Ideology* (Newark: University of Delaware Press, 1984), p. 278.
3. Alfred Owen Aldridge, *Man of Reason: The Life of Thomas Paine* (Philadelphia: J. B. Lippincott, 1959), p. 125.
4. In 1789 Paine was corresponding with Jefferson about events in France. As the American Minister in France, Jefferson provided Paine with some firsthand accounts of the events. On 17 January 1790 Paine sent Burke an enthusiastic report on the Revolution's progress, quoting from a letter Jefferson had written him on 11 July 1789. In *Rights of Man*, Paine makes the January letter and Jefferson's (anonymous) comments an issue, as he does the earlier letter from the Abbé Morellet (see Appendix).
5. David Freeman Hawke, *Paine* (New York: Harper & Row, 1974), p. 229.
6. David V. Erdman, *Commerce Des Lumières: John Oswald and the British in Paris* (Columbia: University of Missouri Press, 1986), pp. 204–8.

7. James H. Billington, *Fire in the Minds of Men: Origins of the Revolutionary Faith* (New York: Basic Books, 1980), p. 35.

8. Ibid., pp. 36, 39–40.

9. Gary Kates, *The Cercle Social, the Girondins, and the French Revolution* (Princeton: Princeton University Press, 1985), p. 207.

10. Erdman, *Commerce Des Lumières,* p. 162. Earlier, in October 1791, the prospectus for *La Chronique* had listed Paine as one of its contributors.

11. Ibid., p. 183.

12. Ibid., pp. 225–26.

13. Ibid., p. 243.

14. Hawke, *Paine,* p. 290.

15. See John Goldworth Alger, *Glimpses of the French Revolution: Myths, Ideas, and Realities* (London: Sampson, Low, and Marston, 1894), pp. 31–36.

16. Aldridge, *Man of Reason,* p. 244.

17. David A. Wilson, *Paine and Cobbett: The Transatlantic Connection* (Montreal: McGill-Queen's University Press, 1988), pp. 67, 71.

18. Richard Price, *Political Writings,* ed. D. O. Thomas (Cambridge: Cambridge University Press, 1991), p. 196.

19. Quoted by Patrice Higonnet, *Sister Republics: The Origins of French and American Republicanism* (Cambridge: Cambridge University Press, 1988), p. 1.

20. Cf. Christ's words in Mark 4:22—"For there is nothing hid, which shall not be manifested; neither was any thing kept secret, but that it should come abroad" (Authorized Version). See also Luke 8:17. Despite Paine's hostility to the Bible in *The Age of Reason* (1794–95) and other publications, he allusively fashions himself into the new Messiah, bearer of the new revolutionary gospel.

21. Aldridge, *Man of Reason,* p. 151.

22. Steven Blakemore, *Burke and the Fall of Language: The French Revolution as Linguistic Event* (Hanover, N.H.: University Press of New England, 1988), pp. 19–30.

Chapter 2. Paine's Revolutionary Comedy: The Bastille and October Days in the *Rights of Man*

1. Burke, *Correspondence,* 6:80.

2. Tom Furniss, *Edmund Burke's Aesthetic Ideology: Language, Gender, and Political Economy in Revolution* (Cambridge: Cambridge University Press, 1993), p. 133.

3. Thomas Jefferson, *The Papers of Thomas Jefferson,* ed. Julien P. Boyd (Princeton: Princeton University Press, 1958), 15:267–73.

4. See n. 4, chap. 1.

5. Jerome D. Wilson and William F. Ricketson, *Thomas Paine* (Boston: Twayne Publishers, 1989), p. 62.

6. See George Rudé, *The Crowd in the French Revolution* (Oxford: Clarendon Press, 1959), pp. 74–75.

7. See J. M. Thompson, *The French Revolution* (New York: Oxford University Press, 1966), p. 104; William Doyle, *The Oxford History of the French Revolution* (Oxford: Clarendon Press, 1989), p. 122.

8. See Paul H. Beik, "October Days," in *Historical Dictionary of the French Revolution,* ed. Samuel F. Scott and Barry Rothaus, 2 vols. (Westport: Greenwood

Press, 1985), 2:733; Thompson, *The French Revolution,* p. 106; Doyle, *Oxford History of the French Revolution,* p. 122.

9. Rudé, *The Crowd in the French Revolution,* p. 62.

10. Burke, *Correspondence,* 6:73–74.

11. Cf. Rudé, *The Crowd in the French Revolution,* p. 77.

12. Thompson, *The French Revolution,* p. 107; Doyle, *Oxford History of the French Revolution,* p. 122; Georges Lefebvre, *The French Revolution,* trans. Elizabeth Moss Evanson, 2 vols. (New York: Columbia University Press, 1962), 1:134.

13. Frans De Bruyn, "Theater and Countertheater in Burke's *Reflections on the Revolution in France,*" in *Burke and the French Revolution: Bicentennial Essays,* ed. Steven Blakemore (Athens: University of Georgia Press, 1992), p. 31; cf. Bernadette Fort, "The French Revolution and the Making of Fictions," in *Fictions of the French Revolution,* ed. Bernadette Fort (Evanston, Il.: Northwestern University Press, 1991), pp. 3–32.

14. *Révolutions de Paris* 1 (no. 13, 3–10 October 1789): 6–10, 15–20.

15. Darline Fay Levy and Harriet Branson Applewhite, "Women and Militant Citizenship in Revolutionary Paris," in *Rebel Daughters: Women and the French Revolution,* ed. Sara E. Melzer and Leslie W. Rabine (New York: Oxford University Press, 1992), p. 82.

16. *Révolutions de Paris:* 20–22.

Chapter 3. Revisionist Patricide: Thomas Paine's *Letter to George Washington*

1. Thomas Paine, *Letter to George Washington,* in *CW* (2:691–723). Hereafter, except for clarification, cited as *Letter* (see Abbreviations).

2. For a longer version of this chapter that explores Paine's initial, eulogistic admiration of Washington, see Steven Blakemore, "Revisionist Patricide: Thomas Paine's Letter to George Washington," *CLIO* 24 (No. 3, Spring 1995): 269–89.

3. Hawke, *Paine,* p. 335. The essay was published in *Le Bien informé,* the newspaper of his friend, Nicolas de Bonneville. After his return to America, Paine never mentioned the article although the Federalist Press did. In 1807 he published another article promoting gunboats as an effective means of defense for American coasts, harbors, and ports (*CW,* 2:1067–72)—an ironic proposal given his 1798 proposal to invade American harbors with French gunboats.

4. Winthrop D. Jordan, "Familial Politics: Thomas Paine and the Killing of the King," *Journal of American History* 60 (September 1973): 294–308.

5. James Thomas Flexner, *Washington: The Indispensable Man* (Boston: Little Brown, 1969), p. 93.

6. Gary Wills notes that *character,* in the eighteenth century, was also commonly "used as a synonym for 'reputation.'" *Cincinnatus: George Washington and the Enlightenment* (Garden City, N.Y.: Doubleday, 1984), p. 96. In this context, Paine's assault on Washington's "character" was simultaneously an assault on his reputation.

7. National gratitude to Washington was both an American and European commonplace in the eighteenth century. Richard Price, for instance, in *Observations on the Importance of the American Revolution* (1785), refers to the "debt of gratitude" that American posterity will feel for Washington: ". . . gratitude to that General, who has been raised up by Providence to make them free and independent, and whose name must shine among the first in the future annals of

the benefactors of mankind." Price, *Political Writings,* pp. 121–22. Paine was, in effect, inverting this cultural commonplace and deconstructing Washington's mythic persona.

8. Jay Fliegelman, *Prodigals and Pilgrims: The American Revolution against Patriarchal Authority, 1750–1800* (Cambridge: Cambridge University Press, 1982), pp. 93–106, 214–19, 250–54.

9. Washington was "first referred to as 'Father of his country' in *The Lancaster Almanack* for 1778" (Fliegelman, *Prodigals,* p. 200). Washington as "father" soon became a standard, formulary title; see John P. Kaminski and Jill Adaire McCaughan, ed., *A Great and Good Man: George Washington in the Eyes of His Contemporaries* (Madison: Madison House Publishers, 1989), pp. 74, 105, 118, 121, 125, 154, 157, 178, 185, 188, 195.

10. Paine's responsive rage is also reflected thematically in references to the "rage" of the enemies of France and himself. In the *Letter to Washington,* he refers to the "rage, terror, and suspicion which the brutal letter of the Duke of Brunswick [July 1792] first started into existence in France"—a good description of his own "brutal letter" to Washington. Likewise, Robespierre and the Committee of Public Safety reached "a pitch of rage and suspicion" (*CW,* 2:696, 699), as does Paine. Cf. 2:919, where he is "persecuted" by the "leaders of the Reign of Terror in America and the leaders of the Reign of Terror in France." Paine's ambivalent identification with Washington can be seen in a letter (circa May 1780), in which he refers to the lack of supplies distressing Washington's army and describes Washington's own "distress" in the same way he later refers to himself: "He feels himself like a man forsaken by the country whose interest he has so much exposed himself to preserve" (2:1185).

11. After the war, the New York Senate awarded Paine the confiscated farm (three hundred acres) of a Tory. In a letter to Washington (28 April 1784), Paine thanks him for "the pains you had taken to promote my interests" and estimates the farm and land are "worth at least a thousand guineas" (*CW,* 2:1248). Paine additionally insisted that the United States Congress should reimburse him for all the expenses he had incurred, dating from his arrival in America (1774). Although, in 1784, he wanted at least $6,000, he received $3,000 in 1785, and in that same year the Pennsylvania Assembly, after being urged by Washington, voted to award him 500 pounds for his wartime services. Despite the fact that he had been paid by Congress and two individual states for his wartime activities (albeit not as much as he wanted), Paine continued to push for a congressional pension, which he felt he deserved, for the remainder of his life.

12. More specifically, it is Washington's "Fabian system of *doing nothing*" (p. 718). Washington was frequently compared favorably to the Roman general Fabius, who wore out Hannibal without ever coming to an open engagement (see Wills, *Cincinnatus,* pp. 20, 35, 162, 199, 249). In January 1777 Paine had asserted that "the names of Washington and Fabius will run parallel to eternity" (quoted by John Keane, *Tom Paine: A Political Life* [Boston: Little, Brown, 1995], p. 142). In the *Letter to Washington,* he again assaults and rewrites Washington's mythic reputation—a reputation he had formerly reinforced—turning the adjective *Fabian* into a pejorative suggestion of cowardly delay instead of its positive sense of strategic defense.

13. In the *Letter to Washington* (2:721), Paine converts the 2,500,000 *livres* to "upwards of one hundred thousand pounds sterling"—substantially reduced from the "two hundred thousand pounds sterling" he cites in the *Rights of Man* (*CW,* 1:407).

14. Flexner, *Washington,* p. 150. Laurens was devotedly loyal to Washington. After the court-martial of General Charles Lee, Washington's rival, Laurens "claimed that Lee had impugned Washington with the grossest abuse and insisted on dueling. Lee mocked him for taking it on himself to defend Washington's honor. . . . [b]ut he agreed to the match." A. J. Langguth, *Patriots: The Men Who Started the American Revolution* (New York: Simon & Schuster, 1989), p. 487. It is ironic that Paine highlights Laurens (and hence himself)—a man who had defended Washington's "honor" against "the grossest abuse" of a rival for his position. Later, Paine claimed that Laurens, diffident about his grasp of economic and political matters, had asked him to accompany him to France, otherwise he might not go (*CW,* 2:1208, 1233, 1490). This is, at best, dubious, since Paine's source was only himself—Laurens having been killed in action in August 1782. After Washington had selected Laurens to go to France, Paine, who had been looking for opportunities to leave America and propagandize for the "cause" abroad, asked Laurens, whom he had known since 1778, if he could accompany him as his secretary—a proposal Laurens agreed to but that Paine's congressional enemies opposed. Consequently, Paine decided to accompany Laurens as a private citizen, paying his own way. In a letter to the United States Senate (21 January 1808), he expected compensation for his "service" (2:1490).

15. See Hawke, *Paine,* p. 115; Flexner, *Washington,* pp. 150, 156.

16. Hawke, *Paine,* p. 119.

17. In 1804 and 1808, Paine claimed that the money made it possible for Washington's army to go to Yorktown (*CW,* 2:959, 1490). This was, however, overstated. The "cargo . . . arrived too late to be of any direct use to the American war effort," and the Continental Congress ordered the money to be turned over to Robert Morris, the new Superintendent of Finance, "who used the funds four months later as capital stock to convert the Bank of Philadelphia into the powerful Bank of North America" (Keane, *Tom Paine,* p. 213).

18. See Robert Middlekauff, *The Glorious Cause: The American Revolution 1763–1789* (New York: Oxford University Press), pp. 562–64; cf. Flexner, *Washington,* 156–58. In a letter to Thomas McKean, president of the Continental Congress, shortly after he had returned from France, Paine could only speculate about the French fleet (see *CW,* 2:1197). In a letter to the United States Senate (21 January 1808), Paine, recounting Laurens' mission, mentions everything but the fleet (2:1490).

19. Audrey Williamson, *Thomas Paine: His Life, Work, and Times* (London: George Allen, 1973), p. 97; Hawke, *Paine,* p. 123. Paine worked for the government from 10 February 1782 until 18 April 1783.

20. In a letter "To the Honorable Senate of the United States" (21 January 1808), Paine again claimed a pension based on his contributions to the country, one of which was his mission with Laurens to France, for which he never received "a cent" (*CW,* 2:1490). On 1 February 1809 the congressional Committee of Claims replied formally, acknowledging Paine's services to America during the Revolution, but rejecting his characterization of Laurens' mission. The Committee found that Paine's written claim had been "unaccompanied with any evidence in support of the statement of facts." Moreover, the Committee noted that the journals of Congress contained no evidence that Paine "was in any manner connected with the mission of Colonel Laurens." Conceding that Paine had accompanied Laurens, the Committee concluded that the records did not substantiate "that he was employed by the Government, or even solicited by any officer thereof to aid in the accomplishment of the mission with which Colonel Laurens was

intrusted, or that he took any part whatever, after his arrival in France, in forwarding the negotiation" (Annals of Congress, 10th Cong., 2d sess., 1780–1781, in Keane, *Tom Paine,* pp. 530–31).

21. David Humphreys, *David Humphreys' Life of Washington,* ed. Rosemarie Zagarri (Athens: The University of Georgia Press, 1991), p. 4.

Chapter 4. From the Beginning: Paine's Obsession with Origins and *The Age of Reason*

1. For the historical context, see J. C. D. Clark, *The Language of Liberty 1660–1832: Political discourse and social dynamics in the Anglo-American World* (Cambridge: Cambridge University Press, 1994), pp. 131–36.

2. Hawke, *Paine,* p. 182.

3. Bernard Fay, *The Revolutionary Spirit in France and America: A study of the moral and intellectual relations between France and the United States at the end of the eighteenth century,* trans. Ramon Gutherie (New York: Cooper Square Publishers, 1966), p. 452; Paul Kléber Monod, *Jacobitism and the English People, 1688–1788* (Cambridge: Cambridge University Press, 1989), p. 202.

4. Aside from Paine himself, I have found only one outside source reconfirming Paine's account: his laudatory nineteenth-century biographer, Moncure D. Conway, who says Robespierre's condemnatory sentence was "found in his Note Book, and reported by a Committee to the Convention" and that the Committee added the notation about Paine's attempt to establish "the liberty of both worlds." Conway, however, provides no documentation. See Conway, *Thomas Paine,* ed. Eric Foner, 2 vols. (1892; New York: Chelsea House Publishers, 1983), 2:78.

5. Edward H. Davidson and William J. Scheick, *Paine, Scripture, and Authority: The Age of Reason as Religious and Political Idea* (Bethlehem, Pa.: Lehigh University Press, 1994).

6. See Frank E. Manuel, *The Eighteenth Century Confronts the Gods* (Cambridge: Harvard University Press, 1959), pp. 230–31; *The Changing of the Gods* (Hanover, N.H.: University Press of New England), pp. 67–68.

7. Cf. John Locke, *An Essay Concerning Human Understanding,* ed. Alexander Campbell Fraser, 2 vols. (1690; New York: Dover, 1959), 3.9.23.120–21. Citations are to book, chapter, section, and page numbers.

8. Cf. Locke, ibid., 3.5.8.48–49.

9. Ibid., 4.16.10.377–78.

10. Ibid., 4.18.3.416–18.

11. Christopher Hill, *The World Turned Upside Down: Radical Ideas During the English Revolution* (Harmondsworth: Penguin, 1988), pp. 262–63; cf. 264–67.

12. Cf. Locke, *Essay,* on "Personal Identity," 2.27, sec. 10 and 11, pp. 448–52; sec. 17, p. 458; sec. 23, p. 464.

13. Just before his death, Paine disclosed "that he believed that in a future state he would be conscious of his authorship" (Aldridge, *Paine's American Ideology,* p. 17). Cf. Locke, *Essay,* 2.27.16.458.

14. François Furet, *Interpreting the French Revolution,* trans. Elborg Forster (Cambridge: Cambridge University Press, 1981), p. 2.

15. Ibid., pp. 81–129, *passim.*

16. Linda Orr, *Headless History: Nineteenth-Century Historiography of the Revolution* (Ithaca: Cornell University Press, 1990), pp. 75, 78, 80.

17. Ibid., p. 158.

Chapter 5. Wollstonecraft and the French Revolution

1. Robert Darnton, "The History of *Mentalitiés:* Recent Writings on Revolution, Criminality, and Death in France," in *Structure, Consciousness, and History,* ed. Richard Harvey Brown and Stanford M. Lyman (Cambridge: Cambridge University Press, 1978), p. 107.

2. Ralph M. Wardle, ed., *Collected Letters of Mary Wollstonecraft* (Ithaca: Cornell University Press, 1979), p. 41; Eleanor Flexner, *Mary Wollstonecraft: A Biography* (New York: Coward, McCann, 1972), p. 195; Margaret Tims, *Mary Wollstonecraft: A Social Pioneer* (London: Millington Books Ltd., 1976), p. 233.

3. Hereafter, for clarity, *FR* in parenthesis. All citations from *The French Revolution* are from vol. 6 of Wollstonecraft's *Works.*

4. Ralph M. Wardle, *Mary Wollstonecraft: A Critical Biography* (Lawrence: University of Kansas Press, 1951), p. 172.

5. Mary Wollstonecraft, *Collected Letters of Mary Wollstonecraft,* ed. Ralph M. Wardle (Ithaca: Cornell University Press, 1979), p. 218.

6. Wardle, *Collected Letters,* p. 218, n. 2; Claire Tomalin, *The Life and Death of Mary Wollstonecraft* (London: Weidenfield and Nicolson, 1974), p. 119.

7. Tims, *Mary Wollstonecraft,* pp. 188–89.

8. Wollstonecraft, *Collected Letters,* p. 231.

9. William Godwin, *Memoirs of Mary Wollstonecraft* (1798; New York: Haskel House, 1927), p. 77.

10. Cf. Daniel Gordon, "'Public Opinion' and the Civilizing Process in France: The Example of Morellet," *Eighteenth-Century Studies* 22 (Spring 1989): 302–28; Keith Baker, *Inventing the French Revolution: Essays on French Political Culture in the Eighteenth Century* (Cambridge: Cambridge University Press, 1990), pp. 167–99.

11. Thomas Paine, *Rights of Man* (*CW*, 1:26); Arthur Young, *Travels in France During the Years 1787, 1788, and 1789,* ed. Jeffry Kaplow (1792; Garden City, N.Y.: Doubleday, 1969), pp. 446–47; Thomas Christie, *Letters on the Revolution of France,* pp. 122, 126–28; James Mackintosh, *Vindiciae Gallicae* (1791; Spelsbury, Oxford: Woodstock Books, 1989), pp. 164, 180.

12. James A. Leith, "Symbolism," in *Historical Dictionary of the French Revolution, 1789–1799,* ed. Samuel F. Scott and Barry Rothaus, 2 vols. (Westport, Conn.: Greenwood, 1985), 2:921; Leith, *Space and Revolution: Projects for Monuments, Squares, and Public Buildings in France, 1789–1799* (Montreal: McGill-Queen's University Press, 1991), p. 217.

13. See *Chronicle of the French Revolution,* trans. Louis Nevin et al. (Paris, 1988; London: Chronicle Communications, 1989), pp. 394, 401.

14. Colin Jones, *The Longman Companion to the French Revolution* (New York: Longman, Inc., 1988), p. 120; D. M. G. Sutherland, *France 1789–1815: Revolution and Counterrevolution* (New York: Oxford University Press, 1986), pp. 281, 314, 343.

15. When the Tuileries was stormed on 10 August 1792, many of the *sans-culottes* "carried pikes or bayonets on which were impaled 'rags'"—pieces of

clothing torn from the bodies of the dead Swiss guards. Aileen Ribeiro, *Fashion in the French Revolution* (London: B. T. Batsford, 1988), p. 85.

Chapter 6. Wollstonecraft, *Macbeth,* and the Death of Louis XVI

1. Wollstonecraft's characterization of Louis XVI reinscribes previous characterizations of Louis XV, suggesting a decadent Bourbon repetition. In pamphlets such as *Les Fastes de Louis XV* (1781), the influence of the king's mistresses (the marquise de Pompadour and the comptesse Du Barry) result in the feminization of both the court and the king, who sinks into a "private, slothful, and voluptuous life." Sarah Maza, "The Diamond Necklace Affair Revisited (1785–1786): The Case of the Missing Queen," in *Eroticism and the Body Politic,* ed. Lynn Hunt (Baltimore: The Johns Hopkins University Press, 1991), pp. 66, 68.

2. See Jacques Revel, "Marie-Antoinette in Her Fictions," in *Fictions of the French Revolution,* p. 118; Madelyn Gutwirth, *The Twilight of the Goddesses: Women and Representation in the French Revolutionary Era* (New Brunswick, N.J.: Rutgers University Press, 1992), pp. 136–37; Lynn Hunt, *The Family Romance of the French Revolution* (Berkeley and Los Angeles: University of California Press, 1993), pp. 50, 103, 106.

3. Not entirely lost. A campaign of character assassination started after the royal family was captured at Varennes (June 1791). The king was said to have impaled and roasted live cats and to have slept with his sister. See Peter Burley, *Witness to the French Revolution: American and British Commentators in France 1788–94* (London: Weidenfeld & Nicolson, 1989), p. 141.

4. Apostrophe, in the sense that Wollstonecraft evokes and addresses both the murdered monarchy and the French nation.

5. Macbeth personally killed Duncan, the legitimate king, and he contrived the murder of Banquo, destined to be "the root and father of many kings" (*Macbeth* 3.1.5–6). Both are hauntingly blurred in his imagination. Cf. Wollstonecraft, *A Vindication of the Rights of Woman:* "Macbeth's heart smote him more for one murder, the first, than for a hundred subsequent ones, which were necessary to back it" (*Works,* 5:244).

6. Cf. Mary Jacobus: "Macbeth's self-alienation, the spectator role which he assumes in the face of his own crimes, is often noted by critics" (*Romanticism, Writing, and Sexual Difference: Essays on the Prelude* [Oxford: Clarendon Press, 1989], pp. 35–36).

7. Shakespeare had traditionally been associated with "nature." Cf. Wollstonecraft's review (*Analytical Review,* December 1791) of a play by Ann Yearsley: "Mrs. Yearsley, taking Shakespeare for her model, has copied like most copyists, and despising method, supposed she imitated the wild notes of nature's darling child" (*Works,* 7:398).

8. In *Macbeth,* Duncan is "the great King" (1.2.52), a phrase ironically reechoed when the first witch applies it to Macbeth (4.1.131). Shakespeare uses the phrase in a variety of his plays.

9. Thomas M. Adams, "Prisons," in *Historical Dictionary of the French Revolution,* 2:782.

10. Wollstonecraft, *Collected Letters,* p. 225.

11. Ibid., pp. 226–27.

12. Ibid., p. 227. There are a notable variety of "Gothic" details in both the apostrophe and the letter.

13. Ibid.

14. Tims, *Mary Wollstonecraft,* p. 175.

15. Wollstonecraft, *Collected Letters,* p. 218.

16. Ibid., p. 227.

17. Ibid.

18. In her subsequent (15 February 1793) "letter" to Joseph Johnson, she laments "the blood that has stained the cause of freedom at Paris" (*Works,* 6:444); in *The French Revolution,* the guillotine's blood "stained the earth" (p. 216).

19. Vergniaud, quoted by Simon Schama, *Citizens: A Chronicle of the French Revolution* (New York: Knopf, 1989), p. 714.

20. Wollstonecraft, *Collected Letters,* p. 227.

21. Cf. Jean-Jacques Rousseau, *Letter to Alembert:* "What do we learn from . . . *Oedipe* other than that man is not free and that heaven punishes him for crimes that it makes him commit?" (*Politics and the Arts: Letter to M. d' Alembert on the Theatre,* trans. Allan Bloom [Glencoe, IL: The Free Press, 1960], p. 32). Throughout her adult life, Wollstonecraft was hostile to the theater (ancient and modern); here her hostility is reinscribed Rousseau (cf. *The Rights of Men* [*Works* 5:16] and her quotation from Rousseau's *Letter to Alembert* [1758]). The fact that she herself writes "out" a tragedy has significant, ironic implications with regard to her attack, in *The Rights of Men,* on Burke's tragic *Reflections.*

22. In chapter two of *Romanticism, Writing, and Sexual Difference,* pp. 33–62.

Chapter 7. The Bastille's Blood: The October Days, Barriers, and Marie Antoinette

1. With all the allusions to Louis XVI's execution and metaphors of revolutionary violence being paradoxically washed clean in sacrificial blood, it is possible that Wollstonecraft had seen the engravings and the account of the king's execution in the radical Parisian journal, *Révolutions de Paris* (no. 185, 19–26, January 1793). In that issue, the newspaper declared that "[t]he blood of Louis Capet, shed by the blade of the law on 21 January 1793, cleanses us of a stigma of 1300 years. . . . Liberty resembles that divinity of the Ancients which one cannot make auspicious and favorable except by offering to it in sacrifice the life of a great culprit" (quoted by Hunt, *Family Romance,* p. 10). In *The Deaths of Louis XVI,* Susan Dunn explores how the king's death has haunted the French political imagination for two centuries and how the shedding of his blood was reconceived as a ritual sacrifice sanctifying the French republic.

2. See Hans-Jürgen Lüsebrink and Rolf Reichardt, *Die "Bastille": Zur Symbolgeschichte von Herrschaft und Freiheit* (Frankfurt: Fischer, 1990).

3. Schama, *Citizens,* p. 412.

4. Ibid., p. 407

5. Godwin, *Memoirs of Mary Wollstonecraft,* p. 77.

6. See Sutherland, *France 1789–1815,* p. 163.

7. Cf. Gutwirth, *The Twilight of the Goddesses:* "The full flavor of the word *Autrichienne,* the last syllable of which forms the word *bitch* in French, cannot be re-created in English" (p. 409, n. 46).

8. See Revel, "Marie-Antoinette in Her Fictions," in *Fictions of the French Revolution,* ed. Fort, pp. 120–22, 200, n. 11; Pierre Saint-Amand, "Adorning Marie Antoinette," trans. Zakiya Hanafi, *Eighteenth-Century Life* 15 (November 1991): 26, 30.

9. See Wollstonecraft, *Collected Letters*, p. 251.

10. Ibid., p. 235.

11. Moira Ferguson and Jane Todd, *Mary Wollstonecraft* (Boston: Twayne Publishers, 1984), p. 84; Joan B. Landes, *Women and the Public Sphere in the Age of the French Revolution* (Ithaca: Cornell University Press, 1988), p. 149; Flexner, *Mary Wollstonecraft*, p. 196.

12. Curiously, most of Burke's respondents did not directly contest Burke's representation of Marie Antoinette's pierced bed. The anonymous author of *Strictures on the Letter of the Right Hon. Mr. Burke, on the Revolution in France* (1791) says that the enraged crowd pursued the bodyguards who had fired on them from inside the palace: "they were determined if possible none should escape, and with their bayonets they pierced the queen's bed lest any of them should have taken refuge and concealment there" (Gregory Claeys, ed., *Political Writings of the 1790s*, 8 vols. [London: Pickering & Chatto, 1995], 2 : 232).

13. Wollstonecraft, I believe, follows James Mackintosh's account in *Vindiciae Gallicae* (1791), where Mackintosh uses the same words "left for dead" to refer to the guard outside the queen's apartments (pp. 185–86). Mackintosh, in turn, follows Charles Chabroud's assessment of the official *Châtelet* report on the October Days, where the phrase *"laissé pour mort"* appears with reference to the queen's bodyguard, Miomandre de Saint-Marie. See *Procédure Criminelle Instruit fait au Châtelet de Paris* (Paris: Baudouin, 1790), part IV, p. 65. Part four (Chabroud's assessment) was commissioned by the National Assembly and affixed to the *Châtelet* report.

14. James T. Boulton, *The Language of Politics in the Age of Wilkes and Burke* (London: Routledge and Kegan Paul, 1963), p. 129, n. 1.

15. Doyle, *Oxford History of the French Revolution*, p. 122; Sutherland, *France 1789–1815*, p. 85; John Hardman, *Louis XVI* (New Haven: Yale University Press, 1993), p. 172. Here, as in other accounts, historians variously place the killing of the guards outside in the courtyard, inside the palace, just outside the queen's apartment(s), or a combination of all three. The queen's suite was apparently divided into four apartments, the last containing her bedroom. See Pierre Dominique, *Paris Enlève le Roi, Octobre 1789* (Paris: Librairie Académique Perrin, 1973), pp. 211–12. Jules Michelet says that a bodyguard was killed near the queen's apartment and that the sister of the queen's femme-de-chambre, Madam de Campan, "having half opened the door, saw a guardsman covered with blood, trying to stop the furious rabble. She quickly bolted the door and . . . put a petticoat on the queen, and tried to lead her to the king" (*History of the French Revolution*, trans. Charles Cocks [Chicago: The University of Chicago Press, 1967], pp. 310–11). Georges Lefebvre notes that several guards were killed outside in the courtyard and that a "mob found its way to the queen's antechamber, but she escaped, fleeing to the King" (*The French Revolution*, 1 : 132–33).

16. Schama, *Citizens*, p. 467.

17. Mackintosh, *Vindiciae Gallicae*, pp. 185–86.

18. Gary Kelly, *Revolutionary Feminism: The Mind and Career of Mary Wollstonecraft* (New York: St. Martin's Press, 1992), pp. 164–65.

19. Mackintosh, *Vindiciae Gallicae*, p. 186; see *Procédure Criminelle Instruite au Châtelet de Paris*, IV, p. 65.

Chapter 8. The Inevitability of Progress: A Revolution Within, Happier Far

1. She sent the manuscript of her book abroad in March 1794. This suggests that she was either finishing or revising her book by the time she moved to Le

Havre in mid-January 1794. Between December (1793) and January (1794), more people had been guillotined than at any other previous point in the Terror.

2. *Letters Written in Sweden, Norway and Denmark,* in *Works,* 6:243–345. Hereafter, *Letters Written in Sweden* (see Abbreviations).

3. Wollstonecraft, *Collected Letters,* pp. 232–33.

4. Ibid., pp. 250–51.

5. Ibid., p. 257.

6. Ibid., p. 264.

7. Ibid., p. 267.

8. Ibid., pp. 279, 280.

9. Mona Ozouf, *Festivals of the French Revolution,* trans. Alan Sheridan (Cambridge: Harvard University Press, 1988), p. 29.

10. Wollstonecraft, *Collected Letters,* p. 263.

11. Ozouf, *Festivals,* pp. 11, 104.

Chapter 9. Helen Maria Williams and the French Revolution

1. F. M. Todd, "Wordsworth, Helen Maria Williams and France," *Modern Language Review* 43 (1948): 456–64.

2. Lionel D. Woodward, *Une Anglaise Amie de la Révolution Française: Hélène Maria Williams et ses Amis* (Paris: H. Champion, 1930), p. 20.

3. Ibid.

4. Ibid., p. 40.

5. The full title of Williams' first volume (published the last week of November 1790) is *Letters Written in France, in the Summer of 1790, to a friend in England; Containing Various Anecdotes Relative to the French Revolution; and the Memoirs of Mons. and Madame Du F_____* (London: T. Cadell, 1790). Hereafter, the entire series (1790–96) cited as *Letters* (see Abbreviations). As Matthew Bray notes, "*Letters Written in France* became vol. 1 of *Letters from France* in later edns., after the publication of 'Volume II' in 1792. Two more vols. followed, succeeded by a new 4-vol. series, *Letters Containing a Sketch of the Politics of France, published in 1795–96.*" "Helen Maria Williams and Edmund Burke: Radical Critique and Complicity" (*Eighteenth-Century Life* 16 [May 1992]: 20, n. 1). The publishing history is complicated, see Chris Jones, "Helen Maria Williams and Radical Sensibility," *Prose Studies* (May 1989): 23, n. 7. All eight volumes (both four-volume series) are available in a two-volume facsimile edition: *Letters from France,* ed. Janet M. Todd (Delmar, New York: Scholars' Facsimiles & Reprints, 1975). All references are to this edition. Because the *Letters* consist of *two* four-volume series, the appropriate volume of the Scholars' Facsimiles edition will be cited, followed by the volume in the appropriate series, and then the page number. Thus 2:3.129 refers to the second volume of the Facsimiles edition, the third volume of the series, page 129.

6. Woodward, *Une Anglaise Amie,* pp. 41–42.

7. Ibid., p. 50.

8. Ibid., p. 151.

9. Ray M. Adams, "Helen Maria Williams and the French Revolution," in *Wordsworth and Coleridge: Studies in honor of George Mclean Harper,* ed. Earl Leslie Griggs (Princeton: Princeton University Press, 1939), p. 104.

10. Laetitia Matilda Hawkins, *Letters on the Female Mind, Its Powers and*

Pursuits. Addressed to Miss H. M. Williams, With particular reference to Her Letters From France, 2 vols. (London: Hookham and Carpenter, 1793), 2:85.

11. Jones, "Helen Maria Williams and Radical Sensibility," p. 11.

12. Woodward, *Une Amie Anglaise,* p. 243.

13. See Steven Blakemore, "Revolution and the French Disease: Laetitia Matilda Hawkins' *Letters* to Helen Maria Williams," *SEL* 36 (Summer 1996): 673–91; Hawkins, *Letters on the Female Mind,* 2:106, 108, 183.

14. Woodward, *Une Amie Anglaise,* p. 128.

15. Benjamin Kurtz and Carrie C. Autrey, ed., *Four New Letters of Mary Wollstonecraft and Helen Maria Williams* (Berkeley: University of California Press, 1937), pp. 45–46, 81.

16. Erdman, *Commerce Des Lumières,* pp. 230–31.

17. Adams, "Helen Maria Williams and the French Revolution," in *Wordsworth and Coleridge,* p. 105.

18. William St Claire, *The Godwins and the Shelleys: A Biography of a Family* (New York: W. W. Norton, 1989), p. 158.

19. Woodward, *Une Amie Anglaise,* p. 132.

20. Adams, "Helen Maria Williams and the French Revolution," in *Wordsworth and Coleridge,* p. 112; cf. Gary Kelly, *Women, Writing, and Revolution 1790–1827* (Oxford: Clarendon Press, 1993), p. 208.

21. Christie had been identified as the author of letter five in the eighteenth century, but for a variety of reasons, most twentieth-century readers have assumed the letter was by Williams herself. I have omitted a lengthy appendix dealing with the above but will send a copy to anyone who is interested.

22. Woodward, *Une Amie Anglaise,* p. 89.

23. Ibid., p. 88.

24. Quoted by Chris Jones, *Radical Sensibility: Literature and Ideas in the 1790s* (London: Routledge, 1993), p. 141.

25. Helen Maria Williams, *A Tour in Switzerland,* 2 vols. (London: G. G. and J. Robinson, 1798), 1:2.

26. Woodward, *Une Amie Anglaise,* pp. 96–97.

27. Ibid., p. 98; Adams, "Helen Maria Williams and the French Revolution," in *Wordsworth and Coleridge,* p. 108.

28. Ibid., p. 109.

29. Jones, "Helen Maria Williams and Radical Sensibility," pp. 18–19; cf. Mary Favret, *Romantic Correspondence: Women, politics, and the fiction of letters* (Cambridge: Cambridge University Press, 1993), p. 51.

30. Helen Maria Williams, *Poems,* 2 vols. (London: T. Cadell, 1786), 2:11, l.16.

31. Williams, *A Tour in Switzerland,* 2:48ff., 50–55, 57.

32. Woodward, *Une Amie Anglaise,* p. 146.

33. Ibid., p. 252.

Chapter 10. Comedy, Tragedy, and Romance in Williams' *Letters from France*

1. Hannah More, *Essays on Various Subjects Principally Designed for Young Ladies,* in *The Works of Hannah More,* 11 vols. (New York: Harper, 1847), 2:335.

2. Woodward, *Une Amie Anglaise,* p. 45. My translation.

3. Gary Kelly, "Revolutionary and Romantic Feminism: Women, Writing, and Cultural Revolution," in *Revolution and English Romanticism: Politics and Rheto-*

ric, ed. Keith Hanley and Raman Selden (New York: St. Martin's Press, 1990), p. 119.

4. Leith, *Space and Revolution,* pp. 36, 43.

5. Rousseau, *Letter to M. d' Alembert on the Theatre,* p. 126.

6. Ibid., p. 133. For other allusions to Rousseau, see Nicola Watson, "*Novel Eloisas:* Revolutionary and Counterrevolutionary Narratives in Helen Maria Williams, Wordsworth and Byron," *The Wordsworth Circle* 23 (Winter 1992): 18–23.

7. Williams was often criticized for her Gallicized diction (e.g., "epocha," "phasis," "meridianal," "centrical," "epuration"). Although she uses the word *comedian* in its English sense, she sometimes seems to use it in the French sense of *comédien*—the common word for "actor."

8. See Blakemore, *Burke and the Fall of Language,* pp. 72–73.

9. Apropos of Marx's comments at the beginning of the *Eighteenth Brumaire,* cf. Jean-Paul Marat's remark in July 1792: "How could Liberty ever have established itself among us. At several nearby tragic scenes, the revolution has only been a web of farcical representations." Cited by Marie-Hélène Huet, "Performing Arts: Theatricality and the Terror," in *Representing the French Revolution: Literature, Historiography, and Art,* ed. James A. W. Heffernan (Hanover, N.H.: University Press of New England, 1992), p. 137. In the *Reflections,* Burke sees the members of the National Assembly acting a "farce of deliberation": "They act like the *comedians* of a fair before a riotous audience" (p. 161, my emphasis).

10. In her study of the Revolution, Lynn Hunt, using Northrop Frye's vocabulary, found that in "the first months of the Revolution, most rhetoric was unconsciously shaped by . . . the 'generic plot' of comedy," culminating in the Festival of Federation. In 1792 the dominant discourse shifted to romance—a mythic confrontation between heroes and villains—and subsequently tragedy during the Terror (*Politics, Culture, and Class in the French Revolution* [Berkeley and Los Angeles: University of California Press, 1984], pp. 34–38). Williams' *Letters* roughly correspond to this schema, although she returns to the cyclical, repetitive comedy of 1789.

11. Cf. Susanne Zantop: in the 1790s

the French Revolution was a fascinating spectacle to the German onlooker. France, or rather Paris, appeared as the stage for scenes of horror or delight, which the German spectators could comment upon, applaud, or boo from what appeared to be a safe distance. The stage effect was underscored by the Revolution's own self-conscious theatricality and by the representation of the Parisian "drama" on German stages and in printed texts. Literary reenactments of the revolution in Germany often took the form of comedy, which distanced the events as it represented them. After 1792, when the Revolution was carried across the border, the German auditorium became, so to speak, center stage, which made detached, amused spectatorship no longer possible, and comedy turned to tragedy.

("Crossing the Border: The French Revolution in the German Literary Imagination," in *Representing the French Revolution,* ed. James A. W. Heffernan, p. 215)

12. Jay Fliegelman, *Declaring Independence: Jefferson, Natural Language, & the Culture of Performance* (Stanford, Calif.: Stanford University Press, 1993), pp. 60–61.

13. Helen Maria Williams, *Peru: A Poem in Six Cantos* (London: T. Cadell, 1784), pp. vii–viii.

14. Williams, *A Tour in Switzerland,* 1:118.

15. See G. J. Barker-Benfield, *The Culture of Sensibility: Sex and Society in*

Eighteenth-Century Britain (Chicago: The University of Chicago Press, 1992), pp. 151, 310–11, 316–17.

16. J. A. I. Champion, *The Pillars of Priestcraft Shaken: The Church of England and its Enemies, 1660–1730* (Cambridge: Cambridge University Press, 1992), p. 42. For the ideological implications of the distinction between history and romance, see Michael McKeon, *The Origins of the English Novel 1600–1740* (Baltimore: The Johns Hopkins University Press, 1987), passim.

17. Woodward, *Une Amie Anglaise*, p. 208.

18. Helen Maria Williams, *Julia*, 2 vols. (London: T. Cadell, 1790), 1:141.

19. Northrop Frye, *Anatomy of Criticism: Four Essays* (Princeton: Princeton University Press, 1957), p. 163.

20. In *The Rights of Men,* Wollstonecraft had criticized Burke for introducing and mixing false, artificial poetry and romance into his false, romantic *Reflections* (*Works*, 5:29).

21. See, for instance, Hannah Arendt, *On Revolution* (Harmondsworth: Penguin, 1973), p. 106; Hunt, *Politics, Culture, and Class*, pp. 34–38; Huet, "Performing Arts," in *Representing the French Revolution*, pp. 135–49; Furniss, *Edmund Burke's Aesthetic Ideology*, p. 131; Schama, *Citizens*, pp. 380–83, 535.

Chapter 11. The Sublime and Beautiful in Williams' *Letters from France*

1. Bray, "Helen Maria Williams and Edmund Burke," pp. 2, 5.

2. Williams, *A Tour in Switzerland*, 2:155; cf. 1:48.

3. Williams, *Julia*, 1:26.

4. Cf. James Mackintosh, *Vindiciae Gallicae* (1791): The Revolution's "attainments . . . console us for the portion of evil that was, perhaps, inseparable from them, and will be admired by a posterity too remote to be moved by these minute afflictions, or to be affected by any thing but their general splendor" (pp. 98–99).

5. Cf. Kelly, *Women, Writing, and Revolution*, p. 63.

6. Cf. Kelly, ibid., p. 50.

7. Gutwirth, *The Twilight of the Goddesses*, p. 234.

8. Cf. Frances Ferguson, "Legislating the Sublime," in *Studies in Eighteenth-Century British Art and Aesthetics,* ed. Ralph Cohen (Berkeley and Los Angeles: University of California Press, 1985), p. 134.

9. Gary Kelly refers to "the immediate, sentimental, epistolary, obviously feminine discourse invented by Helen Maria Williams to feminize discourse and the Revolution." He argues that "the Jacobin Revolution of 1793 was treated by . . . Williams and others as a masculinization of the Revolution" (Kelly, *Revolutionary Feminism*, pp. 153–54; cf. 170). This is true if pejorative "masculinization" is confined to Jacobin power and terror, for Williams was attracted to and valorized chivalric masculine defenders and envisioned both the sublime and beautiful complementing each other. As Matthew Bray notes, "the primary human relationship for Williams, the one that forms the paradigm for her political discussions, is heterosexual love" ("Helen Maria Williams and Edmund Burke," p. 8).

10. Woodward, *Une Anglaise Amie*, pp. 26–27.

11. Williams' strong textual identifications with Burke are striking. In letter seven (misnumbered six) of the third volume (1:3.207–41), she warns that if the Revolution continues to be torn by internal contradictions, then "farewell to all those delightful visions, which we have been lately accustomed to flatter ourselves as realized!" (1:3.236). In *Letters on the Revolution of France* (1791),

Thomas Christie quotes an anonymous French journalist on Burke's romantic, chivalric view of France's Old Order: it is thus natural "for a man who saw France in such a light to detest a Revolution that has so cruelly broken the enchantment" (55). Williams undoubtedly read Christie's *Letters*, and Christie, in the concluding letter of Williams' second series (see n. 21, chap. 9), commendably praises his own book and refers to the *Reflections*, as Burke's "romance on the French Revolution" (Williams, *Letters*, 1:4.145, 218, 221).

  12. Williams, *Julia*, 1:14.

  13. Woodward, *Une Anglaise Amie*, p. 190.

  14. F. M. Todd, "Wordsworth, Helen Maria Williams and France," p. 464.

  15. Todd, ibid., passim; Woodward, *Une Anglaise Amie*, pp. 190–92.

Chapter 12. Feminine Representation: Helen Maria Williams' *Letters from France*

  1. Williams, *Poems*, 2:184–86.

  2. Cf., however, John Stuart Mill, *The Subjection of Women* (1869): "The sayings about women's fickleness are mostly of French origin . . . In England it is a common remark, how much more constant women are than men. Inconstancy has been longer reckoned discreditable to a woman, in England than in France" (*On Liberty and other Writings*, ed. Stefan Collini [Cambridge: Cambridge University Press, 1989], p. 183).

  3. Manon Philipon Roland, *An appeal to impartial posterity* (1795; Oxford: Woodstock Books, 1990), Part 1, pp. 55, 78, 165–67, 182–85; Part 2, pp. 17–18, 40, 59–60, 94, 133.

  4. Patrice Higonnet, "Cultural Upheaval and Class Formation During the French Revolution," in *The French Revolution and the Birth of Modernity,* ed. Fernec Fehér (Berkeley and Los Angeles: University of California Press), p. 88.

  5. Quoted by Lynn Hunt, *Family Romance*, p. 382.

  6. Gutwirth, *The Twilight of the Goddesses*, p. 299.

  7. Ibid., p. 321.

  8. Daniel Arasse, *The Guillotine and the Terror,* trans. Christopher Miller (London: Penguin, 1991), pp. 60–61.

  9. See Linda Kelly, *Women of the French Revolution* (London: Penguin, 1987), pp. 127–28; Darline Gay Levy, Harriet Branson Applewhite, Mary Durham Johnson, ed., *Women in Revolutionary Paris: 1789–1795* (Urbana: University of Illinois Press, 1980), pp. 205–20.

  10. Williams' citation of Lequinio is perhaps ironically authoritative, since he had been an enthusiastic participant and promoter of terror in the Vendée. For the organized murder of women and children in the Vendée, including bayoneting, see D. M. G. Sutherland, "The Vendée: Unique or Emblematic?" in *The French Revolution and the Creation of Modern Political Culture: The Terror,* ed. Keith Michael Baker (New York: Elsevier Science, Inc., 1994), p. 108.

  11. For the campaign to demonize the Vendean women as counterrevolutionary collaborators and "torturers," see Sutherland, ibid., pp. 105–6, 112 n. 31.

Chapter 13. Rewriting the Revolution: Contextual Contradiction in Williams' *Letters from France*

  1. See Doyle, *Oxford History of the French Revolution*, p. 154.

  2. Schama, *Citizens*, pp. 737, 859; cf. p. 783.

3. Dunn, *The Deaths of Louis XVI*, pp. 28, 97.

4. In June 1795, "the very word *revolutionnaire,* the code-word of the whole Jacobin regime, was banned" (Thompson, *The French Revolution,* p. 562).

5. See, for instance, *Peru,* 11.1382–83; *A Tour in Switzerland,* 1:163–66, 2:55; *Julia,* 1:41.

6. After 1795, James Mackintosh, in various of his writings, also contextually repudiated his previous representations in *Vindiciae Gallicae* (1791).

7. Thomas M. Adams, "Prisons," in *Historical Dictionary of the French Revolution,* 2:780–81.

8. Cf. *Reflections* and Burke's reference to the mock bravery of revolutionaries who denounce dead tyrants, "because [the revolutionaries] are safe from the dungeons and iron cages of their old masters" (p. 207).

9. Cf. Wollstonecraft, *The Rights of Men:* "—Thus far shalt thou go, and no further, says some stern difficulty; and the *cause* we were pursuing melts into utter darkness" (*Works,* 5:33); Thomas Christie, *Letters on the Revolution in France* (1791): "It will not be by vague and unmeaning assertions, that 'They have gone too far!' when we neither know with any kind of precision how far they have gone, nor where they stopped, nor why they went so far" (p. 60); Paine, *Rights of Man:* Burke's "cry" against the Revolution is, "[i]t is gone too far" (*CW,* 1:317); Joseph Priestly, *Letters to The Right Honourable Edmund Burke* (1792): ". . . are you, Sir, authorized to say to reformation, *Hitherto shalt thou go, and no farther?*" (in Claeys, *Political Writings of the 1790s,* 2:367). In the Bible (A. V.), God informs Job that He has established limits "[a]nd said, Hitherto shalt thou come, but no further." Later, after God has reproached Job ("Shall he that contendeth with the Almighty instruct him? he that reproveth God, let him answer it"), Job replies, "Once have I spoken, but I will not answer: yea, twice; but I will proceed no further" (Job 38:11, 40:5). In the Second Epistle of Paul to Timothy, Paul, referring to the last days, prophesies that evil men "shall proceed no further: for their folly shall be manifest to all men" (3:9). The maxim enjoined prohibition and restraint and was used that way by traditionalists in subsequent centuries. In contrast, the maxim was condemned by British dissidents. In *An Essay Concerning Human Understanding* (1690), Locke criticizes maxims that are supposedly self-evident first principles. One of his criticisms is that people often use maxims as conventional, indisputable truth to stop investigation and the discovery of real truth and knowledge: the Schoolmen, for instance, laid down maxims "beyond which there was no going—when in their disputes they came to any of these [maxims], they stopped there, and went no further; the matter was determined. . . ." The maxims were used in disputes to stop "wrangling," but were "not of much use to the discovery of unknown truths, or to help the mind forward in its search after knowledge" (IV.vii.11; cf. Francis Bacon, *Magna Instauratio* (1620), in *Essays, Advancement of Learning, New Atlantis, and Other Pieces,* ed. Richard Foster Jones [New York: The Odyssey Press, 1937], pp. 246, 267, 300, 316). The Abbé Sieyès opens his famous pamphlet *What is the Third Estate?* (1789) with an anonymous epigraph: "As long as the Philosopher does not go beyond the boundary of truth, do not accuse him of going too far." He then formulates the response of the "privileged order" to the Third Estate: "No matter how useful you are, you can go so far and no further" (*What is the Third Estate?* trans. M. Blondel [New York: Praeger, 1964], pp. 51, 55). The maxim, "thus far and no further," was used by the intellectual left to suggest timidity and conformity, and Sieyès is perhaps behind Paine's, Wollstonecraft's, Williams', Christie's, and Priestly's references.

10. Likewise, an evil "spirit of change . . . is gone abroad" (*Reflections,* p. 110). The allusions are to Shakespeare's *Julius Caesar* (3.2.249; 5.3.94); the counter context is *Hamlet,* 1:1.157–64. In *The Rights of Men,* Wollstonecraft had allusively reversed Burke's reference to the revolutionary spirit that "walks abroad": Burke need not frighten himself with revolutionary spirits, since "another [reactionary] spirit now walks abroad to secure the property of the church." Referring again to Burke, she asks why the imagination is "appalled by terrific perspectives of a hell beyond the grave," when "Hell stalks abroad"—the concrete "lash" that whips the slave's back, the political system that neglectfully starves and kills people (*Works,* 5:37, 58). Similarly, Mackintosh, *Vindiciae Gallicae* (1791): ". . . murder and rapine, if arrayed in the gorgeous disguise of acts of state, may with impunity stalk abroad" (p. 174). In *A Tour in Switzerland,* Williams refers to "revolutions . . . abroad in the earth" (2:36).

11. Lee Sterrenburg, "Mary Shelley's Monster: Politics and Psyche in *Frankenstein,*" in *The Endurance of Frankenstein: Essays on Mary Shelley's Novel,* ed. George Levine and U. C. Knoepfilmacher (Berkeley and Los Angeles: University of California Press, 1974), p. 145.

12. Emmet Kennedy, *A Cultural History of the French Revolution* (New Haven: Yale University Press, 1989), pp. 207, 208–209.

13. Williams, *A Tour in Switzerland,* 2:129.

14. Cf. Michael Walzer, ed. *Regicide and Revolution: Speeches at the Trial of Louis XVI* (Cambridge: Cambridge University Press, 1974), p. 207.

15. In his introduction to Burke's *Reflections,* Conor Cruise O'Brien notes the similarity between Burke's "tremendous, unformed spectre" rising "out of the tomb of the murdered [French] monarchy" and Marx's "specter of communism" haunting Europe at the beginning of *The Communist Manifesto* (1848). Conor Cruise O'Brien, Introduction to *Reflections on the Revolution in France* (Harmondsworth: Penguin Classics, 1986), p. 9. Marx apparently plays on conservative European fears of revolutionary Communism, conjuring up the haunted language of counterrevolutionary discourse.

16. Plutarch, "Romulus," in *The Lives of the Noble Grecians and Romans,* trans. John Dryden (New York: The Modern Library, 1939), p. 39.

17. Ibid.

18. Ibid.

19. Jean-Clément Martin, *La Vendée et la France* (Paris: Le Seuil, 1987); Reynald Sécher, *Le génocide Franco-Français: La Vendée-Vengée* (Paris: Presses Universitaires de France, 1986); Rene Sédillot, *Le Coût de la Revolution Française* (Paris, 1987).

20. Cf. Hayden White, *Metahistory: The Historical Imagination in Nineteenth-Century Europe* (Baltimore: The Johns Hopkins University Press, 1973), pp. 49–53.

21. Leo Damrosch, *Fictions of Reality in the Age of Hume and Johnson* (Madison: The University of Wisconsin Press, 1989), pp. 8–9.

Epilogue

1. See, for instance, J. L. Talmon, *The Origins of Totalitarian Democracy* (New York: Praeger, 1960).

2. Darnton, "The History of Mentalitiés," in *Structure, Consciousness, and History,* ed. Brown and Lyman, p. 108.

3. François Furet, *Interpreting the French Revolution,* p. 6.

4. Gilles Deleuze, *Difference and Repetition,* trans. Paul Patton (New York: Columbia University Press, 1994), *passim.*

Appendix

1. Thomas W. Copeland, *Our Eminent Friend Edmund Burke: Six Essays* (New Haven: Yale University Press, 1949), pp. 146–82.

2. *The Correspondence of Edmund Burke,* ed. Thomas W. Copeland et al., 10 vols. (Chicago: Chicago University Press, 1958–78), 6.70–71.

3. Photostat, American Philosophical Society, Philadelphia, PA. In the letter, Paine mentions that he has enclosed a letter from the Abbé Morellet, "which will shew what was the disposition of the French Ministry a year ago."

4. Quoted by Alfred Owen Aldridge, "Thomas Paine, Edmund Burke, and Anglo-French Relations," *Studies in Burke and His Time* 12 (1971): 1853.

5. Quoted by the editors of Burke's *Correspondence,* 2:425.

6. Albert Goodwin, *The Friends of Liberty: The English Democratic Movement in the Age of the French Revolution* (Cambridge: Harvard University Press, 1979), p. 101.